T0348094

Mark Falcoff

A Culture of Its Own

Taking Latin America Seriously

Routledge
Taylor & Francis Group

LONDON AND NEW YORK

First published 1998 by Transaction Publishers

Published 2017 by Routledge
2 Park Square, Milton Park, Abingdon, Oxon OX14 4RN
711 Third Avenue, New York, NY 10017

First issued in paperback 2017

Routledge is an imprint of the Taylor and Francis Group, an informa business

Library of Congress Catalog Number: 98-13734

Library of Congress Cataloging-in-Publication Data

Falcoff, Mark.
   A culture of its own : taking Latin America seriously / Mark Falcoff.
     p. cm.
   Includes bibliographical references and index.
   ISBN 1-56000-361-8 (alk. paper)
     1. Latin America—Civilization—20th century. 2. Latin America—Relations—United States. 3. United States—Relations—Latin America.
4. Latin America—Relations—Europe. 5. Europe—Relations—Latin America. I. Title
F1414.2.F35 1998
980.03'3—dc21   98-13734
                                CIP

ISBN 13: 978-1-138-50715-9 (pbk)
ISBN 13: 978-1-56000-361-8 (hbk)

For Ambassador Henry E. Catto, Jr.

Contents

Part V: Latins and Europeans

Introduction

Foreign areas have a way of finding and recruiting their own specialists. In my own case, it all began with the study of Spanish at the age of fourteen, a precocious age for the United States, where our ignorance of foreign languages is so deep-seated that anyone who can string a few sentences together in another tongue is said to be "fluent" in it. Very soon after discovering, to my horror, that I would have to master two different versions of the verb *to be*, I stumbled upon the more agreeable fact that to learn a new language is to enter an entirely different cultural universe. While the Spanish-speaking world lacks the strength, self-assurance, or complexity of what the French call *la francophonie*, its constituent parts are nonetheless more closely linked, at least in literary and cultural terms, than their English-speaking equivalents.

It is a world with its own historical memory, its own sensibility, and its own peculiar weaknesses. It exults in some of the same victories and mourns many of the same defeats. It practices particular virtues and vices, and it has its own notion of the good life. To enter it through the door of language, even in a hesitant, stumbling way, immediately puts one on a wholly different frequency from one's fellow citizens, who tend to casually associate Spanish with the speech of domestics, day-laborers, or migrant agricultural workers. How often in recent years have I had to sit, patiently and (I confess) sometimes a bit condescendingly, through the excited observations of provincial Anglo-Saxons who discover this world for the first time, usually at a point too late in their lives to seriously contemplate taking out a linguistic passport.

But the confusion (or ignorance) of what lies on the other side of the frontier is not confined to what one might call the populist-chauvinist side of American culture, many of whose sins are, when all is said and done, unintentional. People who study Latin America professionally, which is to say, the men and women who teach Latin American history, politics, sociology, and litera-

1

ture at our universities and colleges have rather more to answer for. With all the information at their disposal, they often labor under a delusion of their own—namely, that the region as a whole is constantly in a state of revolutionary or pre-revolutionary turmoil, largely due to the nefarious policies of the United States and the multinational corporations, often regarded as one and the same thing.[1]

This mindset has produced two curious anomalies. The first is that, since anti-Americanism is (for them) the measure of both political respectability and cultural authenticity, movements that in other parts of the world would be clearly recognized as fascist or fundamentalist, are in Latin America embraced as wholesome expressions of Enlightenment values. The other is that by pretending that these countries are merely picturesque extensions of American power, rather than societies with lives of their own, rich in contradictions and conflict, they end up by trivializing whole societies and pushing them aside. Thus by a rather curious detour, Latin American studies in the United States have often ended up being yet one more expression of our national narcissism, our lack of genuine curiosity about anything different from ourselves. Perhaps it is not surprising, then, that so many of our leading "experts" on Latin America do not speak Spanish at all well, and some—difficult as it is to believe—hardly speak it at all.

I have often reflected upon how this parlous situation came about. Before 1959, which is to say, before Fidel Castro took power in Cuba, Latin American studies as a field hardly existed in the United States. Then overnight, the prospect of a revolutionary contagion in our own hemisphere, sponsored and subsidized by the Soviet Union, unleashed a national panic. Once the region was suddenly declared of acute geopolitical importance, all our institutions—government, universities, philanthropic foundations—in typical American fashion, rushed pell mell to overcompensate for past neglect.

It must be difficult for today's crop of graduate students, faced with extremely problematic prospects for future employment, to imagine the abundance of resources that existed thirty years ago. In my own case, I recall with pleasure and no small amount of nostalgia an entire summer spent in far off Chile, courtesy of the Ford Foundation. Since the provincial university at which I supposed to study was shut down by a student strike, I was left with nothing to do but read the local papers (including the imaginatively edited Communist daily *El Siglo*), practice my Spanish, travel up and down that narrow country in buses and antiquated British trains, and discover Chile's excellent wines. Even now I can recall my morning breakfasts in a café in the main plaza, watching middle-aged men sipping coffee and brandy, huddling together against the cold in their heavy overcoats and black berets—a scene uncannily evocative of the descriptions of Spain's Basque country which I had already read in the novels of Pío Baroja. I returned home via Argentina and Uruguay, hopelessly smitten.

The burst of national interest in Latin America, which made possible my career and that of hundreds of others, had a curious and even paradoxical outcome. Far from minting a pliant corps of specialists at the service of the American empire, it created a dissident intelligentsia. In part this was so because the boom in Latin American studies overlapped the Vietnam War, which in turn created a climate of cultural disaffection in American universities that quickly swept over, and continues to dominate, those branches of international studies dealing with what used to be called the Third World.

But there was another factor as well. When we Americans went into the field to do research for our dissertations, we had to come to terms with Latin America's ultra-politically correct academic institutions, where to get along you had to go along. A lack of progressive credentials, particularly for a U. S. citizen, led to the most debilitating stigma of all: to be branded an agent of the CIA. Over time most of us were beaten down, though not merely as the result of social and professional pressures. In many cases left-wing intellectuals and politicians (often the same people) were the only Latin Americans we got to know at all well, so perhaps it is not surprisingly that so many of us readily absorbed their world view.

In my case, I can recall the exact moment at which I ran straight into the brick wall of reality. It occurred two years after my Chilean experience, when I was living in neighboring Argentina and researching my dissertation on the ideological origins of Peronism. One of my friends was an Anglo-Argentine of my own age who came from a well-to-do (but not, I suppose, strictly speaking, "oligarchical") family, and his parents occasionally invited me to dinner at their spacious penthouse overlooking the elegant suburb of Belgrano. Late that evening, after everyone else had gone to bed, the father of the family and I got to discussing agricultural policy under various Argentine governments. This subject was of more than academic interest to my host, since he owned and operated a large *estancia* in the southern part of the Province of Buenos Aires.

The conversation amounted to a lightning bolt illuminating a hitherto darkened landscape. Conventional wisdom—that is, the notions regnant in the intellectual circles I frequented—had it that Argentina's landowning class had been a particular beneficiary of *de facto* governments which had ruled after Perón's overthrow in 1955. Or stated another way, "popular" governments were hard on the landowners, whereas "oligarchical," "military," or "anti-popular" governments were particularly solicitous of their interests. My host insisted that since 1945 *no* government in Argentina, whether civilian or military, whether democratic or dictatorial, had been sympathetic to the interests of agriculture, which they regarded as a milch-cow to be squeezed for the benefit of industry. When I insisted that surely this could not be the case with the current (military) government, one of whose principal figures came from one of the country's oldest and most prominent landholding families, he insisted that it was. He even added a wealth of detail about bag taxes and other disincentives to productivity that left me frankly flabbergasted. (Later I was to read a more systematic, or as Argentines would say, "scientific" exposition of the same point in Carlos Díaz-Alejandro's *Essays in the Economic History of the Argentine Republic.*)

When I returned to the United States, I recall discussing the issue with one of the then rising stars of Latin American studies. He was not a bit interested in facts as they pertained to Argentina, or indeed anywhere else. His view was that the landowning classes in Latin America had mismanaged their patrimony, and that it was time that their land be taken from them. It was not the last of such conversations I was to have. Some years later, delivering a paper on land reform policies in Chile at Stanford University's Center for Latin American Studies, I discovered a similar disinclination. Nobody in the room questioned my facts; they preferred not to grapple with them. "I don't like this," one academic present said with admirable candor. "I can't say exactly why I don't like this—but I don't." That was that.

Thus, by gradual degrees, and in some ways without even realizing it, I became one of the "bad boys" of Latin American studies in the United States. As the old saying goes, if you have a lemon, make lemonade; and once liberated from any sense of obligation to orthodoxy, I found myself free to write about the subjects I was really interested in, and to write about them in my own way. Needless to say, this has not always evoked the deep appreciation of my colleagues, some of whom have taken the trouble to read me out of the field. But it produced a gratifying result as well, namely, that people who were not interested in Latin America at all—or at least, who supposed that they were not—suddenly discovered that there was something in it for them. It was not merely a question of an unconventional political outlook, although that was certainly there, but an approach more common to European or Asian studies, one which takes the social sciences seriously without being overwhelmed by them, and expands the boundary of a field to encompass the totality of its cultural expression. This book is a kind of display case of my method.

It consists of essays, lectures, and reviews written over the past fifteen years, covering five major areas. The first deals with issues that, though intrinsic to Spain and Latin America, have become important battlefields in our own domestic cultural wars. In particular I have singled out the frivolous debate over Columbus, which accompanied the observance several years of the 500th anniversary of his founding voyage. I have also discussed the growing presence of a Spanish-speaking (or Spanish-identified) population in the United States, and its role in the ongoing debate over multiculturalism. In this connection, I have included a short essay on Carlos Fuentes, just to show how a Mexican intellectual attempted to manipulate both subjects for a public television audience in the United States. The piece on politics and literature in Latin America shows how the process works in reverse—how, that is, revolutionary romanticism in the United States threatens to shape (or misshape) Latin America's literary patrimony.

A second section deals with three outstanding figures of Spanish and Latin American culture—Victoria Ocampo, José Ortega y Gasset, and Federico García Lorca, each illustrating in a different way the role of the intellectual in society. I have dealt here as well two outsiders, one English, another American, both of which have interpreted Spain and Spanish-America to the Anglo-Saxon world, one for good, the other for ill. The former is the late British Hispanist Gerald Brenan, whose magnificent *Literature of the Spanish People* I was lucky enough to discover as an undergraduate, but which today would be regarded as hopelessly out of date. In consigning Brenan to the black hole of memory, today's critics are not merely rejecting his old-fashioned approach, however, but an entire notion of literature. The latter is Carlton Beals, the first of a genre—the "committed" American journalist, driven by private demons, riding his revolutionary hobbyhorse in Latin America. Though Beals has been dead for decades now, his like is, alas, with us still.

The third section deals with Cuba and its revolution, which given the crucial role both played in the development of Latin American studies, hardly requires justification. However, at issue here are deeper methodological issues. Far from ratifying the "anti-imperialist" perspective, my studies of U. S. relations with Cuba (as indeed with Nicaragua, Haiti, and other client states in the Caribbean) has convinced me that far too little attention has been paid to the limits of American power. More often than not, the application of American pressure has produced results that were not sought in the first place, or at any rate, has led to outcomes very different from Washington's original intentions.

The point is not inconsequential. Even today, many otherwise well-educated people in the United States imagine that the emergence of a communist regime in Cuba the logical product of our supposed uncritical support of the dictator Fulgencio Batista. Many also believe that by our alleged uncomprehending reception of the Castro revolution, we "pushed" Cuba into the arms of the Soviet Union. Remarkably enough, some of these same people now embrace a new myth, namely, that the lack of freedom on the island today is not due to the totalitarian logic of its political system, but—to the U. S. trade embargo.

How people in the United States think about the Cuban revolution may, of course, tell us less about their knowledge of the island than their feelings about their own country. For if Castro has failed in his original objective to "turn the Andes into the Sierra Maestra," he has at least succeeded in conscripting to his enduring advantage the surviving remnants of anti-Americanism throughout the world, not just in Europe or Latin America, but in the United States itself. Indeed, these feelings have even affected the way many Americans view the Cuban-American diaspora, by any standard one of the most successful immigrant groups in the United States.

The fourth section deals with Argentina, a country with which I have had a long and intimate association. In some ways it provides a perfect counterweight to Cuba, since it was developed largely by British capital and for many decades prided itself on its cultural, economic, and political independence from Washington. Freedom from American influence did not, however, assure Argentina's admission to the progressive Kingdom of Heaven. Argentina's once orderly political life was shattered in 1930 and again in 1943, 1955, and 1976–1982, the product of party rivalries, a troubled civil-military relationship, reckless economic policies, and a profoundly divisive political mass movement, Peronism, which was a curious combination of European fascism and the American New Deal.

The chapters in this section approach the topic from rather unconventional, even oblique angles. First, I offer a personal memoir of a long morning spent with General Perón himself in Madrid in 1968. This is followed by two other essays on Argentina's more recent misfortunes—war in the South Atlantic, and the contending terrorist forces' struggle for control of the state in the 1970s. This latter episode is also relevant to U.S.-Argentine relations, since the commission appointed by President Raúl Alfonsín (1983–89) to investigate the "dirty war" against the Left identified the United States as its intellectual author. Coming as it did from so authoritative a source, this was an accusation that deserved serious attention and analysis.[2]

Like the United States, in many ways Latin America is an extension of European culture and civilization, however much Europeans persist in denying the fact. In the final section I have attempted to illustrate the ways in which this unacknowledged relationship has played itself out in widely differing locales. The final chapter, "Why Europeans Support the Sandinistas," would at first glance seem to be outdated, since the controversy of which it treats no longer exists. However, Europe's continuing sympathies, whether overt or covert, for the Castro regime in Cuba, derive from the same sources—jealousy of the United States and condescension towards Latin Americans, particularly Latin

American democrats. Moreover, some of my observations about European society, though written a decade ago, seemed upon re-reading, to be admirably prescient in the light of present-day trends.

Another chapter which appears in the first section, "The Only Hope for Latin America," may also seem to have lost currency, since it was written before Latin America was overtaken by the current wave of free-market economic reforms. It is well, however, to look back to the period before 1989, both to see exactly what it is that the reforms have replaced, and to understand why, in spite of their vast social costs, there is no real possibility of turning back.

Collections of essays are notoriously bad risks for publishers—or so I am often told. That makes my gratitude all the greater to Irving Louis Horowitz, President of Transaction Publishers, for suggesting this project and for pushing forward with it in spite of some reservations expressed by others. And I thank also my assistants Gwendolyn Wilber and Daniel Green, who addressed themselves to the arduous task of preparing the manuscript for publication.

Mark Falcoff
Washington, DC, March 1997

Notes

1. At the end of section 1, "Orphans of Utopia," I have included an account of a recent meeting of the Latin American Studies Association which affords some idea of the atmosphere which still prevails in the field. For a review of some recent literature, see my "Brilliance and Bunk in Latin American Studies," *Orbis* (Winter 1997), pp. 119–130.
2. An even more bizarre version of this point of view is offered in the American film *Apartment Zero*.

Part I

Ideas and Ideologies

1

Was 1492 a Mistake?
Did Columbus Go Too Far?

Until quite recently, Columbus's arrival in what is now the Dominican Republic on 12 October 1492, was unambiguously regarded as one of the most important and fortuitous events of human history. And Columbus himself, part mystic and dreamer, part man of science, part arbitrageur, has long embodied qualities that are particularly attractive to Americans. One hundred years ago, President Benjamin Harrison called him "the pioneer of progress and enlightenment," opening the celebrations which marked the fourth century of his voyage.

What followed in 1892 was a vast orgy of self-congratulation which lasted a full year, punctuated by brass bands, the Columbian Exposition in Chicago, even the commissioning of Antonin Dvořák's *New World* Symphony. Every age tends to rewrite history according to its own needs and prejudices, so we cannot expect nowadays to commend Columbus's voyage in quite so uncritical a fashion. But given the temper of our times and the particular drift which elite culture has taken lately in this country, that was hardly to be expected. Even so, some of the indisputable consequences of Columbus's voyage—things like the sudden radical enlargement of geographical knowledge, the exchange of plants and animals, the incorporation of a huge portion of the earth's surface into a larger economic system, the generation of new nations and cultures, not to mention the widening of the political and moral horizons of humanity—these things would seem to me to be worthy of some appreciation by even our most skeptical contemporaries. In fact, though, we haven't quite entered the quincentennial year, and already Columbus and his

January 1992 Bradley Lecture at the American Enterprise Institute.

legacy have come under what might be called a "preemptive attack" by a coalition of religious, cultural, and racial groups.

The struggle over historical meaning began, as these things so often do, with words. The term "discovery" has suddenly become suspect, since that makes it sound as if the indigenous peoples of this hemisphere existed only once the Europeans were aware of them. When you state it that way, who could disagree? But finding another word to substitute for it proved surprisingly difficult. After extensive negotiations, the Columbus Quincentenary Commission in the United States finally convinced its critics to accept a compromise. We are now to regard what happened in 1492 not as a discovery at all, but an "encounter." *Encounter*: a curious word, which sounds agreeably neutral, since it places both the discoverer and the discovered on a presumptive plane of cultural equality. But I think most people would agree that it does fail to convey the full richness of the event; we have the sense that something is clearly missing. Cultural critic John Leo put it very well recently when he said, "Encounter: as in 'my car has encountered a large truck going eighty miles an hour.'"

Clearly the struggle over terms masks deeper and more vehement emotions. After all, those who have succeeded in consigning the word "discovery" to oblivion did not set out merely to establish cultural parity between two worlds. Rather, they hoped to advance a more radical social and historical vision. The United Nations, which on these matters is almost always politically correct, discovered this as long ago as 1986, when after four years of impassioned debate, it abandoned altogether any attempt to celebrate the fifth century of America's appearance on the world map.

Here in the United States, the lead has been taken by the National Council of Churches, which refers to 1492 and all of the events which followed as "an invasion and colonization with genocide, economic exploitation, and a deep level of institutional racism and moral decadence." With an even broader brush, the American Library Association classifies the entire period of the European discovery and colonization of the Western hemisphere as the Native American Holocaust, and now urges its members to approach the Columbus celebrations from an authentic Native American perspective, dealing with topics "like cultural imperialism and colonialism."

Author Kirkpatrick Sale, whose new biography of Columbus, *The Conquest of Paradise*, appeared just in time to benefit from the new revisionist wave, prefers to condemn the great mariner for "ecocide": the destruction of the delicate balance between man and nature which presumably existed in this part of the world before his arrival. Not surprisingly, leaders of indigenous communities in the United States have had much to contribute to this discussion. According to Russell Means of the American Indian Movement, "Columbus makes Hitler look like a juvenile delinquent." Jan Elliot, a North Carolina Cherokee and editor of the monthly *Indigenous Thought* agrees and adds that "the discovery of America is nothing to celebrate, unless you want to celebrate all the lives of our people who died." An officer of the Morning Star Foundation, who happens also to be a member of the Cheyenne and Arapaho Indian nations, urges us to commemorate instead, the 500th anniversary of 1491 which she calls "the last good year." Gary Wills recently said, "A funny thing happened on the way to the quincentennial celebration of America's discovery: Columbus got mugged. This time the Indians were waiting for him." A newspaper headline summarizes the situation telegraphically: COLUMBUS, A RUTHLESS RACIST NOW, SAILS TOWARDS PUBLIC RELATIONS REEF.

It would be logical to assume that the sudden tidal wave of resistance to the Columbus celebrations is the product of new information about the man, his life, his works, findings which justify a radical reevaluation of all three. But the truth is that on those subjects we know today most of the important facts which earlier generations knew one hundred and even possibly two hundred years ago. There are still recurrent arguments about Columbus's ancestry, as well as whether he was really the first European mariner to discover the hemisphere. Lately there have been new assertions that not Columbus, but African sailors, first established the transatlantic link between the two hemispheres. But the circumstances of Columbus's voyage, as well as the short and longer term impact, have never been in doubt, including all of its unlovely aspects. These latter I will mention here, so that we get them right out of the way: the virtual obliteration of some Indian populations, the enslavement of others, and the subsequent decision to import African chattels to supplement the colonial labor force. Nor is the controversy over the moral dimension of the European conquest all that new. Actually, it is more than 300 years old, and was initiated by a Spaniard, Bartolomé de las Casas.

A soldier and a settler in Cuba and Hispaniola before taking Dominican religious orders, Las Casas was the first person in Western history to clearly raise the rights of conquered, non-Western peoples. As a demographer he left something to be desired. But as a propagandist he displayed uncommon imagination, verve, and what we would call today public relations sense. He managed to get a special hearing at a levée of the Spanish court, which was specifically convoked in Valladolid in 1550, the purpose of which was to resolve the most controversial issue of that day, namely, whether the Indians of the newly discovered lands possessed immortal souls, and therefore, ultimately deserved the same treatment as other men.

In Valladolid, Las Casas took on one of the most learned advocates in Europe, Juan Ginés de Sepúlveda, who had been retained by the Spanish settler community in America to articulate their interests. That great debate ended in a draw, but under Las Casas's influence, the Spanish monarchy eventually abolished Indian servitude in its overseas provinces, a command which was predictably unenforced, and also, unfortunately, ultimately unenforceable.

Las Casas's real contribution, however, was not legal, but ideological and historic. His *Brief History of the Destruction of the Indies*, a massive work published in 1551, is the first human rights report in history. And like a few too many such reports, it was full of tales which lost nothing in the telling. It recounts in lurid detail incidents of torture, murder, and mistreatment of the native population by ruthless Spanish adventurers, accusing his fellow countrymen of nothing less than genocide. Translated almost immediately into the major European languages and published under a new title (*Tears of the Indies*) his book became an international bestseller. Outside the Iberian peninsula, it generated an entire literature of indictment of Spain and of all things Spanish. In fact, it forms the cornerstone of the Black Legend, which is a shorthand term for the enduring notion, particularly in northern European countries, but also in the United States and also to some degree in Latin America, that Spaniards are uniquely cruel, bigoted, tyrannical, obscurantist, lazy, fanatical, greedy, and treacherous.

Las Casas's work thus marked the point of departure for another singularly Western phenomenon, a penchant for certain strains of national self-criticism to pass, sometimes imperceptibly, over into national self-hatred. Nor, finally, is the notion of pre-Columbian America as Paradise Lost something only now being discovered by our environmentalists.

Columbus's own journals make reference to the innocence and primeval charm of the Indians who approached his boats, "naked as their mothers bore them," as he writes in his diary, and the generosity and abundance of the natural environment. The concept of the Noble Savage dominates Las Casas's work, and even Spaniards who actually participated in the conquest of Mexico thought much the same, at least at first, fascinated by the complexity and sophistication of the societies which they encountered. Bernal Díaz del Castillo, who left an immortal account of the conquest of Mexico, found himself grasping for metaphors in order to describe what he saw, often drawn from the Spanish books of chivalry, which were the closest thing that his contemporaries possessed to what today would be either utopian literature or science fiction.

But it was actually in France and England that the concept of the Noble Savage and the Edenic innocence of America corrupted by Europeans probably attained its fullest expression. "Time and again," the art historian Hugh Honour has written, "the native peoples of America were dragged into court, to give evidence in theological, philosophical and political disputes, few of which had any direct reference to them." This was not because these Europeans were particularly interested in American Indians, or even America, but because they regarded the New World and its pre-Columbian civilizations as a mirror. Perhaps, more actually, the proper term would be a photographic negative, one which reflected or contrasted certain features of their own societies. By no means did all of these writers subscribe to the notion of America as Eden. For some, the native communities of the New World proved that in a state of nature, man's existence was, as Hobbes put it in his *Leviathan*, "at once solitary, poor, nasty, brutish, and short." But quite a few, including Michel Eyquem de Montaigne, and some of the French philosophes a generation or two after him, felt that such communities provided an admirable counterexample of naturalness, purity, and social harmony, as opposed to the excessive luxury and artificiality of their own court societies.

The basic brief was laid out as long ago as 1559, in a long poem by Pierre de Ronsard, which described the Indians of Brazil, as "wandering innocently, completely savage, completely naked" (interesting how often Europeans return to this aspect!) "as free from clothes as from malice, who know not the words virtue and vice, senate and king, who live according to their pleasures, satisfying their appetites, and who have in their hearts none of the terror of the law which makes us live in fear." Ronsard was particularly impressed with the fact that these Indians were apparently ignorant of the institution of private property, and therefore, he thought, untormented by the vice of ambition. "Leave them alone," he urged, "for now is their golden age."

To judge by their sheer longevity, certain ideas, however wrongheaded, must serve some very important purposes. The myth of the Noble Savage, or what I would rather call, more accurately, the Nobler Savage, seems to be open of these ideas. Echoes of Ronsard, with some intriguing modern embellishments, reverberated last year in a full-page advertisement in the *New York Times*, whose purpose was to solicit funds for a national museum of the American Indian. Those who placed this ad were not satisfied to argue, as indeed they might well have done, that these cultures constitute a vital and indispensable part of our national heritage and patrimony. Instead they insisted on attributing to the Chippewas and the Apaches, the Iroquois and the Sioux, "insight into the delicate balance between man and nature, offering us a timely environmental message. Their ethic of sharing provides an inspirational model for today's society. Their systems of governance paralleled many of the concepts used to frame the Constitution. And their views of the universe and insights into astronomy, may well help us chart our future in space."

Now, it is easier to forgive eighteenth-century Europeans for playing hard and fast with the facts about pre-Columbian America, because after all they did not have the benefit as our contemporaries now do, of the modern disciplines of history, anthropology, and archaeology. In his *Brief Relation*, Las Casas claimed that the Spaniards had killed twenty million Indians in the process of settling Hispaniola and the other islands of the Caribbean archipelago. Today we know that Columbus and his men could not have done this even if they had tried. As historian Philip Wayne Powell pointed out a few years ago in a remarkable book entitled *Tree of Hate*, "if each Spaniard listed in Bermúdez Plata's book *Passengers to the Indies*, for a whole half-century after the discovery had killed an Indian every day and three on Sunday, it would have taken a generation to do the job."

The issue here is not one of numbers alone, though perhaps it bears repeating here, however ponderous or pedantic the point may be, that exterminating the Indians was decidedly not the purpose of the conquest. The Spaniards had no interest whatever in reducing the numbers of their potential labor force, or, for that matter, the number of potential converts to Catholic Christianity. But in arriving at his figures Las Casas, and many others who followed in his tradition, did not and generally do not allow for the diminution of the indigenous populations by sheer circumstance; specifically, the lack of immunity to European disease, warfare with other tribes, culture shock, or even miscegenation, that is to say, the gradual process of integration into the newer and larger, racially mixed communities, which were created by Spanish settlement in the late sixteenth and early seventeenth centuries.

Nor do what we now know about some of the more important Indian societies provide us with much reassurance, at least for those who claim to hold in high regard such things as harmony with nature or respect for cultural or political pluralism. The Aztecs were a people of remarkable attainments, authors of a civilization, which even now, nearly four centuries extinct, invites our fascination and even our admiration. But they were an imperial race who had conquered and subordinated most of the other peoples of the Valley of Mexico, and waged relentless war upon their neighbors to extract victims for human sacrifice.

Let the record show that this form of ritualized murder was not practiced only on occasional holidays. Their cosmology told the Aztecs that the end of the world was only a matter of time, and that it could be postponed only by continually appealing to the gods with gifts of human flesh. Indeed, it was precisely the Aztecs' cruel but impersonal treatment of other peoples which rendered them uniquely vulnerable to European interlopers.

Stated baldly, Cortéz could never have destroyed the city state of Tenochtitlán with a few hundred Spaniards equipped with horses, swords, long-bows, and extremely primitive artillery. He succeeded only by grasping certain crucial geopolitical facts and striking a military alliance with the Tlaxcalans, another particularly fierce people which had never reconciled itself to subordinating itself to the Aztecs.

By the time the Spaniards reached what is now Central America, the Mayan civilization there had been in decline for several hundred years. The apparent sudden disappearance of a federation of Mayan temple cities until very recently mystified archaeologists, since they took as a given that as a people, the Mayans were a peaceful and philosophical folk—accomplished artists, poets, and astronomers.

We now know, since the first commemorative stones have been deciphered, that this is far from the case. There was no federation in the first place, nor could there be one, because the Mayans were every bit as aggressive and warlike as the Aztecs. Initially, they engaged in bizarre sadomasochistic military rituals, which recognized sharply circumscribed limits, but at one point, things veered out of control, and stylized warfare between kings degenerated into large-scale attacks on each others' cities, devastation of agricultural fields, and the wholesale murder of innocent civilians. Inscriptions on a large wall at Dos Pilas in remotest Guatemala where they were deciphered three or four years ago, bespeak the terror of a people in fear of annihilation. When asked recently by *Harper's Magazine* what the Mayans were worried about, one of the archaeologists said, "they were worried about war, ecological disaster, deforestation." And he added, "I think the population rose to the limit that technology could bear. They were so close to the edge, if anything went wrong, it was all over."

The Indians of North America were far less sophisticated than the Aztecs and Mayans, and human sacrifice as such did not play a role in their religious life. But it cannot be said that they were particularly respectful of the environment, except insofar as their small numbers and their primitive level of technology made it difficult to leave much of an impress on the lands which they occupied. The latter explains why so many lived a semi-nomadic existence as hunter-gatherers, moving on after the most obvious and immediate natural resources were exhausted. Nor were they, by and large, respectful of other Indian peoples, whom they viewed as every bit as alien as the white man. From what we know about these societies, and actually we know quite a lot, ideas like minority rights and pluralism played no role whatsoever in their political, or perhaps I should say, their prepolitical organization. With the best will in the world, it is simply not possible to be historically honest and at the same time credit them even in a parallel fashion, with the achievements of our founding fathers in Philadelphia.

It hardly needs to be said that nothing we know and nothing we are likely to yet learn, will ever justify to our contemporaries the conquest of other peoples, no matter how primitive or brutal. That is the primary point which was first made by Father Las Casas, and it is no small contribution to the development of the modern Western sensibility. But to debate these issues as if they were part of ongoing events completely upsets what I would call the apple cart of context. Las Casas wrote at a time when there was still some hope of shaping native policy in Spanish America. Today Columbus's controversy, or the Columbus controversy, is not about what to do, but at least by indirection, what should have been done.

To morally repeal the work of five centuries is quite a project, but far from being humbled by its magnitude, the revisionists rush ahead, hell-bent, forcing the rest of us to follow their argument to its logical or illogical conclusions. So let's do that for a moment. If the European discovery of America was indeed, again quoting the National Council of Churches, "an invasion and colonization, with genocide economic exploitation, and a deep level of institutional racism and moral decadence," then there can be only one historical conclusion. 1492 was a mistake. Columbus went too far. And only one historical solution: we must all mount our boats and return from whence we came.

So far of course, no revisionist has been bold or foolhardy enough to say this openly, although having been through much of the literature, I am sure it has occurred privately to more than one of them. Obviously such an undertaking would be impossible, from an economic, logistical, and human viewpoint. But there is another, more important reason for avoiding the issue. Columbus not only discovered, for at least Europeans, a new hemisphere, but in so doing, facilitated the creation of an entirely New World— new in the sense of having no prior existence. When we speak today of the United States, Canada, Mexico, Chile, Argentina, Brazil, or for that matter Cuba and the Dominican Republic, we are talking, not merely about political sovereignties which were created in the nineteenth century, but societies in the fullest sense of that term. And there is simply no way of deconstructing them into their constituent pre-and post-conquest parts.

To say that we must return from whence we came would raise the nagging question of who "we" are. And once that is done, the revisionist case loses whatever moral clarity it at first seems to possess. It also implies, and not very subtly, that the Indian peoples of the Americas, past and present, constitute a peerless repository of virtue, or rather virtues, which, when you examine them more carefully, turn out to be Western virtues, and uniquely Western virtues at that. That surely, for example, is the message of Kevin Costner's updated horse opera, *Dances With Wolves.* It is an indiscreet question, but the revisionists really don't allow us to avoid it. Are non-Western peoples better practitioners of Western values than the West? Alas, there is not much evidence that they are or were, and it is as unfair to them as to us to pretend otherwise.

Finally, there is a troubling contradiction in the critics' bill of indictment, what I would call an inexplicable lack of proportionality between the punishment and the crime. How seriously can we take accusations of genocide and ecocide and other disasters nothing short of cosmic, when the remedies to which we counseled are at best ameliorative and incremental? Here is a random list. Reading lists on the Native American Holocaust. An hour of silence at Columbus Square in New York City. Three ships to be sent back to Spain from Latin America, this time named the *Resistance*, the *Base Community* and *Liberation Theology*, instead of the *Niña*, the *Pinta*, and the *Santa María*. Efforts to repatriate Montezuma's armor from the Vienna Museum. A seminar on Women in the Americas at the Smithsonian Institution, one of whose panels is (I'm not making this up) "The Convent as a Catalyst for Autonomy." Indeed, the best that the more serious-minded can manage is a year-long program of reflection, repentance, and promises to sin no more. In this spirit, Professor Franklin B. Knight of Johns Hopkins University instructs us "to educate ourselves about a Brave New World, devoid of the arrogance and ethnocentrism of the past, in which all people are taken on their own terms, and accorded dignity and respect, the rich as well as the poor, the developed as well as the underdeveloped, the mighty and the weak, the large and the small." As the Aztecs might say, "Pretty small beer."

These and other incongruities do not trouble Columbus's contemporary critics because they are not really much interested in what happened in 1492, or even in the century or two thereafter. Theirs is a distemper with the world in which we live today. And having failed thus far to sell on the open market their political agenda, which I take to be slow-growth or no-growth, an incomes policy based on grievances rather than productivity, and redistribution of resources based on racial spoils—having failed, as I say, to sell this in the political arena, they are now trying to bludgeon it home on the cultural battlefield. In that context, the Columbus controversy is merely the latest engagement in this war.

By selecting this particular issue—let us concede the point—the revisionists and their allies have shown a certain panache. They have already managed to turn what might have been a rather dull and pro forma observance into something more controversial and even newsworthy. And before this quincentenary year is over, they will doubtless have done yet more—by leveraging the machinery of our sensitive political system, by intimidating university administrators, museum directors, and librarians, by threatening unseemly public demonstrations, and by writing large checks on this country's apparently inexhaustible fund of patience, tolerance, and basic decency. But will they succeed in what is after all their larger objective—to change the way we feel about ourselves, our country, and the larger civilization of which we are a part? Not bloody likely.

But in spite of themselves, they have already succeeded in raising some questions which are entirely appropriate to the quincentennial year, and also, I must say, to the ongoing cultural debate in our own country. According to what standards can the West be held accountable for the actions which accompanied the discovery and settlement of the Americas? The only possible answer would seem to be, its own. Do we know something today, something we did not know yesterday, that puts in a morally different light, different in the sense of inferior, the spread of European culture to the Western hemisphere? We do not. In a larger sense, has the spread of European civilization around the globe, not just in this hemisphere, been on balance a positive factor in world history? I would submit that there can be no doubt of it.

Let me take each of these points in turn. In its particulars, the Iberian conquest of the Americas was in no way different from the course of other empires in world history. Replete with murder, exploitation, the forced relocation of populations, and the destruction of whole cultures. But its moral framework was radically dissimilar. Yes, it was Spaniards who committed the abuses and crimes of the conquest, but it was also Spaniards, as the distinguished Peruvian novelist and statesman Mario Vargas Llosa has reminded us, who were the first to condemn them and demand that they be brought to an end. As Vargas Llosa puts it, "abandoning the ranks, in order to collaborate with the vanquished."

And not Spaniards by accident. Say what one will about the pre-Columbian cultures, there is simply no way that this defection could have taken place among them, where the individual had no identity apart from the collectivity, and no rights against it. "The first culture to interrogate and question itself," Vargas Llosa adds, "the first to break up the masses into individual beings, who with time gradually gained the right to think and act for themselves, by some surrealistic logic"—here, the novelist's special touch—"arrived on the sword points of invading treasure hunters, bringing to the Americas in spite of themselves, the Judeo-Christian tradition, the Spanish language, Greece, Rome, the Renaissance, the notion of individual sovereignty, and the chance of living in freedom."

Vargas Llosa thinks that it would be useless to ask whether it was good that it happened in this manner, or whether it would have been better for humanity if the individual had never been born in this part of the world, and instead, "the tradition of the ant-like societies had continued forever." I would add, not merely useless, but logically incoherent, since it calls upon us to compare two objects which are inherently unequal. On one hand, we have societies fixed once and for all, on the other, a culture which because of an inborn penchant for self-examination, is constantly evolving. That is what we are celebrating this year, not the arrival to these shores of the fifteenth-century version of Western civilization, but what it has become since, and what it may become in the future.

Even the harshest critics of our societies in this hemisphere cannot deny that over the past five hundred years, and particularly over the last two hundred, we have not precisely wallowed in a bath of complacency and self-satisfaction. After all, the Americas were the birthplace of the revolutionary idea, of political self-determination and the economic autonomy of the individual, and those who imagine that these are antiquated nineteenth- century notions which have outlived their relevance, must face the fact that today they are spreading around the world like wildfire, even to such unlikely corners as Albania and China. Now admittedly, this is not what Columbus had in mind. He set sail from Palos in southwestern Spain thinking he would eventually drop anchor in the harbors of the Great Khan in Asia. But without his journey in the first place, the history of humanity would have been very different, and I submit, very much darker.

Nor is this merely a matter of historical speculation. We do in fact have a way of testing the proposition. The entire period since 1945 has been one long orgy of anticolonialism throughout much of Africa and Asia, and milder forms of anti-Western sentiment in much of Latin America. And what we have learned from recent experience in these places, is that the decline of the West, that is, a country's withdrawal from or expulsion of Western influence, does not in fact, lead to the rise of the not-West. Quite the contrary. It leads to less freedom, not more; less human dignity, not more; less food, not more; less health not more; less education, not more; not progress, but regression.

The failure of anti-Western ideologies on the ground, in Cuba and Angola, in Vietnam and Mozambique, in Algeria, Syria, and Iraq, ought to give greater pause to the critics of Western civilization, currently trying to hitch a free ride home on Columbus's caravels. The case of Algeria is particularly instructive. Having gained its independence from France in 1962, today that hapless country lives off the remittances of its people fortunate enough to have found a home in the former colonial metropolis. While the winds of political liberalization sweep the globe, Algerians are forced to take shelter behind a ramshackle Marxist dictatorship, itself the perversion of a Western ideal, in order to ward off the threat of something even worse: a particularly ugly form of Islamic fundamentalism. On one point, however, the critics of Columbus are not wrong. His voyage is indeed a proper metaphor for the spread of Western influence throughout the world. That influence is once again on the rise, this time not on the sword points of treasure hunters, but under its own flags, and by the sheer force of its ideas. As Western civilization becomes, increasingly, a universal ideal, the distinction between discoverers and discovered will become meaningless. And a hundred years from now, the Columbus controversy will seem even more bizarre and incomprehensible than it does to us today.

2

Beyond Bilingualism

The United States of America is the most powerful exponent of the English language in the world today; paradoxically, it is also one of the major forces for the diffusion of Spanish. Although exact statistics are hard to come by, between 13 and 14 million people within our borders speak Spanish as a first language, and perhaps just as many can use it at home to address their parents and grandparents. This means that in raw statistical terms the United States is more important in the constellation of Spanish—speaking countries than Uruguay, Ecuador, or Chile, or the five Central American republics and Panama combined. In sheer numbers it is only slightly less important than Argentina.

But numbers alone do not tell the whole story. Today some of the most important television and radio transmissions in the Spanish language originate in the United States. We have a vigorous daily, weekly, and monthly Spanish-language press. The importation of books in Spanish is growing by leaps and bounds, although some major American publishers are setting up to print Spanish-language novels, essays, and works of nonfiction for direct distribution to mainstream bookstores. Finally, in a country so persistently incurious about other cultures, at any given day nearly 3 million students are agonizing over the difference between *ser* and *estar*. By several orders of magnitude Spanish is, in fact, the most widely studied foreign language in the United States.

Yet in North America a deep current of Hispanophobia pervades Anglo-Saxon culture. It predates the independence of the United States by almost two centuries, a legacy of the English and the Dutch, who did so much to promote the Black Legend of Spanish cruelty as part of their own efforts to seize for themselves Spain's extensive colonial empire. Anti-Spanish attitudes in the American colonies were nourished as well by the militant Protestant theology that so sharply defined the Puritan communities of New England. As early as the late seventeenth century, we find Puritan divines like Cotton Mather and Samuel Sewell studying Spanish—with a view to winning converts to their version of Protestantism. Sewell spoke of "bombing [sic] Santo Domingo, Havana, Puerto Rico, and Mexico itself" with the Spanish Bible, and Cotton Mather even wrote a book on Protestant doctrine in Spanish, published in Boston in 1699, intended for—as he might say—the darker regions of Spanish America.

Disillusionment with Southern Neighbors

The emergence of an independent American republic reinforced these anti-Spanish notions, notwithstanding the fact that Spain had been an ally in our struggle against Great Britain. The American revolution was if nothing else a protest against the monarchical principle, against a state church, large standing armies, primogeniture, and the colonial principle. As one of the three pillars of the Holy Alliance, Spain set itself up as a frontline state in the defense of these institutions. Second, when the new republic felt sufficiently consolidated to think of expansion south and west, it ran up against what one historian called the Spanish-American frontier—in the Old Southwest, in the Floridas, in the Mississippi Valley.

By declaring their independence from Spain, the Spanish-American republics momentarily redeemed themselves in the eyes of their North American counterparts. But as their efforts to consolidate these new states faltered, and the institutions inherited from Spain periodically reasserted their hegemony, North Americans became disillusioned with their southern neighbors. Indeed, one might say that the image of Latin America went back and forth throughout the nineteenth century, according to the perception of who was winning in the cultural civil wars there, Rosas or Sarmiento, García Moreno or Montalvo—in effect, the Inquisition or the Enlightenment. To some degree this ambivalent attitude toward Latin America continues to the present day—complicated by the question of illegal immigration.

Anti-Spanish attitudes in the United States reached something of a paroxysm during the war in Cuba in 1898. But, paradoxically, once the conflict ended and our quondam Cuban allies turned out to be something less than impressive when viewed at close range, we suddenly discovered the nobility and dignity of our defeated adversary. The Spanish admiral who went to Newport, Rhode Island, to escort home naval prisoners of war was received with so much cordiality by his hosts that he went home disoriented and confused. Of course, by then the United States could afford to be generous, since it had just liquidated the remnants of Spain's colonial empire and had effectively occupied and colonized the former Spanish territories in the South and West of the North American continent. In places like California and New Mexico the Spanish language was in full retreat.

The Disaster of 1898

For Spaniards 1898 was "the disaster" that set into motion a major movement of reflection, self-criticism, and self-examination. The political and ideological consequences of this movement were by no means simple; in effect, it forked off into at least two major variants, which for reasons of convenience we might call "conservative" and "liberal," although perhaps the terms traditionalist and renovating might be more exact. For the former, Spain's decline was the consequence of its betrayal of a glorious heritage and of excessive pandering to the intellectual and social trends of Northern Europe. Only by remaining true to its own historic identity could Spain recover the hold it once had over the imagination of half the known world.

But for the liberal variant, Spain's failure to embrace wholeheartedly the values of science, modernity, and progress were the precise cause of its backwardness and the loss of its influence overseas. Over time, the prescriptions offered by each side became diametrically opposed and found their expression—first, in the creation of the Second Republic and then in the Spanish civil war (1936–1939).

Americans, of course, had no trouble recognizing in the concept of *Hispanidad*, the forces that their ancestors had rejected from the seventeenth century. At the same time, the more enlightened, liberal version of Spanish patriotism—*Hispanismo*–and its most concrete expression, the Second Republic, found ready acceptance and sympathy in the United States. Indeed, if the civil war did nothing else, it forced Americans to consider the possibility that Spain contained within itself sharply divergent political and cultural syntheses. For a brief moment Spain even became a focus of utopian sensibilities, particularly after the Republic adopted some of the styles, language, and customs of the militant international left.

The victory of the insurgent side extinguished this utopian vision or consigned it to the area of nostalgia and fantasy. In the future, such urges found outlet in Cuba and (briefly) in Allende's Chile and in Sandinista Nicaragua. In the immediate aftermath of the civil war, the vision was replaced by the romance of defeat, best expressed in Hemingway's novel, *For Whom the Bell Tolls*. As time went on, however, and the Franco regime consolidated its iron grip, Hemingway's writings on Spain—like those of lesser American writers such as Barnaby Conrad—became increasingly apolitical. This trend is foretold in *Death in the Afternoon*, where the tension between *Hispanidad* and *Hispanismo* (between "bad" Spain and "good" Spain) is replaced by a kind of cheap *costumbrismo:* castanets, bullfights, Carmen, and the cult of danger, against an inviting backdrop of good weather, good wine, and bargain prices for tourists lucky enough to draw their salaries in dollars.

Of course, Hemingway was far from the first Anglo-Saxon writer to romanticize Spanish distinctiveness (or backwardness, or both). But his doing so is remarkable in light of his own earlier political trajectory and underscores the degree to which the Franco regime and the circumstances of cold war politics forced those with a continuing interest in Spain to choose between loathing and denial. By the time of Franco's death, Spanish cultural issues had ceased to play any important role in the United States, so thoroughly indeed that Spain's transition to democracy—a drama utterly central to people living under authoritarian regimes of a similar stripe—went virtually unnoticed.

Washington's Shifting Interests

Meanwhile, the focus of U.S. attention to the Spanish-speaking world shifted south. In the run-up to the Second World War the Roosevelt administration fashioned something called the Good Neighbor Policy, which was intended to conscript America's Latin neighbors into a quasi-alliance in exchange for concessions on trade and promises of nonintervention. But once the war was won, Washington's interest shifted elsewhere, and its concern for its southern neighbors was limited to the quality of their anticommunism.

The next defining event was the Cuban revolution, which frightened American élites (and the American public as well) with the prospect of a continental movement with potentially catastrophic geopolitical consequences. The Kennedy administration's response to this challenge included not merely a massive program of economic, technical, and military aid, but increased funds for language teaching, the creation of the Peace Corps, and intensified cultural exchange.

While this project was eventually derailed by the Vietnam War, it created an entire generation of American specialists in Latin America, some of whom are serving today in the highest positions of the Clinton administration, the foreign service, the academy, and the media. It also offered immediate employment to thousands of Cuban teachers who, fleeing the Castro regime, colonized the Spanish departments of American universities.

A Flood of Immigrants

Another watershed was the gradual loosening of restrictions on immigration from the Western Hemisphere. Until about 1961, U.S. entry quotas were based on an explicit commitment to replicate the ethnic makeup of the country as it had been in 1920—which is to say, a society made up largely of people of British, German, and Scandinavian origin. By the 1960s, however, economic growth in Western Europe had caused many of those quotas to go unfulfilled. Meanwhile, the United States was critically short of many skills that were abundantly available in Latin America: hence the decision to open our borders, starting with qualified immigrants like physicians, scientists, and educators.

As is the case with most government policies, what started out as a trickle eventually became a flood. Every immigrant admitted under special dispensation had not merely a wife and children, but parents, aunts, uncles, cousins, all of whom wanted to come too.

Meanwhile, the economic growth of the American Southwest, particularly its agricultural sectors, led to a rising demand for cheap labor of a type no longer available locally. Most of it ended up coming from Mexico, to such a dramatic degree that one Mexican diplomat not long ago referred (somewhat indiscreetly, to be sure) to the massive Mexican repopulation of regions lost in the war of 1848 as *la reconquista*.

The political and economic turmoil of Latin America has produced large spurts of outmigration to the United States. The Cuban diaspora began in the 1960s and, though it has known moments of remission, has never really ceased. Today there are at least 1.5 million Cubans living in the United States, with the present administration committed to taking an additional 20,000 a year for the indefinite future. In the case of Mexico, the periodic financial crises that unfailingly come at the end of every six-year presidential term there redoubled the numbers that would normally have come to work in agriculture.

Disorder and repression during the 1970s brought large numbers of immigrants from such nontraditional sources as Argentina, Uruguay, and Chile. At the end of the decade, civil wars in El Salvador, Nicaragua, and Guatemala transferred a significant number of Central Americans to the United States. Even countries with happier political conditions like Costa Rica have come to export most of their exchange students and many of their more ambitious professionals. As of this writing, Los Angeles is now the second city of Mexico, Guatemala, and Costa Rica, while Miami is the second city of Cuba, Panama, and Haiti and is in active contention with Los Angeles and New York for the same position with respect to Colombia, Venezuela, and many other places.

A New Spoils System

The civil rights revolution in the United States has led to a new politics of racial and ethnic spoils, or what I like to call "leveraged victimhood." This policy was originally crafted to compensate African-Americans for past discrimination but has been extended since to cover other groups who can advance some plausible historic grievance. In this they have been assisted by the U.S. Census Bureau, which now classifies Americans into a half-dozen racial or ethnic categories to assist social engineering.

Hence we now have something called a "Hispanic," which describes not someone born in a Spanish-speaking country, nor someone who speaks Spanish well or badly, nor even someone with a Hispanic surname, but someone who identifies himself as such. This of course covers a wide range of possibilities, from expatriate members of the Spanish nobility or former plantation owners in Cuba to the most recently arrived agricultural laborer or unemployed migrant. In between is a vast ocean of Americans who may speak Spanish at home and English outside of it, or Americans who are of Latin American origin (recognizably or not) but whose habits, food preferences, language, and lifestyles in no way resemble those of their grandparents.

Moreover, differences in social and educational level produce a troubling linguistic paradox: immigrants drawn from the professional classes in Latin America tend to speak the best Spanish, but at the same time their children also learn English better and more rapidly and integrate more completely into American society. The poorer strata from Mexico and Central America speak Spanish with a very limited vocabulary—sometimes as little as 2,000 words—and are often functionally illiterate but resist linguistic assimilation more firmly and more successfully. Their children often speak both English and Spanish with an accent.

These complexities help to explain the inconclusive nature of the current conflict over bilingualism in the United States. On one hand, the widespread use of Spanish here is a reality that cannot be changed, even over the longer term, because the Spanish-speaking population is being continually replenished by newcomers faster than that population is being assimilated. On the other, the shortage of people who can teach in proper Spanish, combined with the pressures of the marketplace and America's trashy but pervasive popular culture, provides more than ample assurance that English will remain the dominant language of the United States for the indefinite future. Advocates of unilingualism may win symbolic victories, such as the exclusive use of English on ballot papers or government forms, but short of a major change in immigration policy—sustained over at least two decades—Spanish will continue to be the most widely spoken second language in the country.

Unlike other countries with more evolved bilingual cultures, however, such as Canada, Belgium, or Switzerland, the United States has no stable intellectual class to maintain a consistent level of quality in the country's second language. What we have instead are expatriate academics recruited to teach Spanish to (largely inattentive) Anglophone students at colleges, universities, or secondary schools. At the same time, Spanish is not, regrettably, taken seriously as the source of a great literary tradition in its own right.

A Short Cultural Memory

This reflects, in the first instance, the life experiences of children of Spanish-speaking families. Their parents tend to come from countries where they were cheated out of a decent secondary education and where books were an expensive and apparently useless luxury. At the same time, the cultural memory of many of America's Spanish-speaking citizens is remarkably short. This point was forced upon me some years ago while teaching a course on the history of Mexico at a West Coast university. All the Mexican-American students in the class were astounded at the goings on in nineteenth-century Mexico: the conflict over church lands, civil-military rivalries, the struggle to secularize education, the Indian question, Maximilian and Carlota—it was all new to them. They thought that Mexican history was "about" Villa and Zapata! The sentimentality surrounding these two figures for younger Mexican-Americans masks an inconvenient fact, namely, that the glorious revolution of which they are so proud was responsible for 2 million deaths, many of them from hunger, and may well have provoked their grandparents' decision to emigrate to the United State in the first place.

Moreover, unlike, let us say, Greek-Americans or Italian-Americans or Irish-Americans, the "Hispanic" has no country of origin. His identity is a creation of Anglo-America, which fails to differentiate between Cubans and Mexicans, Panamanians and Argentines, Bolivians and Hondurans. This expresses Anglo-America's geographical ignorance, racial prejudices ("they all look alike"), and lack of interest in anything different from itself. But not too much should be made of the chauvinistic aspect, because the United States today is not the same country it was in 1898 or even 1953. Over the past thirty years Anglo-America has suffered a serious crisis of cultural self-confidence, and no longer believes in the value of its own traditions or heritage. Spaniards who deplore our ignorance of Cervantes and Lorca can take some comfort—cold comfort though it may be—that our children today can hardly identify Shakespeare or Whitman. Meanwhile, our social and cultural elites regard manifestations of national pride as evidence of bad taste and lack of sophistication.

The "Hispanic" is also a creation of professional "Hispanics," which in most cases are either Mexican-American or Puerto Rican politicians and activists, seeking to intermediate permanently between the "white power structure" (as they would call it) and populations who still feel a sense of cultural and economic powerlessness. Some of the things they do—such as fight discrimination in employment or housing, or demand greater access to public services, or help immigrants adjust to a new life in the United States—are commendable, although other organizations, such as trade unions, ethnic business associations, and the Roman Catholic and Pentecostal churches actually do a more effective job at all three.

Permanent State of Limbo

But just as there is no *patria* for the Hispanic, neither is it clear exactly what his purpose may be in the United States—except, ultimately, to resemble the rest of us. Even the most militant Mexican-American does not favor the partition of California and the Western United States and their return to Mexico. Indeed, the logic of most of "Hispanic" demands for greater access to economic opportunity leads ineluctably to greater integration, including linguistic integration and the diluting of a distinctive "racial" or cultural identity. For the moment, at least, the "Hispanic" leaders in the United States do not have to confront this contradiction, since for every "Hispanic" who is becoming integrated into Anglo-America, one is every day beginning the long journey all over again.

To keep our Spanish-speaking population in a permanent limbo of semi-powerlessness, the professional "Hispanics" are assisted by the Anglo-American liberal. For him "Hispanic" is a social or political category, not a cultural one (or it is cultural only to the extent that culture is "about" deprivation, oppression, or discrimination). He is led to support a "Hispanic" agenda—let us say, bilingual education—not because he has some grasp of the great traditions of the Golden Age or knows the splendid novel of manners of the nineteenth century or the sublime poetry of Rubén Darío or Antonio Machado, but out of guilt, snobbery, or a desire to differentiate himself from our xenophobic populist right.

Taking Spanish Culture Seriously

Four points stand out in this vast canvas. First, whatever else can be said about the seventeenth-century American Puritans, at least they took Spanish culture seriously. They recognized it as a complete civilization in its own right, an alternate pole of attraction for roughly half our hemisphere. They bothered to learn its language to better confront it. While we can smile at their religious prejudices and exaggerated sense of cultural self-assurance, our present-day doubts about ourselves have not made us more curious about others, except insofar as they send back negative refractions of our own image.

Second, the diffusion and widespread use of Spanish in the United States today in no way constitutes a threat to the use and—dare I say it?—the hegemony of English. While there are centrifugal forces at work in American society today, language is not one of them. The status of Spanish in the United States is different from that of, say, Catalan in Spain, since it lacks territoriality, a coherent literary-intellectual class, and an imaginable political project. While a combination of leftish social engineering and political opportunism have created a new protected category of citizen, his identity is determined not by language but by surnames, physiognomy, or self-definition.

Third, there is no dominant definition of *Hispanidad* or *Hispanismo* in the United States, nor is there likely to be in the future. Here the contrast with French is instructive. It is Paris and the French Academy that define Frenchness in the world, including received pronunciation— all other manifestations of the language and culture are seen as subordinate variations. The irrelevance of Madrid and the Spanish Academy to our Spanish-speaking populations reflects the historic rupture between the peninsula and Spanish America in the nineteenth century, but it also bespeaks the increasing diversity of America's immigrant communities.

"Hispanic" has become a political, not a linguistic or cultural category, to which language is purely incidental. Like so much else in American political life, the issue of cultural diversity has been trivialized and made a toy of the bureaucratic process. In some countries the existence of two vigorous languages side by side provides an interesting tension, and in the Canadian case, even a crucial element of national self-definition. The United States is apparently large enough and rich enough to ignore its own linguistic geography. And so Spanish remains a foreign language in more ways than one, bringing a centuries-old cultural rivalry to a sharp and unexpected conclusion.

3

The Only Hope for Latin America

As the twentieth century nears its final decade, the forces which have shaped the entire postwar era appear at long last to be in definitive decline. At any rate, it seems virtually certain that in the coming years various regions and powers will play roles very different from the ones they have played for nearly half a century. The United States—somewhat recovered from Vietnam but apparently lacking the political will to continue as a great power—debates what role its resources will allow it to play. Within three years, the countries of the European community will open their borders to one another, creating what may well be the world's largest and most powerful economic unit. The imminent end of the cold war has been announced, and major trends in West German opinion suggest the revival of an idea at least as old as Bismarck, namely, that Germany's interests lie to the East, not the West. Japan, defeated and humiliated by the United States in 1945, now holds the key to New York's financial markets, and therefore the entire economic well-being of its erstwhile conqueror. Korea, once a ward of American charity, has become a major industrial power in its own right, expanding its hold on some of the most competitive (and lucrative) Western markets.

In the so-called Third World, the picture is radically different. There, at least to judge by reports in the press, the characteristic motifs are internecine conflict, social regression, and sharp economic decline. This is most dramatically evident in Latin America, whose real per capita Gross Domestic Product (GDP) has declined by at least 1.5 percent since 1980. In every rubric used by international agencies or development organizations to measure well-being—consumer price levels, investment, exports, imports, or the proportion of external debt to exports—the region as a whole has moved backward, in some cases precipitously so. It is perhaps the only Westernized region of the world with good reason to fear the twenty-first century.

This is a fairly astounding development when one reflects upon the fact that these figures subsume not merely backward tropical republics like Honduras or Paraguay but sophisticated urban societies like Brazil, Argentina, Colombia, and Venezuela—nations which ranked in the second tier of powers after the Second World War; which registered fairly respectable rates of growth for the first six or seven decades of the twentieth century; and which still produce large numbers of talented and energetic scientists, engineers, physicians, technocrats, intellectuals, and skilled workers, many of whom have quit their places of origin for Western Europe or the United States, or are in the process of doing so.

The loss of international status has been both relative and absolute, and over the years a new rhetoric has come into existence to explain the current state of affairs, as well as to make certain that the blame is placed as far from home as possible. During the 1960s, the dominant themes of public discourse in Latin America were the allegedly "unequal terms of exchange" of goods and services or the supposed machinations of the "transnational corporations." In the 1970s, all ills, economic and otherwise, were attributed to the lack of democratic government, due, supposedly, to the export of militarism and "McCarthyism" by the United States. In the 1980s, the new explanation has become the burden of Latin America's huge public and private debt. This is certainly not negligible; in 1988 it was estimated at somewhat in excess of $400 billion, the service on which represented slightly more than 42 percent of the value of exports. "The status quo is intolerable," states one report by a multinational commission. "As long as Latin America must pay out substantially more in interest than it obtains in new loans, the region will remain stuck on a treadmill of austerity, stagnation, and rising debt," the report continues, and concludes that the weakest performing economies of the region "require outright relief from a significant share of their obligations."

Some Latin American political leaders have gone considerably further than this, demanding not merely debt relief or debt forgiveness, but the massive transfer of new resources, such as those which the Soviet Union and the United States will presumably possess as a result of the new nuclear weapons agreement with the Soviet Union and the general disarmament process. As Vice President Julio Garret Ayllon of Bolivia—by no means a man of the Left—recently stated, it would be terrible if funds excised from Western military budgets ended up being utilized by the industrialized countries to "improve and increase their technological development, thus postponing the aspirations of the underdeveloped countries which are greater in number and have the highest mortality, unemployment, and illiteracy rates."

Thus in a mere twenty years the political agenda in Latin America has gone from the need to liberate oneself from foreign economic influence and U. S. "imperialism" to asserting the obligation of the quondam imperialists to rescue societies on the verge of economic collapse. In times past, even quite irrational economic demands could be made more palatable by invoking the larger security imperative; in the post-cold war world, the Latin Americans may find it significantly more difficult to get Washington to return their calls, much less to earmark for them larger portions of its dwindling budget for overseas assistance.

In no country is this dilemma placed in sharper relief than Peru, where the rate of inflation in 1988 reached 1,722 percent, more than ten times its previous record (158.3 percent) just three years ago. Personal income has declined steadily over the last ten years, and is now at the level of 1968. Massive strikes, often degenerating into violence, have become a commonplace, and only the sure conviction that a coup would lead to international isolation and sanctions by the U.S. Congress has prevented the armed forces, which gave up power to civilians in 1979, from seizing it once again. As if this were not enough, Peru is afflicted with a peculiar guerrilla movement, the so-called Shining Path (*Sendero Luminoso*), which probably constitutes no more than 3,000 persons, but is capable of blacking out Lima, the capital, or other Peruvian cities at will, and posing a serious security threat in many areas of the countryside.

As in most Latin American countries, in Peru the contrast between rich and poor, between haves and have-nots, is enormous, though not for lack of attempts at a radical solution. In fact, Peru has already had its revolution, complete with land reform, self-governing "industrial communities," expropriation of foreign oil companies, expulsion of the U.S. military mission, and the purchase of arms from the Soviet Union—all under a leftist military junta which was in power from 1968 to 1975. These policies bore a remarkable resemblance to those of Marxist Salvador Allende in neighboring Chile (1970–73). Indeed, the results were much the same—the only difference being that, having a military government to start with, the experiment ended not in a coup but in the surrender of authority to hapless civilians.

As far as Peru has gone, this would appear to some to be not far enough. The current president, Alan García Pérez, is a firebrand of the Latin American populist Left who took office in 1985 determined to square accounts with the United States and the International Monetary Fund, both of whom he held responsible for his country's problems. During the first two years of García's term, Peru reduced payments on its foreign debt (then estimated at $14 billion) to 10 percent of its export revenues; for a brief period the country enjoyed a modest consumer boom before it became apparent that debt service was only a small part of its economic problems. García's popularity, which was 67 percent at the beginning of his term, now hovers in the low teens, and sophisticated observers have reason to think that he has been actively conniving at a coup of his own as the only way of assuring his political future six or seven years hence. At this juncture, the Marxist mayor of Lima, José Barrantes, appears the most likely successor to García in next year's elections, though Barrantes may not successfully turn aside a mounting challenge from the novelist Mario Vargas Llosa, a political newcomer who is perhaps the most famous living Peruvian. If Barrantes does win, it will be interesting to see if an explicitly Marxist president can go farther than his predecessor in hurling the country backward toward the sixteenth century.

Peru would seem, then, to be a case study in the apparently limitless capacity of Latin American societies for self-mutilation. However, this may be true only at the level of public (that is, explicitly political) life. Beneath the surface there is another reality which holds out some hope for Peru's future and that of societies like it. Such, at any rate, is the import of Hernando De Soto's new book, *The Other Path*, which has already captured the imagination of readers in nearly two dozen Spanish-speaking countries, and is now available in English.[1] On one level, *The Other Path* is a study of how the Peruvian economic system actually works, to whose benefit, and at what cost. But on another level, De Soto's book amounts to a countermanifesto to what passes for "development economics" in Latin America (as well as the United States and Western Europe), and an alternative theory of economic history. This is a great deal to ask of a single volume, yet De Soto carries it off with surprising success. At any rate, the study, which was conducted by the Institute for Liberty and Democracy (ILD) in Lima, a think-tank which De Soto heads, raises questions that will be difficult to ignore, and presents data that must either be refuted, or provoke some radical rethinking at places like the U.S. Agency for International Development and other bodies charged with the allocation of assistance to Third World countries.

The Other Path shows that there are two ways of looking at societies like Peru—either by measuring their economic performance in terms of the amount of wealth generated by enterprises licensed by the government (the "formal sector"), or by looking at their underground economies (the "informal sector"). In the case of Peru, it is De Soto's contention that in recent years fully 48 percent of the economically active population, representing 61.2 percent of all hours worked, has been engaged in informal activities which have contributed 38.9 percent of the GDP recorded in the country's national accounts. Without this informal sector, Lima today would have almost no housing and virtually no public transportation.

Like most Third World capitals, Lima has mushroomed into a sprawling metropolis over the last forty years, largely as the result of migration from rural areas. On paper, this growth has been strictly controlled by laws governing zoning and licensing. In fact, virtually the totality of the postwar city has been created in defiance of the law, successive portions having been gradually incorporated into the existing system through a succession of amnesties and recognitions purchased by pledges of political support to a succession of governments of the most varied ideological complexions.

Like most Latin American governments, one regime after another in Peru has come to power committed to "affordable housing." According to ILD calculations, between 1960 and 1984, the state invested $173.6 million in housing, much of it presumably from foreign assistance. Yet this amounts to a mere 2.1 percent of the resources put into housing by the informal sector. In 1984 the total value of informal housing—that is, housing built without a permit—in Lima was in excess of 58 billion, and what is perhaps more to the point, equivalent to 69 percent of the country's long-term external debt in the same year.

Clearly, there is still a housing shortage in Lima, but not from lack of energy, capital, or commitment on the part of Peruvians, who have managed to circumvent the state and outperform it—spectacularly so.

The story is the same in public transportation. De Soto's group discovered that in 1984 fully 91 percent of the facilities in Lima were being operated informally, by a fleet of buses, minibuses, and taxis, representing 41.2 percent of all public investment in Peru. Again, the contrast with the state is instructive. In 1973 the "reformist" military junta attempted to create the Metropolitan Federation of Transport Cooperatives. Though by the end of 1982 the Federation had received $12.9 million in subsidies, its fleet had actually declined in size—from 285 to 189 vehicles. Were President García (or his successor) to decide to outlaw the vast pirate armada of vehicles which provides the capital with transportation, he would have to come up with $620 million in replacement costs, leaving aside an additional $400 million in infrastructure (gas pumps, repair shops, and so forth).

These figures point to a fact often missed by journalists, diplomats, international civil servants, and humanitarians, namely, that the structure and dimensions of employment in Peru (and, presumably, other countries like it) are very different from those set forth in official figures. Quite apart from the people engaged in construction and transport, De Soto's group has found that fully 314,000 people in Lima are dependent upon street vending, which in 1985 represented $6.2 million worth of sales a week, $322.2 million a year. The net per capita income from street vending was $58 a month, which may not seem like much to Americans, but is nearly four times the legal minimum wage. Technically, street vending is either illegal or subject to a welter of regulations tending to limit its extent, and various Peruvian governments have tried to circumscribe it by building markets where small-scale commercial transactions can take place. There are in fact some 57 of these markets in Lima, but the ILD has discovered that there are another 274 which officially do not exist—four out of five.

One might well ask why so large a part of the Peruvian economy is underground. The answer is that over the last two generations at least, every government, whether civilian or military, Left, Right, or Center, has enacted a welter of regulations whose effect is to stifle enterprise. In order to document the full dimensions of this problem, the Institute for Liberty and Democracy actually undertook to "walk through" a series of operations. Its researchers found that to get a building permit required eighty-three months of applications, litigation, and waiting. It took twenty-six months to obtain approval of a minibus route. To build a market, an average of seventeen years was required, De Soto reports, "from the formation of a mini-market until the market proper comes into operation." If someone were foolhardy enough to stay the course until a small industrial firm were finally established legally, which would take quite literally years, he would discover that to remain formal would cost 347.7 percent of the firm's after-tax profits and 11.3 percent of its production. "In other words," De Soto notes, "for every $100 that a small industrial firm must pay in order to remain legal, $22 goes to taxes, $73 to other legal costs, and $5 to utilities...The company's prosperity depends less on how well it does its work than on the costs imposed on it by law." Small wonder that so many people have deserted to informality.

An even more interesting question is why the Peruvian state would wish to stifle enterprise in the first place, particularly since the main effect of such a policy is to shrink its own tax base. The answer is that the organizing principle of all government activity in Peru (and indeed, in almost all Latin American countries) is to distribute income—and unearned income at that—rather than generate it. This, according to De Soto, has "transformed us into a democracy of pressure groups." He goes on:

> A legal system whose sole purpose is redistribution....benefits neither rich nor poor, but only those best organized to establish close ties with the people in power.
> It ensures that the businesses that remain in the market are those that are most efficient politically, not economically....
> Thus, redistributive laws ultimately politicize all sectors of the population. which try to organize in order to live at the other's expense. Consumers press for prices below competitive levels, wage earners press for wages above them, established businesspeople try to prevent or delay any innovation that might damage their position, and employees exert pressure to keep their jobs and avoid replacement by more efficient workers.

> The system has forced all of us to become experts in obtaining protection or advantages from the state.... Some of the country's best talent and... best hours are spent on waging redistributive wars instead of achieving real progress.

This point becomes clearer when one turns to the specifics. The reason Lima has almost no legal public transportation is that over the years the government has imposed a series of controls on fares which are, to put it mildly, economically irrational. After these regulations drove several companies out of business, the state took them over, pumped millions of dollars into subsidizing them, and the fleet still shrank in size. However, the larger political purposes of the government were served—it could prove it was "caring" because it refused to buckle under to pressures to raise fares. The dirty secret is that if all Peruvians had obeyed the law, the city of Lima would have come to a total standstill.

There are many ways in which the explosion of Peru's informal sector can be regarded as a sign of the fundamental health of the society—its capacity to negotiate past irrational obstacles; the working energies of its people; the entrepreneurial skills which require no injection of "foreign aid" to blossom; the sheer power to create wealth by people who are, inevitably, very poor by Western standards. But as De Soto points out, two economic systems operating at cross purposes exact an unusually high price. The informals must disperse employees among a number of smaller and less visible workplaces, preventing the creation of critical mass or economies of scale. They cannot advertise their goods and services. They are fearful of entering certain markets. They are undercapitalized because they have no access to major sources of credit: even if they did, they would be hesitant to invest in certain major capital improvements lest they attract government attention.

There is also a point beyond which informal enterprises cannot expand. Because they are not legally recognized they cannot transfer their property easily; they cannot sell shares; they cannot convert debts into shares; they have great difficulty obtaining insurance; they must spend substantial amounts defending their possessions. In matters such as housing, there is a strong temptation to invest disproportionately in moveable objects (household electrical fixtures, for example) rather than in piping, drainage, and roofing. There is a tendency to rely upon word-of-mouth and personal recommendations rather than allow production, labor, and capital markets to remain wide open "and so achieve both economies of scale and increasingly efficient specialization."

Even so, the informals are hardly irrelevant to the formal system. That is, though they do not pay direct taxes on operations, they transfer resources to the government and other formal institutions through indirect taxation, inflation, and differences in the interest rate which they must pay to private and small-scale lenders. In 1985, for example, the ILD estimates that $1.367 billion—or 9.5 percent of the GDP—was transferred to the state from the informals. As De Soto points out, "This would have more than covered the central government's entire investments for that year, which came to $465 million."

De Soto's description of the Peruvian economy is redolent not of socialism but of the corporate state, with one major difference—successive governments have not succeeded in making the official structures coterminous with the system as a whole. Instead, there are really two Perus, one whose objective is to redistribute wealth, no matter how much this reduces the actual amount of wealth available (the formal sector), and another which operates according to the normal law of supply and demand, but given the legal context, must limit its scope and reach, lives in fear of discovery, and inevitably contributes less to society and to the state than it otherwise might do (the informals).

What De Soto suggests is that Peru is living in two historical times at once—officially, it inhabits a period similar to that of Western Europe during the reign of mercantilism; unofficially, it is battering down the walls that separate it from the modern world. In order to illustrate the metaphor, De Soto devotes an entire chapter to comparative history, reminding us that for a very long period countries like England and France were organized in ways not very different from contemporary Peru. They too "had to support a large number of unproductive bureaucrats and lawyers, who served only to wrap, unwrap, and rewrap [their] countries' subjects in laws which controlled, distributed, redistributed, and assigned the privileges which strengthened the state and favored certain entrepreneurs." This approach was perhaps understandable in a period when most societies were isolated from one another; when levels of technology were abysmally low;

when life expectancy was short; and when the notion of a finite universe was a logical response to the perceived environment. No such excuses can be provided to any state in the contemporary world, least of all in Latin America.

De Soto goes even further, and provides an entirely new twist to Marx's theory of historical development. He argues that the degree to which European societies have succeeded in making the transition to modernity and democracy depends directly upon their capacity to make the jump from mercantilism to capitalism. This provides him with a continuum, with England on one end, France in the center, and Russia on the far side. "The lesson to be learned from Europe," he writes,

> is that a declining mercantilist government which resists the necessary institutional changes is opening the door wide to violence and disorder. It may delay the final outcome at the cost of repression and considerable suffering, but sooner or later the contradictions will probably be solved either by a Communist dictatorship or by coexistence within a democratic system and a market economy.

Some may find this affirmation a bit too sweeping. Economic historians of Western Europe will no doubt quibble over some of his interpretations of British, French, or Russian history, but clearly De Soto is onto something very important, at least as far as Peru is concerned. One of the ways in which the issue has been confused in that country has been the tendency of beneficiaries of the official system (owners of large-scale businesses benefiting from government subsidies, direct or indirect)—in other words, the political Right—to adopt the language and ideological stance of their confrères in modern Western countries. This leads the traditional Left, not unnaturally, to confuse the two systems and conclude that "although private ownership of the means of production predominates, the development the country needs has not been achieved, proving that capitalism has failed and that a collectivist model is needed." In short, in Peruvian politics both Left and Right are debating the merits of a system which exists only at the margins.

Actually, there is very little private property in Peru, in the sense that most people have no legal right to the wealth they have created. De Soto shows how some groups, particularly urban settlements, have used partisan politics to negotiate recognition of what they already enjoy in usufruct. Nonetheless, most people enjoy only what he calls the "expectative rights of property." If the system were opened up, and the right to property made universal, this would have the effect of freeing vast productive forces currently either underground or not yet congealed into wealth, propelling Peru toward a capitalist revolution of a type not yet seen in Latin America.

De Soto has never made any claims that his book does anything more than describe what the Institute for Liberty and Democracy found in Peru. Yet since *The Other Path* was published, he has been flooded with mail, phone calls, and visits from people from Mexico, Ecuador, Colombia, Venezuela, and Argentina, all of whom have assured him that "if you change the names of the towns or the names of organizations, you have [my country]." These include industrialists, labor leaders, even the vice president of a South American country. If they are right, then important political choices lie ahead. Will the region be able to make them? It is a tall order—given, particularly, the continuing domination in every country of a political class trained only in the jurisprudence of the old system. This class lives in a parasitic fashion on the diminishing wealth created by the formal system, and is egged on by the vast infrastructures of development organizations favoring an international welfare state.

The truth is, however, that no vast international transfers of wealth are likely to take place in the 1990s: the only hope for the survival of democracy in the region is the diffusion of property and the enfranchisement of those who actually work and create wealth. The Latin American politicians are right about one thing: the current economic crisis is undermining the stability of the region, and raises the very real specter of a plunge into a full-dress collectivism. But the answer to this is more economic freedom, not less. "We have to call things by their real name," President Felipe González of Spain recently said. "Their economic system doesn't work. The explanations their leaders give for the poor results are no longer convincing." He was referring to the socialist states of Eastern Europe, but his remark might just as easily be addressed to his colleagues in Latin America. Hernando de Soto has given them a road map to the future; one can only hope they will prove capable of taking it.

Note

1. Translated by June Abbott (New York: Harper and Row, 1989).

4

Literature and Politics in Latin America

The task of the writer in Latin America has never been an easy one. In some countries literacy hardly surmounts functional levels; in others, where it far exceeds them, there still is not much of a public for which one can write. There are few serious universities or literary reviews, and the book trade is one of the most perilous occupations imaginable, subject to the anomalies of paper supplies, exchange controls, price controls, and a minuscule market. It is perhaps unflattering to say so, but Latin Americans are not great readers of books: instead they consume huge quantities of newsprint, cafe gossip, and conspiracy theories. This is so not withstanding the fact that the region has also produced some world-class writers, and shows every indication of continuing to do so.

In some ways, of course, the foregoing merely describes the situation of literature in any area of the Third World. But in one important regard, Latin America is quite different from, say, Africa, the Middle East, or southern Asia: Latin Americans are more firmly situated within the Western literary tradition. Even so, one should not make too much of this: in some ways, the region has more in common with other non-Western areas than we think. This leads to much confusion on the part of American and Western European readers, who are often taken in by false labels, and misunderstand the spirit underlying much of Latin American literary work. Nonetheless, Latin American literature has succeeded in gaining a foothold in mainstream Western culture, as a kind of exotic cousin whom we feel obliged to admit to our table. The relationship is sometimes based more on courtesy, guilt, and misunderstanding than on genuine affinity, but the writers themselves would be foolish indeed not to take advantage of it.

The subject of literature and politics in Latin America, is, of course, extraordinarily broad. Yet a few ruthless generalizations will serve as a point of departure. The image of the writer as an independent critic of society and power, or as a voice in the wilderness defending humanistic and liberal values against an established order of violence and greed, is greatly exaggerated. Indeed, most writers in Latin America have been unusually drawn to power, for reasons both of economic necessity and cultural predisposition. Further, at least since the turn of the century, they have been particularly attracted to non-liberal or anti-liberal ideologies. More recently, their anti-liberal bias has been positively encouraged by the literary establishments in Western Europe and the United States. And finally, a new generation of liberal voices has succeeded in making itself heard in Mexico, in Peru, in the Southern Cone republics. But the future of this generation remains extremely problematic. Here I propose to comment at length on each of these propositions.

Popular tradition places the roots of censorship in Latin America deep in the colonial period, when the Spanish authorities forbade the importation of works of creative imagination. It is true that Latin Americans were expected from the very start to subsist on a steady diet of sermons, writings of the Church fathers, and lives of the saints (some of which, actually, were very nearly pornographic). There was also, however, from the very beginning an underground trade in other books; the first copies of Cervantes's *Don Quixote*, for example, were smuggled to the New World in crates supposedly containing bottles of wine. This serves as a useful illustration of the limits of censorship, which—like almost every other aspect of government in the region—has never worked the way it is supposed to.

To be sure, over the years there have been instances in which individual titles have been prohibited, or even physically destroyed, sometimes with considerable brio. These episodes have captured the momentary attention of the Western cultural public. For example, copies of Mario Vargas Llosa's first novel, *The Time of the Hero* (1963), were publicly burned at the military academy in Peru where much of its action takes place. The incident was seized upon by its American publisher to promote the work of a (then) unknown writer. The junta in Chile staged a widely reported (and photographed) book-burning episode shortly after the coup in 1973, and has seized and destroyed several book shipments since then. Despite such incidents, however, censorship has been a less serious threat to literature in Peru, Chile, and elsewhere than other things, including indifference, popular taste, and economic constraints. Only in Cuba and (until yesterday) Nicaragua has literature been conscripted into rigorous service to the state.

Dramatic individual instances of censorship mask a more important fact about the literary state of Latin America—namely, that in most cases the relationship between writers and power has been symbiotic. During the first century of independence, literary skills of any kind were a monopoly of urban elites who dominated national affairs. Many writers were also presidents, generals, ministers, ambassadors, or prefects. While individual writers were persecuted and sometimes driven into exile, this was due to their affiliation with the party out of power, not to the allegedly subversive content of their work.

Moreover, in the absence of a broad economic base to support an independent or semi-independent intellectual calls, writers had no choice but to recur to the State for economic subsistence. This point is particularly well established in Doris Meyer's recent anthology, *Lives on the Line: The Testimony of Contemporary Latin American Authors*.[1] Starting in the nineteenth century, but continuing well into the twentieth, many Latin American governments maintained writers on the national budget, often as consuls or even ministers at overseas legations; for example, Rubén Darío, the greatest voice of Spanish-American poetry, was happy to edit the official daily of the oligarchical regime in neighboring El Salvador, and, later, to represent the dictator of his own country in Madrid. "He lived side by side with idiotic and reactionary politicians," Cuban novelist Alejo Carpentier later observed, "whoring generals whom he found agreeable and even interesting." (The comment loses none of its impact by the fact that Carpentier himself later did exactly the same thing for Fidel Castro, for whom he served as ambassador to France.)

The Peruvian poet José Santos Chocano served as diplomatic agent for the Mexican bandit-cum-revolutionary Pancho Villa, and even more deplorably, for Manuel Estrada Cabrera, ruthless dictator of Guatemala from 1905 to 1920. Successive Chilean governments maintained another great poet, Pablo Neruda, by offering him minor diplomatic posts in the Netherlands Indies and in Spain, and they did the same for his colleague, also a Nobel laureate, Gabriela Mistral. Jorge Luis Borges for years worked at the Buenos Aires Public Library, and subsequently became the Director of Argentina's National Library.

The phenomenon is by no means limited to "conservative" Latin American governments or to military dictatorships of the Right. Indeed, the first Latin American government to recruit writers and artists systematically for specifically political purposes was a government of the Left—revolutionary Mexico of the 1920s and 1930s. The Mexican phenomenon deserves more than passing reference because it embodies the finished model to which so many other Latin American governments and political parties secretly aspire: a one-party state that dominates both its military institutions and its labor movement; that elevates corruption to a system; that deftly conjugates a left-wing foreign policy with a right-wing domestic policy; and that preemptively eliminates criticism from abroad by accusing skeptical foreigners (particularly Americans), of racism, imperialism, or "lack of mutual respect."

In some respects what historians call the Mexican revolution (1910–1940) was not notably different from other struggles for power in that country save for its duration, geographical extent, and the degree of physical and human damage inflicted upon a helpless population. But the new Mexican authorities understood (as their predecessors did not) that in order to create enduring institutions, it was necessary to conscript cultural workers, particularly writers and artists. These in turn could be used to create a façade of broad philosophical meaning or what in many ways was nothing but a pillaging expedition which culminated in the creation of a new class of "revolutionary" millionaires.

By nationalizing large sectors of the nation's economy, the new government evidently acquired vast control over culture; no newspaper, could survive without advertising from state enterprises, or even go to press without newsprint from paper companies that were also now "socially owned." But the revolutionary political class in Mexico went well beyond negative sanctions—it created new opportunities for writers on state-subsidized literary magazines and periodicals, or for government agencies. It also created a state publishing house (*Fondo de Cultura Económica*), the first such in the history of Latin America.

Most important of all, the Mexican government mastered the use of house intellectuals in order to counteract unfavorable news stories abroad. The efficacy of the new system was first demonstrated in 1929, when José Vasconcelos, one-time minister of education (who was, in fact, responsible for creating many of the revolution's new cultural institutions), was defeated for the presidency of Mexico. Himself an honest man who abhorred violence and corruption, Vasconcelos was labeled by the regime as a "reactionary"—a damning accusation which had immediate resonance on both sides of the border. After a fraudulent election, his followers all over Mexico were set upon; many were murdered, and several dozen were buried in a mass grave. The candidate himself was lucky to escape the United States with his life.

The intellectual class, however, kept silent or repeated the allegations of the government, while the American liberal community (*The Nation* and *The New Republic*) saved its disapproval for Vasconcelos, whom it saw as a backslider who had abandoned his revolutionary faith. Since then, Mexico has enjoyed a unique immunity from criticism by American liberals otherwise so interested in the conduct of other repressive Latin American governments. This undoubtedly reflects, at least in part, the lengthy quiescence of Mexico's own literary and intellectual community—the crowning achievement of the triumphant revolutionary state.

While no other Latin American country has fully replicated the Mexican model, elements of it have appeared and reappeared periodically across the continent. Perón in Argentina (1946–55) and Allende in Chile (1970–73) used control of the economy to bankrupt potential advertisers in the opposition press (the latter failing to extinguish the independent *El Mercurio* only because of a covert subsidy from the CIA). Another recent example is the self-styled "left-wing" military government of Peru (1968–79) which in 1974 "transferred to the national majorities" all of the daily newspapers of Lima, throwing five hundred journalists and press-workers into the streets for having allegedly worked for the "oligarchy" and "imperialism." For novelist Mario Vargas Llosa, this was the moment of a great epiphany; up to that time he thought of the intellectual as a kind of moral reserve of the nation. Instead,

I recall my stupefaction upon seeing with what indecent haste legions of lawyers and philosophers, literati and sociologists jumped at the chance [for employment on the papers]. Among their number there was, naturally, the usual quota of rogues and professional opportunists, hacks that had served other, no less shady employers in times past. And there was also a tiny group of militants of the Communist party granted permission by their leaders to prostitute themselves—to infiltrate these places of power and put them to their own use before the adversary could do so.

To a man (and a woman) they accepted "the lie of the 'transfer to the social sectors' and went to work in the dailies to fulfill a function about which, from the very first, there could be no doubt whatsoever." No doubt some were driven by sheer economic necessity, Vargas Llosa continues, but given the wretched salaries they were paid, this can hardly have been their principal motivation. At issue was an appetite for power, "a fascination even greater in a country like ours, where, given the cultural poverty of the environment, intellectual life tends to be replete with frustrations."

These developments in Peru are characteristic of the explosion of urban centers in Latin America since the Second World War, an explosion that expanded the number of writers (or potential writers) well beyond the capacity of any state to absorb or co-opt fully. Even with greatly enlarged government payrolls, the safety valve of emigration to Western Europe or (particularly) the United States, the ubiquitous grants from foreign foundations and United Nations agencies, the supply still far exceeds the demand. Vargas Llosa's point remains valid, however: the difference between "ins" and "outs," "haves" and "have-nots," divides the literary community far more than any devotion (or lack of it) to democratic principle, commitment to freedom, tolerance for other people's ideas, or preference for an open political and social order. This does not prevent individual writers from producing very good work, often of no particular political import; but in their public role as repositories of the national culture, they are not, as a group, democratic exemplars.

If further proof were needed, there is the evident attraction that anti-democratic and anti-liberal ideologies have long held for the Latin American literary class. In the nineteenth century the reigning notion was positivism, which in its Latin American version justified rule by the enlightened few—the *científicos*, as they were known in Mexico; in the twentieth, it has been fascism, communism, or both. Some have moved from one extreme to the other without difficulty; the most notable case was Argentine novelist Julio Cortázar, an early supporter of Franco who switched sides in the 1950s, participated in the Russell Tribunal on "American War Crimes" in Stockholm, and subsequently supported leftist police states in Cuba and Nicaragua; another example is Nicaragua's José Coronel Urtecho, a former admirer of Mussolini who until recently was the chief literary apologist for Comandante Daniel Ortega.

The number of Latin American writers who have been attracted to Marxism at one time or another, or have actually joined Communist parties, is legion, including Neruda, Guatemala's Miguel Angel Asturias (another Nobel laureate), Brazil's Jorge Amado, Argentina's Ernesto Sábato, Cuba's Nicolás Guillén. As in Western Europe and United States, most of these men made their commitment in the 1930s and 1940s, under the double impact of the Depression and the Spanish civil war; some abandoned communism later on, out of disillusionment with either the Hitler-Stalin pact or the Khrushchev revelations of the crimes of the Stalin era. But unlike Marxism in Western Europe and the United States, they did not necessarily gravitate toward a liberal democratic vocation; more often, their Marxism became a bit like other people's Catholicism—a religion one continued to profess but no longer practiced. Paradoxically, with the exception of Neruda (and not always him) their work reflects little familiarity with the canons of socialist realism; rather, they tended to borrow their aesthetics from Zola and the French naturalists.

Another generation emerged in 1968, inspired by the Cuban revolution, the Vietnam War, and the example of Che Guevara. These writers could be regarded more as "New Left" than Marxist or Marxist-Leninist; while their work is more explicitly political in content, it is demagogic or melodramatic rather than doctrinal in tone, utilizing setpiece techniques of social protest, nationalism, and anti-Americanism, often writing with an eye to the European and American book-buying public than to national audiences. By and large it has produced fewer writers of genuine quality—the best-known being the Uruguayan Eduardo Galeano (just now being discovered in translation by New York's radical-chic literary community) and his compatriot Mario Benedetti, Chile's Ariel Dorfman, and Nicaragua's Omar Cabezas and Sergio Ramiréz. Of course, the most famous member of this group is Nobel laureate Gabriel García Márquez of Columbia. Unlike the others, however, García Márquez's novels have no political content whatsoever—in spite of this, however (or perhaps because of it), his political pronouncements (on behalf of Castro and, later, the Sandinistas) are unusually shrill.

The generation of 1968 also reflects a more cosmopolitan trend in Latin American letters—the internationalization, as it were, of certain formerly local themes, which in this case are protest, revolution, repression, solidarity, and also the supposed "authenticity" of native cultures threatened by North American consumerism. The "dirty war" against urban guerrilla subversion in Argentina (1973–1982), but even more, the coup which deposed Allende in Chile, followed later by the Sandinista revolution in Nicaragua and the struggle of the Farabundo Martí National Liberation Front (FMLN) guerrillas in El Salvador, led an emerging generation of Western Europeans to discover a special affinity with what they imagined Latin America to be. The point of convergence was a common hatred of the United States and the conviction that the real enemy of humanity was not communism but a renascent fascism and American economic interests and mass culture (seen as one and the same thing). Of course, not all Latin American writers responded to this situation by plunging into political themes; but the more ambitious (or unscrupulous) among them could not help noting that revolutionary posturing was the most expeditious route to success in the North Atlantic publishing and literary worlds.

Again, Vargas Llosa gives us the best picture of this new kind of Latin American writer:

> Although he rarely belongs formally to a revolutionary party or engages in the difficult sacrifices required of a genuine militant, he calls himself a Marxist and on all occasions broadcasts to the four winds that American imperialism—the Pentagon, the monopolies, Washington's cultural influence—is the source of our underdevelopment.

> He has a keen sense of smell, which allows him to detect CIA agents, whose tentacles he finds everywhere, including Boy Scout camps, tours of the Boston Symphony, Walt Disney cartoons, or anywhere or any time someone questions state-controlled economies or one-party states as a social panacea.

> Meanwhile, while polluting the air of his own country with these sulphurous pronouncements, he is a permanent candidate for grants from the Guggenheim and Rockefeller foundations (which he almost always receives), and when—thanks to local dictatorship—he is exiled or chooses to exile himself, it would serve no purpose to seek him in the countries he supposedly admires and broadcasts as models for his own—Cuba, China or the Soviet

Union—since the place he selects to continue his revolutionary struggle is New York University, or the University of Chicago, or California, or Texas, where he is a visiting professor only pending his appointment to a richly endowed permanent chair. Who is this person? This, dear friends, is the progressive intellectual.

The proliferation of such "progressive intellectuals" says even more about development in the United States over the last twenty years—and particularly, developments in American culture and higher education—than about Latin America. It is obviously unfair to require a minimal coherence between thought and action by intellectual visitors to the United States, when native practitioners of philosophy and letters see no reason for it themselves. It is also unrealistic to expect writers in countries with limited economic resources to be insensitive to demands of the international market. It is perhaps worth noting, however, the degree to which the "long march through institutions" has created an alternative American culture, with its own requirements which at least conceivably shape the composition and design of its imports.

In any event, certain expectations on American university campuses (derived mainly, it seems, from such often-exhibited movies as *State of Siege, The Battle of Chile, Missing,* and *Salvador*) must be met. For example, one Chilean novelist (himself a former supporter of the Allende regime) experienced some difficulties on an American lecture tour in 1980; the discovery that he had accepted an airplane ticket and per diem expenses from the United States Information Agency (USIA) profoundly troubled several students and faculty in one university in the San Francisco Bay Area at which he spoke; but the fact that he resided in his own country—to which he had finally been permitted to return from Spain the previous year—rather than in exile was what finally convinced some in the audience that his anti-Pinochet *bona fides* were not in order. It may be a coincidence, but so far his novels, though well-known and highly regarded in Spain, France, and West Germany, have yet to appear in the United States.

Not only are many Latin American writers not political at all; others have become intensely anti-political as the result of their own experiences, particularly with "revolutionary" governments in Cuba and Nicaragua; still others—a small but distinguished company—have made the journey back from the authoritarian left to the democratic center. The late Argentine novelist Manuel

Puig (*Kiss of the Spider Woman*, 1979) is perhaps the best example of the first. As a student of film-writing in Rome in the 1950s, he was astounded to discover that intellectual circles in Italy were pervaded by a kind of left-wing McCarthyism. "Emotionally, I was split. On the one hand, a popular cinema of protest appealed to me; but on the other, I also liked cinema with a story, and this apparently classified me as a die-hard reactionary." Puig persisted, though, and eventually developed his own style and themes, which have to do with the confusion of sex roles and cultural models that afflict contemporary Argentine society—a subject so daring as to prevent his first novel, *Betrayed by Rita Hayworth* (1968) from being published in Argentina until after it had already succeeded in a French translation.

Other novelists had their fling with revolution, and lost their taste for it. The best example is Guillermo Cabrera Infante, a rising star of Cuban literature, who worked on *Lunes de Revolución*, the cultural supplement of Castro's official daily, until he ran into problems with the censor. He eventually defected from his post as cultural attaché in the United Kingdom, and continues his work in England today. His novelistic work reconstructs Havana in the late 1940s and early 1950s—the last moment of the old regime—and maps the parameters of cultural dislocation, in this case, the enormous influence of American culture in Cuban life, against the impossibility of fully replicating the foreign model. Though Cabrera Infante has done much to puncture the balloons of the English literary Left in their love affair with Castro—his remarks, when interviewed, are extremely astringent—he could hardly be said to have any strong political views of his own.

Chilean novelist José Donoso introduces a special variant, which might be called "post-political." His newest work, *La desesperanza* (1985; English version, *Curfew*, 1988) recounts the experiences of a left-wing folk singer who returns to Chile after spending nearly a decade in Western Europe cashing in on European guilt and solidarity; he discovers that many of the people on the Left who stayed behind and faced the dictatorship in its most ferocious period are resentful of his success. For his part, he discovers a Chile entirely different from the one he left, exhausted spiritually from the ideological wars of the 1960s. Donoso's narrative style is droll and ironic, reflecting a cynical worldview evocative of Cabrera Infante. A somewhat similar spirit pervades the magnificent novel of his compatriot Jorge Edwards, *Los convivados de piedra* (1978), which provides a long and somewhat skeptical perspective on Chilean political life, moving back and forth between the prewar and the Allende years.

The most important development in recent Latin American letters has been the emergence of a new group of writers who have made a decisive liberal and democratic commitment, explicitly denouncing totalitarian regimes and utopian ideologies. The most important, and certainly the best known, is Octavio Paz, the Mexican poet, anthropologist, diplomat—and now Nobel laureate—whose magazine *Vuelta* has become the vehicle whereby a new generation of Latin American writers dare to experiment with dangerous ideas—dangerous, that is, to the Latin American literary-cultural establishment and its numerous and well-placed foreign allies.

Paz himself has been a dominant figure in Mexican letters for two generations. His own left-wing credentials leave little to be desired. His father was the Washington representative of the famous revolutionary General Emiliano Zapata; he himself rushed to Spain in the 1930s to demonstrate his solidarity with the beleaguered Second Republic; and in the later part of the decade he was close to the Trotskyite movement in Mexico. In 1968, he resigned his post as ambassador to India to protest the shooting of students at the Plaza of Three Cultures in Mexico.

For some years now, however, Paz has been moving away from his earlier militancy. As early as 1950, he wrote an article condemning the concentration camps in Stalinist Russia—a daring act for an intellectual in Mexico, where the enemy of one's enemy is automatically one's friend. As it was, the piece had to be published in Victoria Ocampo's literary quarterly, *Sur*, in faraway Argentina. He was almost alone among Mexican intellectuals in expressing reservations about the Cuban revolution during the 1960s and 1970s. And he publicly objected to his country's support of a 1976 United Nations resolution equating Zionism with racism; since his view happened to coincide with that of the United States, he was widely accused of treason to the Mexican nationality.

Neither then nor now, however, could Paz be regarded as a man of the Right. He has denied ever being an "anti-Communist," and in fact *Vuelta* conspicuously opposed U.S. policy in

Vietnam, publishing pieces by Noam Chomsky and I.F. Stone. At a forum at Harvard University in 1972, he declared that given Mexico's dependence on the United States, its "transformation into a more just, freer, and more human society—a democratic socialism founded on our history—is inevitably linked to the United States." As such, he told his audience, "your struggle is our struggle. Our friends are your friends because your enemies are ours...We must join together—Mexican and American dissidents, to change our two countries!"

The major turning-point in his thinking seems to have been reached a little over ten years ago. As he told a Mexican journalist,

> The situation of 1977 is very different from 1937. After thousands of accounts by eye-witnesses—from Trotsky and Victor Serge at one extreme, to Souvarine and Solzhenitsyn at the other, with Khrushchev's secret speech in the center—it is impossible to close our eyes... It seems to me inexcusable to ignore or remain silent in the face of the reality of the U.S.S.R. and the other "socialist" countries.

Even more to the point, while still embracing socialism as "the only rational solution for the West," this could only be the case if it were "inseparable from individual liberties, democratic pluralism, and respect for the rights of minorities and dissidents." In any event, he continued,

> for Latin America, socialism is not on the agenda. Socialism is not a method of developing more rapidly, but a consequence of development. Socialism in underdeveloped countries, as the experience of our century demonstrates, is rapidly transformed into state capitalism, generally controlled by a bureaucracy that—in the name of an idea—governs in a despotic, absolutist manner.

From here it was but a small step to openly condemns the Sandinista regime in Nicaragua as an effort to establish "a bureaucratic-military regime inspired by the Cuban model" in a now-famous speech at the 1984 Frankfurt Book Fair. That speech—which had repercussions throughout Western Europe and Latin America—did nothing more than state the obvious; nonetheless, since then, Paz has found himself accused of being a right-winger. His political and economic views are still somewhat to the left of center, but his liberal democratic convictions are no more in doubt than they ever were. Most revealingly, when asked to enumerate the obligation of Mexican writers to their country, he replied, "I do not believe that writers have specific obligations to their country. Their obligations are to the language—and to their consciences." Contrast that with the statement of Nicaraguan writer Claribel Alegría in *Lives on the Line*: "If there is no place [in Central America] for 'pure art' and 'pure literature' today, then I say so much the worse for pure art and literature."

Mario Vargas Llosa is some twenty years younger than Paz. He belongs more properly to the generation of 1968, but has, evidently, separated himself from it. Unlike Paz, he was unreservedly enthusiastic about the Cuban revolution in its earlier days; conversely, he has moved further away from his original ideas. In the first volume of political essays published under the evocative title *Against Wind and Tide* (*Contra viento y marea*, 1986), he reproduces at the very beginning an article on Cuba which originally appeared in the early 1960s in French, as a way of charting the ideological distance he has since traveled.

The articles in *Against Wind and Tide* suggest a very gradual process of movement. The great watershed seems to have been his appointment by President Fernando Belaúnde Terry to a national commission to investigate the conduct of the Peruvian army after an encounter between it and the Shining Path guerrillas in the high Andes. The commission eventually absolved the army of charges of wanton abuse of human rights, and Vargas Llosa defended its findings in an article in *The New York Times Magazine*. Since then he has customarily been referred to as a "right-winger," a label which no longer bothers him.

Like Paz, Vargas Llosa claims to have been influenced by the conduct of Marxist regimes in practice; as he has said, "policies designed to correct injustices are significantly less effective than [those inspired by] liberal and democratic doctrines and ideas—that is to say, those who do not sacrifice freedom in the name of justice." Unlike Paz, however, he has actively embraced liberal economics, and recently ran for the presidency of Peru as an advocate of drastic reform along free-market lines.

Pablo Antonio Cuadra is the grand old man of Nicaraguan letters—one of the most highly regarded poets in Latin America. For some years he has also been the editor-in-chief of *La Prensa*, the voice of the Nicaraguan opposition under both the Somoza dictatorship and the Sandinista regime. A self-confessed Nicaraguan nationalist, Cuadra is also an outspoken defender of liberal values. As he told a radio interviewer recently, "I think a nation has a basic human right: the right to the truth." When asked "what do you think the news media law should be?" he replied, "I have been asked that question for fifty years...The answer is very simple: The best news media law is the one that does not exist." As for the "situation of contemporary literature in Nicaragua," he replied,

> Our work is to publish someone else's works, particularly independent writers, and—in way that could be described as negative—create the proper climate for true, apolitical literature. To strip literature of political influence is one way to restore its freedom.

Nicaragua, of course, is one country in which literature has recently been understood to have a concrete political purpose. As Cuadra's compatriot Claribel Alegría—one of the Sandinistas' favorite literary figures—puts it, "I do not know a single Central American writer who is so careful of his literary image that he sidesteps political commitment at this crucial moment in our history, and were I to meet one, I would refuse to shake his hand." Though the Sandinistas were often praised in the foreign press for such cultural innovations as poetry workshops for the army and police (!), during their decade of rule political or anti-political writers had considerable difficulty getting published. As Cuadra told an Associated Press reporter two years ago, "Some of our best young poets are in exile—in Texas, in Venezuela." In *Lives on the Line* he adds an ironic observation: "several of my friends who flaunted their independence in front of the right-wing dictatorships have happily bent over backwards to all the demands of the [Nicaraguan] revolutionary leaders."

All of that may change in Nicaragua now, as it has in Mexico, where a new generation of writers now has at least the opportunity to be heard. Significantly, there is now a South American edition of *Vuelta*, edited in Buenos Aires by the Uruguayan writer Danubio Torres Fierro, who spent a number of years as a political exile in Mexico, where he came under the influence of Paz and his circle.

Though not a novel, Jorge Edwards's book *Persona non grata* (1977) deserves mention in his context. Though primarily a writer, Edwards was for many years a career diplomat in the Chilean foreign service. Because of his socialist convictions, he was selected to be Allende's chargé d'affaires in Havana in the first months of 1971. A long-time sympathizer with the Cuban revolution, he had made short trips to the island in the past, and even served on prize committees for Castro's state publishing house, Casa de las Américas. Nonetheless, the experience of living there and witnessing the regime's treatment of individual Cubans, particularly his writer friends, was a shattering experience. *Persona non grata* is a compelling memoir of his months in Cuba, and, with Milovan Djila's *Conversations with Stalin,* ranks as a classic contribution to the literature of disillusionment. Significantly, Ariel Dorfman, who understandably did not like *Persona non grata,* could think of no greater insult to Edwards than to accuse him of treason to—of all places—Chile. Edwards remains a social democrat—closer in his views to Octavio Paz than to his friend Vargas Llosa—hugely admired by the democratic forces in Chile, whose man-of-letters laureate he has, perforce, become.

How successful will this tendency be? In large part, it depends on two developments, one proceeding from abroad, the other at home. The death of socialism (or, rather, the death of the idea of socialism), particularly in Europe, has so far not made much impact upon Latin American intellectual life. Old habits die hard; so does the notion of the writer-as-militant. As Paz recently wrote, "Their grandfathers swore by St. Thomas and they swear by Marx, yet both have seen in reason a weapon in the service of Truth with a capital 'T,' which is the mission of intellectuals to defend...Thus there has been perpetuated in our lands an intellectual tradition that has little respect for the opinion of others, that prefers ideas to reality, and intellectual systems to the critique of systems." It remains to be seen how long such a concept of intellectual citizenship can endure an ideological vacuum or a crisis of faith. Insofar as Marxism is concerned, one or the other (or both) are coming, whether or not the Latin American intellectuals are prepared for it.

It remains to be seen, also, what trends prevail in American intellectual life, particularly as they are reflected in the New York publishing world. Not to put too fine a point on the matter, the titles offered to American readers reflect to a disproportionate degree the ideological preferences of editors in the major book publishing houses, as opposed to either judgments of literary quality or the interest of readers. As a result, there now exists something of an artificial market for Latin American literature, one that encourages writers to produce work mainly with an eye to a public that will read them in translation. As the Mexican critic Enrique Krauze has shown in a controversial study of Carlos Fuentes, this threatens the authenticity of their work. It is easy to imagine a situation in which Latin American literature could exist in a kind of ideological cocoon for some years to come—or, perhaps, artificially maintained on a life-support system made up of, say, *The New York Times Book Review, Harper's Magazine,* and Pantheon Books. It would constitute the literary equivalent of the current situation of higher education in the United States—a series of cultures scattered across a society which actually have little or nothing to do with it. In short, if revolutionaries wielding machetes and spouting the clichés of liberation theology is what the American book-buying public is thought to want, it is hard to imagine they will not get it. At any rate, they may not be able to buy any other kind of Latin American literature at their local bookstore.

In the end, everything depends upon events within Latin America itself. If, for example, there is a new round of right-wing military governments, a new generation of leftist writers will certainly emerge in response, with or without the quasi-incentive of foreign translations. At the same time, if the region succeeds in joining the liberal economic revolution spreading in Eastern Europe, that will change the local environment in many important ways, including literacy, patterns of consumption, and, inevitably, the role of the writer in society.

If, however, the republics simply continue on their present course, avoiding either reform or revolution, but failing to hold their ground as viable economic entities, then Latin American writers may find themselves in the position of their counterparts in the Arab world, where themes of suicide, frustration, and death repeat themselves in endless (and monotonous) variation. In that event they would not constitute a serious threat to liberal society, but then, there would be little for them to threaten. One can only hope that the future, for both Latin America and for its republic of letters, holds out a more hopeful prospect.

Note

1. Berkeley and Los Angeles: University of California Press, 1988.

5

Orphans of Utopia

Suppose they gave a Latin American revolution and nobody came? Well, from 4–9 April 1991 the people came, but the revolution never quite got off the ground. The scene was not Bolivia, Peru, or El Salvador, but the Hyatt-Regency in Crystal City, Virginia, where 2,500 people gathered for the Sixteenth International Congress of the Latin American Studies Association (LASA). Founded twenty-five years ago, LASA is very much a child of the 1960s. At previous meetings this much was obvious in details small as well as large. The uniform of choice tended to be radical fancy-dress (jeans and boots for both sexes; long, unkempt hair likewise; grubby native accessories); the principal activities were revolutionary theater and political posturing, the regnant ideology an undifferentiated mixture of Marxism, anarchism, and anti-Americanism.

This year, however, some things were different. Suits, ties, and dresses were everywhere in evidence. ("This is the first year," one Chilean academic mumbled, "that the women look like *women*.") Voices were low and so, by the way, were the energy levels. Civility was the order of the day: there were no catcalls or jeers at Bernard Aronson, who addressed a large meeting in his capacity as the State Department's chief Latin American policy official. Even two American army officers at a panel on low-intensity conflict in El Salvador escaped unscathed.

Not that *everything* has changed: in the race for LASA's presidency, Marxist economist Carmen Deere (of the University of Massachusetts at Amherst and also of farm-machinery fame), an adviser to the Cuban and Sandinista governments, defeated the "liberal" candidate, William Leogrande of American University (but who also likes the Cubans and the Sandinistas). But probably not too much should be made of this: while the program this year confirmed that Latin American studies remains in many ways a "left" or even, in places, a "far left" field, it is gradually but perceptibly becoming less so. Still there were examples of the old animus. For example, Beth Sims of the Inter-Hemispheric Education Resource Center assured a roundtable on the 1990 elections in Nicaragua that the United States had virtually "bought" the victory of Violeta Chamorro—this in spite of the fact that, as Charles Lane of *Newsweek* pointed out from the floor, it was obvious to any observer that the Sandinistas outspent UNO at least three to one.

The Old Faith was also manifest in dozens of booths representing a wide range of radical and revolutionary causes, including the vicious Shining Path guerrilla movement in Peru (cheek by jowl with the Fulbright Commission!), and various organizations who make and distribute radical films. Nonetheless, the auditorium-sized room where some of these films were on continuous display was often completely empty. This could serve well as a metaphor for the conference as a whole: much of the traditional menu was available, but appetites were a bit tepid.

Part of what's happening here is that the greening of academia is turning to the graying: as in other fields, the current generation in Latin American studies is getting older, and—given the coming economic crunch in higher education—probably will not be replaced. With fewer jobs available teaching, say, Andean history at Fort Gloch State College, potential graduate students are going instead to law school or for their M.B.A. A kind of middle-age calm, combined with a soupçon of ideological exhaustion, has settled over LASA's membership, and thus over its deliberations.

But there is something else that accounts for the shift and that was very much in evidence at the LASA conference: the Latin American intellectuals themselves have changed their worldviews. The point is an important one, because as a field Latin American studies has always had a strong sense of constituency—Americans who wrote about the area often did so with an eye to the approval of their foreign colleagues. During the 1960s and 1970s, in fact, no North American (in the social sciences at least) could move successfully in Latin intellectual circles without incorporating at least partly the reigning orthodoxies, including the superiority of central planning to the market, the superficiality (not to say the perversity) of "bourgeois democracy," and the

United States as the first cause of all the evils that afflicted the Southern hemisphere.

Over the past two years, however, the Left in Latin America has been profoundly shaken by the collapse of communism in Eastern Europe and the revelations of *glasnost*. At the same time, in Argentina, Chile, Uruguay, and Brazil a process of reflection and self-examination that began long before Gorbachev's innovations has led to the embrace of democracy as a positive value in itself, not merely a gimmick to be manipulated in the service of other social or economic goals. As for the United States, never has its stock in the region been higher, especially among democratic socialists and social democrats, many of whom have personally benefitted from Washington's unambiguous support for democratic transitions, and the persistent curiosity of our Congress in the matter of human rights performance.

The result at Crystal City was a muted but discernible confrontation between the Latin American Left and their longtime counterparts in the American academy. Entirely emblematic of this phenomenon was a session on the first year of Chile's newly elected government, where Sergio Bitar, President Allende's former minister of mines, courteously but firmly took issue with two American *marxisant* academics, one of whom had grandly declared that what Bitar's country had was not a democratic government at all but "a military government administered by civilians."

The real moment of truth occurred at a session which brought together three Soviet scholars of Latin America to discuss the impact of *perestroika* on their field of study. The first two papers were full of anodyne generalities. The quiet buzz of platitudes was suddenly interrupted by the third speaker, Vladimir Stanchenko from the Institute of World Economy and International Relations in Moscow. Reading his paper in excellent American-accented English, Stanchenko tore into the entire course of Soviet policy in Latin America for the last three decades. It was no secret, he confided to the audience, that since the Cuban revolution the Soviet Union sought to exploit unrest in Latin America as a way of "weakening U.S. interests and constraining Washington's global position." This is what led both Soviet military planners and ideologists to establish a military and naval presence in Cuba (which he called "a hostage to Soviet military power"). Later, euphoric with the "strategic parity achieved with the United States after Vietnam," Brezhnev purposely increased tensions in the region as a way of "harassing the sleeping giant, the United States." Among other things, Brezhnev used "the dictatorship in Cuba" to manage and direct Third World movements and also to advance Soviet interests in the English-speaking Caribbean (Grenada and Guyana), a region to which he, Brezhnev, "attributed great importance."

As for Central America itself, Stanchenko observed that there could be "little doubt" of a Soviet involvement through Cuba: Nicaragua's military build-up under the Sandinistas, as well as arms, assistance, and advice to the FMLN and "other Marxist groupings," bore witness to Soviet involvement. In effect, until recently Soviet policy in Central America has contributed unnecessarily to the deterioration of relations with the United States," while working to impose "totalitarian regimes" in hapless Third World countries.

There it was—everything down to the T-word! When Stanchenko finished, it seemed as if all the air had been sucked out of the room. Hands rose rapidly. "What you are saying," gasped one woman, "is what the Right in the United States has been saying for some time"—which, as far as it went, was certainly a valid observation. Another demanded to know if Stanchenko had been born before 1959—surely not all of these events in the region began only when the Soviets put their hands in the pot. Then one man in the first row stood up and said, "When President Reagan called the Soviet Union 'the evil empire,' some of us tried to explain to our classes that the Soviet Union wasn't like that at all. Now, however, we hear voices from the Soviet Union repeating arguments of the extreme Right in the United States." Then, moving in for the kill, he said, "Don't you people have something of a problem of credibility? Why should I believe you now? Were you telling the truth before, when you wrote in a very different vein?" (Scattered but determined applause.)

Stanchenko assured the audience that he had indeed been born before 1959—"that's why I know more about some of these things than many of you here." As to his own credibility, he informed the audience that he had only begun to publish since *perestroika*. "Other colleagues may have written the opposite." Nonetheless, he went on, he could very specifically affirm that Soviet arms shipments to the region occurred before Ronald Reagan came to power in the United States. "Either you believe the facts—or you don't believe the facts."

Perhaps the most characteristic response came not from the hard Left but from the soft. "I am concerned about the United States as an international police force for hire, and the Soviet Union not able to do anything about it," one voice from the back of the room wailed. "What will it mean for world peace?" Wasn't the cold war, with all its warts, better at least in that way? Stanchenko didn't think the cold war was all that good for world peace. There were discontented rumbles as the session broke up; the speakers were surrounded by angry academics. When Stanchenko finally broke free to go to lunch, he was heard to remark to and American colleague, "Well, I have to tell the truth, don't I? What else can I do?"

Part II

Pictures from an Exhibition

6

"An aristocrat in the public square": José Ortega y Gasset

The role of the intellectual in "backward"—that is, largely non-industrial—societies has been one of the major themes of the twentieth century. This is not surprising, since no previous period of history has opened the road to power to so many practitioners of ideas—though in societies in which literacy has been rather problematical. As a matter of fact, one of the principal ways the "underdeveloped" (or, as we now say, the "developing") world differs from Western Europe and the United States is the almost sacerdotal role assigned to individual writers, poets, playwrights, historians, and philosophers. The contrast between that situation and our own could not be starker, and it provokes much anguish in our literary papers. Look at Senegal, we are typically reproached by critics of our own (rather less philosophical) political class. *There* they have (or had) a poet for a president! Or at Nicaragua, whose vice president is Sergio Ramírez, a novelist!

But in fact the greater deference due certain individual intellectuals in particular countries should not be viewed with unrestrained enthusiasm. In places where ideas are regarded as weapons, those in power typically feel the need for a monopoly of force. This explains why non-Western societies ruled by poets and novelists more frequently engage in censorship than those governed by the cultural laity, or why they are more inclined to jail, persecute, or exile their intellectuals. In those countries, an intellectual's youthful militancy often dies in disillusionment and the embrace of actively antipolitical attitudes; what begins as commitment ends in withdrawal. Thus, after a lengthy detour, the sacerdotal, non-Western intellectual often ends up as dislocated and powerless as his conferee in the West—but with some additional, quite drastic, personal inconveniences.

This syndrome is in many ways anticipated by the career of the Spanish philosopher José Ortega y Gasset, whose hundredth anniversary has just been observed and who is now the subject of a major intellectual biography by Rockwell Gray.[1] Spain is, evidently, a European country in strictly geographic terms, but as late as the 1920s and 1930s it was regarded by Britain and France as being as backward culturally and socially as many Third World nations today, and many of the issues raised there have a certain contemporary relevance for Africa and Latin America. It was during those very years that Ortega became known in the United States for two books, *Invertebrate Spain* and *The Revolt of the Masses.* Both works touched on themes sufficiently broad to attract people not particularly interested in Spain or even in philosophy as such. His later books, which were written in the 1940s and early 1950s but appeared in this country a decade or more later—*Man and People, Man and Crisis, History as a System, The Dehumanization of Art*—appealed to rather smaller circles—academic philosophers or litterateurs deeply involved in tracing the development of ideas on the Spanish peninsula and in Spanish America.

Gray gives these aspects of Ortega's career all of the attention they deserve (indeed, perhaps a bit more than they deserve), but he also establishes quite firmly his subject's role as an archetype of the involved public intellectual—what Ortega himself called "an aristocrat in the public square." It is this aspect which invites greater analysis and discussion. Above all, Gray's book helps us to place Ortega in the context of Spanish intellectual history—between the generations of 1898 and 1914, between the decline of positivism and the ascendancy of Marxism. He allows us to see Ortega as an exemplar of a kind of liberal conservatism (or conservative liberalism) subsequently superseded by other, less lovely, ideological currents that prevailed in the Spanish civil war (1936–39) and after.

Ortega was born in Madrid in 1883. His father was a prominent journalist; his mother, the daughter of the owner of the great liberal daily, *El Imparcial.* After private schooling he entered the University of Madrid, from which he received a doctorate in 1904. He then went to study in Germany—an unusual decision for Spaniard in those years—eventually settling in Marburg, where he specialized in Kant. Returning to Spain four years later, he received an academic appointment at a teacher-training institute, and in 1910 he won (by competitive examination) the chair of metaphysics at his alma mater.

Between 1911 and 1936 Ortega became one of Spain's truly towering personalities. He contributed regular articles to *El Imparcial* and also to its successor, *El Sol*. He established what later became the Espasa-Calpe publishing house, which made available to Spainiards for the first time accurate, inexpensive paperback translations of the major works of Western European science, philosophy, history, and belles lettres. (The series, incidentally, is still being published). In 1923 he founded *Revista de Occidente*, Spain's first truly substantial journal of books and ideas, and the following year a publishing house of the same name, to bring out foreign (largely German) philosophical treatises.

But Ortega was something more than merely an intellectual figure—he was also an active, eloquent critic of Spain's corrupt, decrepit political system. During the 1920s the monarchy had undermined much of what remained of its prestige by plunging Spain into an apparently endless colonial war in Morocco; it had discredited the parliamentary system by sponsoring a quasi-dictatorship under General Miguel Primo de Rivera; and it had acted as a brake on needed reforms in education, transport, land tenure, and civil-military relations. Through his newspaper columns Ortega did much to turn the Spanish middle class against the monarchy, and after the abdication of Alfonso XIII in 1931 he was elected to Parliament on an independent ticket (rather remarkably labeled Agrupación de Intelectuales Independientes al Servicio de la República).

Ortega's service in the new constituent Cortes was brief and disillusioning; he withdrew from it in 1932 to devote himself to teaching, serious writing, and journalism. An early critic of leftist and anti-clerical excesses which eventually doomed the Republic, he was nonetheless regarded as one of its founders, and therefore anathema to its enemies. Not surprisingly, when the Army of Africa rose up against the authorities in Madrid in the summer of 1936, Ortega was forced to flee for his life. After a brief stay in Paris, he took ship to Buenos Aires (where he lived from 1939 to 1942), subsequently relocating in Estoril, Portugal (1942–48). After 1949 he divided his time between his home in the suburbs of Lisbon and Madrid, where he established a residence, but the environment (and the attitude of the Franco regime) was such that he never fully reentered a Spanish intellectual life. Instead, he became a kind of ambassador-at-large of European culture, welcome as a supreme adornment to conferences and celebrations almost everywhere except in his own country. By the time he died in 1955, he was regarded as the last paladin of an earlier, golden age of Spanish liberalism, and not without reason. Yet within a decade a new generation of Spanish intellectuals won over to Marxism had relegated him to their dustbin of history—an ironic coda to a career begun and brought to fruition in the service of Enlightenment ideals, and prematurely truncated by the victory of clerico-fascist forces in the Spanish civil war.

As an intellectual biographer, Gray sets for himself the task of elucidating both Ortega's person and his oeuvre—a formidable undertaking for a career which spanned more than fifty years on two continents and involved both prolific public and literary activity. Nonetheless, three major themes emerge quite clearly.

The first is the need for Spain, in Gray's words, to "define itself by standards established beyond its frontiers"—in other words, to submit itself to the norms of Western European culture. In and of itself, the idea was not new: since at least the eighteenth century the Spanish intellectual community had been divided between those who considered the country backward and those who merely regarded its Western neighbors as heretics beyond the pale.

But controversy had become more explicit after defeat in the war with the United States over Cuba and the Philippines in 1898. The "disaster," as it was always called, forced a new generation of writers—Ángel Ganivet, Miguel de Unamuno, Azorín—to rethink the comfortable pieties that had sustained their fathers and grandfathers. Eventually the so-called "generation of '98" divided into conservatives and reformers, or perhaps better said, into nationalists and cosmopolites (*hispanizantes* and *europeizantes*)—those who believed that Spain must return to its preternatural essence (whatever that might be), on one hand, and those who, on the other, frankly called for the Spanish people to relinquish, in Gray's phraseology, "their arrogant notion of being the chosen people of the Christian world, and embrace a more distinctly secular view of things."

Broadly speaking, Ortega associated himself with the latter group, and even invented a term—"invertebration"—to describe his country's lack of rigorous social and cultural standards. He was not questioning the value of hierarchy as such, merely the functional utility of Spain's prevailing institutions—Church, throne, army, aristocracy, parasitic political class. The problem, he held, was that the established order, judged against the background of other European countries, simply did not work. His critiques, at times deeply wounding, were difficult to ignore. "The intellectual level is sinking so far and so rapidly at this point in our own decadence," he wrote, for example, just after his return from Marburg, "that shortly there will be neither academies nor theaters, rather, we Spaniards will sit around enormous café tables and tell each other risqué stories."

In both *Invertebrate Spain* and *The Revolt of the Masses*, books which became international bestsellers, Ortega inveighed against the logical product of Spain's dysfunctional system: the "mass man" who refused to accept proper cultural authority and leadership. At times this message was seriously misunderstood, as if it somehow implied an antipathy to democracy, or was embraced by people (including the dictator's son, José Antonio Primo de Rivera, later founder of the Falange, Spain's most successful Fascist party) with whom Ortega could have little in common politically. As Gray points out,

> the traditional notion of social classes inherited from nineteenth-century social thought is notably absent from the book [*The Revolt of the Masses*], which divided society between cadres of elite leadership and the mass man who rejects them.

It is clear from Ortega's writings that "mass man" was emphatically not a class phenomenon: he could be found at any point on the social scale. Indeed, the central part of Ortega's critique of the Spanish system was that it logically promoted the wrong kind of people. Many of Spain's military, clerical, and political leaders of the 1920s—including, by the way, its aristocracy and high society—were what Ortega had in mind when he spoke of "mass man."

Nonetheless, there was a central tension in Ortega's thought with stark political implications. "Clearly a liberal in his devotion to education and self-realization," Gray writes, Ortega nonetheless

> feared the invasive force of mass taste, which, he believed, threatened to reduce all models of excellence to its own base level. With the noblesse oblige of the liberal who is not at heart a democrat, he seemed at once

committed to raising men's rights and fearful that success in this effort
might ultimately elude him and the elite leadership of which he dreamed.

Ortega's cultural messianism may seem a bit precious for the
contemporary reader, but it grew out of an elitism far more dis-
interested and constructive than the alternative advanced by the
Spanish traditionalists of the day—José Calvo Sotelo, José Maria
Pemán, Pedro Saínz Rodriguez, individuals who would emerge
as major "cultural" figures of the Franco regime. *Their* source of
inspiration was Ramiro de Maeztu (1876–1936), who had long
argued (most notably in *Defensa de Hispanidad*) that Spain's decline after 1700 was due to the supposedly rampant invasion of
secular humanism and a corresponding decline in militant Catholicism. Ortega's call for higher cultural standards, if under an
enlightened leadership class, presupposed important changes in
the structure of Spanish society and education—in other words,
was fundamentally "liberal" in the context of the time, and understood as such.

The second theme of Gray's book, very much related to the
first, is Ortega's insistence on the continuing vitality of European culture. This was a particularly important note to strike in
the 1920s, when Spenglerian notions of doom and apocalypse
were popular in Germany and France, and some Spanish left-
wing intellectuals preferred to find their models in more exotic
locales—the Soviet Union, or even the charade of revolutionary
Mexico. In contrast, in the pages of *Revista de Occidente* educated
Spaniards could find what Gray calls "a kind of cultural topogra-
phy of Europe," including abundant attention to history and sociological theory, a defense of modern art (though not
Surrealism), and an up-to-date summary of the major literary
trends in several European languages. (After 1931, Ortega's
magazine devoted considerably more attention to specifically
Spanish issues.) The depth and strength of Western culture—particularly as manifest in England, France, and pre-Hitlerian Germany was a theme to which Ortega returned with renewed vigor
after the Second World War. By then the notion was gratuitous
in the United States or Western Europe, but in Spain itself—locked
once again in self-imposed isolationism—it had come to be regarded as eccentric when not downright pernicious.

Gray's third theme, which links the other two, concerns the
role of the intellectual in society. Like many educated comso-

polites in backward countries, Ortega oscillated on the proper role of persons like himself: at times, he saw them as the proper harbingers of modernization, the natural architects of reform; at other times, he advocated their total withdrawal from the corrupting influences of public life. In any case, Gray writes, Ortega tended "to distrust the partisan blindness occasioned by *engagé* commitments." By the end of his life, in fact, Ortega was openly critical of the cult of "commitment" practiced by certain kinds of political intellectuals—particularly Heidegger and Sartre, with many lesser copies to follow. As Gray paraphrases it, "for him, this...was the very contradiction of a genuinely philosophical attitude, which consisted in the 'negative capability' not to commit oneself, but to remain open to further analysis."

Not surprisingly, then, the heyday of Ortega's role as a public intellectual was the late 1920s—during the last season of the Bourbon monarchy. Once the new Republican order was in place, and ideas had to be translated into action, Ortega discovered how ill-equipped he was to compete in the public square, particularly with a whole new class of intellectual mediocrities suddenly raised to prominence—men like Manuel Azaña on the Left, or José María Gil Robles on the Right.

Though elected to Parliament for the province of León on a program which advocated, among other things, unionization of workers of both sexes, mild socialization of private capital, and separation of church and state, Ortega quickly found himself outclassed by leftist demagogues within the republican coalition. He correctly foresaw serious problems for institutions founded on fanaticism and revanchism. The anti-clerical provisions of the new republican constitution particularly disturbed him, as did the tendency to look to imported models of revolutionary change or an excessively ideological approach to economic issues. As he told one audience:

> Ladies and gentlemen, I am not a Catholic, and since my youth I have taken care to formalize in a non-Catholic fashion even the humble details of my private life. But I am not about to have imposed on me the wild figureheads of an anarchical anticlericalism.

A few weeks later he had retired from politics, and the civil war which followed four years later (as well as the victory of the anti-republican coalition) effectively precluded any reconsideration on his part. In Argentina and Portugal he was an outsider subject to the goodwill of local authorities; and thought he was permitted (after 1948) to return to Spain, he found it prudent to limit his remarks there to the most abstruse philosophical topics. Long after the final collapse of the Republic, Ortega maintained only the most tentative of truces with the Franco regime—and vice versa. The Falganist press heaped scorn upon even his most innocuous comments in such rare public seminars as he gave during the late 1940s. For his part, he refused to accept the state pension due him on his seventieth birthday in 1953. Nonetheless, the regime made a half-hearted attempt to appropriate his memory at the time of his funeral in October 1955, a backhanded admission that this man—whom it had driven into exile and pushed onto the margins of an intellectual life he had once so greatly enriched—had represented the best of the Spain it had extinguished. Ironically, had Ortega remained in Madrid throughout the war, and had the forces of the Republic triumphed, it is just possible that he would have fared no better, and possibly worse.

So much has changed in Spain since the death of Franco in 1975 that it is difficult to place Ortega on the current intellectual scene there. In the fashionable, prevailing circles of the Left, he is regarded as somewhat bourgeois and passé; the Right, now dispersed and demoralized (as much by the consumer revolution as by political change), feels no more affinity with him than it did a generation or two ago. His legacy lives on, somewhat modestly, in the *Revista de Occidente*–both the journal and the publishing house—which his son reopened in 1963. Overseas, Ortega's influence outlasted him by about twenty years. In Argentina he inspired a whole generation of philosophers and writers who have only recently departed the scene. And in Mexico, a country Ortega never visited, his influence was strongly felt through the pedagogical activities of former students—Spanish republican émigrés who found shelter at the Casa de España (later the Colegio de México). Some three million copies of his works have been sold in Spanish, a language in which his prose is regarded—quite rightly—as a model of clarity.

Ortega's life was a long, strenuous exercise in logic, rational discourse, and moderation. His reward—during his lifetime and thereafter—was not great. But one cannot help feeling that the particular position he eventually comes to occupy in the cultural pantheon of Spain and Spanish America will tell us a great deal about the prospects for those countries, whose destinies have been thwarted (or self-thwarted) for so long.

Note

1. *The Imperative of Modernity: An Intellectual Biography of José Ortega y Gasset* (Berkeley and Los Angeles; University of California Press, 1989.)

7

Victoria Ocampo's *Sur*

The problem of culture in South American countries is eminently political, in the sense that writers and artists have no choice but to decide early on where they fit in the broader context of Western civilization. During the period of the Iberian conquest, the issue could hardly arise: a politico-military order, imposed from the top, created a sharp hierarchy of values, in which proximity to the culture of the rulers—in this case, either Spanish or Portuguese—defined one's own position in society. The coming of the Enlightenment to Latin America in the late eighteenth century upset such certainties. For the local elites, the Iberian model was successfully challenged by France, creating a permanent schism between the culture absorbed, as it were, at one's mother's knee, and what one now knew to be "culture" in the highest sense of the word. One of the principal frustrations of the Latin American intellectual then became—and has since remained—the lack of immediate correspondence between the cultural values imported from abroad and the raw materials— human and otherwise—immediately available at home.

Since the First World War, however, some have risen to question the value and relevance of Western culture to what are, after all, only imperfectly Western societies. This cultural nationalism holds that Western institutions and values are exotic imports which have nothing to do with what these societies are all about.

In some ways this debate echoes the controversy between "Westernizers" and "Slavophiles" in late imperial Russia, but with three crucial differences. First, the range of cultural alternatives Latins have been free to explore has been much greater than it ever was for the Russians. Second, in certain places—Argentina, Chile, Uruguay, and the southern provinces of Brazil—the prospects for replicating Western society have been much greater than any other conceivable synthesis. And third, intellectuals in Europe and the United States, unlike their nineteenth-century predecessors, have tended to encourage a rejection of their own institutions, ostensibly to encourage the Latins in their search for "authenticity" but actually to service their own exoticism, utopianism, or self-hatred.

All of these issues and more are helpfully illuminated in a major new monograph, by the British scholar John King, on the Argentine literary review *Sur* (1931–1970) and its remarkable founder, Victoria Ocampo (1891–1979), who sustained *Sur* as a major force in Argentine and Hispanic letters for more than forty years.[1] Apart from making accessible for the first time to the English speaking reader an enormous amount of material on Argentine culture and politics Mr. King also reveals some of the agendas which inspire Latin American studies in Western Europe. and very specifically in the United Kingdom. But more on that anon.

Monographs on extinct literary journals are usually interesting only to specialists—if to them. Typically, they establish the phylogeny of alliances, schisms, and regroupings of small cliques of writers whose importance is difficult to grasp today. What makes this study different is the fact that the journal upon which it is based was party to a major cultural and political controversy in Argentina. Most of the issues in Mr. King's book are, in fact, of continuing importance in the other Latin American republics, as well as a number of other countries of the Third World.

In the mid-1960s, when I was living in Argentina as a graduate student, it was simply impossible not to notice the way that the very name of Victoria Ocampo or her journal divided any social gathering into two warring camps. What somebody thought of Ocampo, *Sur*, and its group of writers anticipated a great deal of information about them, as well as about their views on Argentina and a wide range of other subjects.

In *Sur*'s final decade, Victoria Ocampo was something of an institution in Buenos Aires—particularly revered by those Argentines for whom the best period of national life had been before the first government of General Juan Perón (1946–1955). These might be reactionary society ladies who remembered those years as ones in which "you could get a servant for a favor"; but they might just as easily be schoolteachers or other less exalted personalities whose nostalgia was not for a world they had lost but for a world that might have been—Argentina as a democratic nation, with a rich, tolerant, and diverse cultural life. Ocampo's enemies were likewise disparate: they included Peronists and populists of other descriptions, also Marxists of a certain stripe ("Trotsko-Peronists"). These people despised her for her supposed wealth, her aristocratic origins, her friendships, her flamboyant personal style, above all for her notion of literature as something apart from—and superior to—politics, especially Argentine politics.

She was always "the controversial Victoria Ocampo"—a remarkable sobriquet for a woman who saw herself as basically nonpolitical (and who in fact is taken to task by Mr. King for being just that). For the irreverent, particularly cabaret comedians, she was an easy target, a relic from prehistoric ages, when the light went out from Paris to tell the Argentines what time to get up in the morning. One personal recollection perhaps illustrates this point. In the mid-1960s, there was a Fulbright professor in Buenos Aires from one of the minor universities in the mid-Atlantic area. He was a pleasant academic hack—a type which in retrospect seems unobjectionable compared to the kind of people who probably dominate his university today. Although his Spanish was atrocious, Ocampo, discovering that he was an American professor of philosophy, insisted on capturing him for her salon.

This was a sort of *thé-dansant* which met at her home in the elegant suburb of San Isidro on Sunday afternoons, admission to which was not easily obtained. The building itself was an architectural folly of a type which was once quite common in Argentina—a full-scale copy of the Petit Trianon at Versailles. The crème of Buenos Aires literary society—or rather, of a certain section of it—was there, but the poor professor could not communicate very well with his fellow guests, for the ground rules called for everyone to converse in French, a language which he had never learned to speak or understand. The learned professor, it thus turned out, had nothing to say.

The story—which was supposed to speak volumes about the superficiality of the circle surrounding Señora Ocampo—made the rounds of the small American academic community in Buenos Aires, mostly graduate students. None of *us* had been invited; our *Schadenfreude* was complete. Only in later years did it occur to me that the incident may never in fact have occurred.

The history of *Sur* begins and ends with this woman because it is impossible to imagine that remarkable literary enterprise without her. Born to one of the country's most distinguished (and wealthiest) families in 1891, she received the conventional education of a young woman of what was then the most rigid and pretentious aristocracy in Latin America. This included French and English governesses; trips to Europe at an early age; music; poetry; deportment; and preparation for an early marriage and motherhood. From the very beginning Victoria was precocious, and to some degree rebellious as well. In 1913, at the age of twenty-two, she married a man she did not love, apparently as a means of escaping the stifling atmosphere of her father's house. When her spouse proved equally oppressive, she left him and established a household of her own, to the horror of her elders and the envy of her contemporaries. She was the first woman of her class to drive her own car and smoke a cigarette in public.

In 1938 she went to Europe as a wealthy, footloose divorcée, living for most of the time in Paris, where she came into contact with the elite of French literature and art. A stunning beauty—she remained so well into middle age—she was also extremely generous with her resources, and therefore welcome in the most exclusive salons and studios of the French capital, as well as in literary cafés. It was here, too, that she got to know many of the Russian émigrés in Paris, particularly Stravinsky, whom she was later to bring to Argentina. In 1931, she returned to Argentina, determined to start a literary review of her own.

The two personalities who seem to have inspired her in this enterprise were the Spanish philosopher José Ortega y Gasset and the American writer Waldo Frank, both friends whom she met in Europe and who remained on *Sur's* editorial board to the end of their lives. Ortega had already visited Argentina in 1916 on a lecture tour, and returned in 1929, where he was the subject of much attention, particularly from women. In those days Buenos Aires society was a huge consumer of European culture, from lecturers to opera singers, much the way New York is today. This was facilitated by its vast wealth—the peso was on par with the dollar, and Argentina was ranked fifth or sixth among the countries in the world—and also by the fortuitous reversal of the seasons: the North Atlantic summer is the height of the Argentine social and cultural season.

According to Mr. King, Ortega's influence on Victoria Ocampo and *Sur* was felt in two critical ways. He believed that intellectuals should remain apart from politics; and that one of the primary tasks of any intellectual was to establish links with his counterparts in other countries; "autarky," he held, "could only spell obscurantism." As a corollary, Ortega asserted that the gap between the elite and the masses of any society was unbridgeable, and that the intellectuals of all countries had far more to say to one another than to their own peoples. These views reflected Ortega's own disillusionment with Spanish politics, and to some extent with Spanish culture; but they were well received in Argentina—a new country populated by immigrants from Spain and Italy but ruled by an aristocracy of landowners whose claim to prominence was partly based on the cultural distance between themselves and the hoi polloi. On the other hand, *Sur* never explicitly subscribed to Ortega's views (or any other elitist doctrines); thus, it was perfectly possible for serious democrats to feel at home with *Sur*'s approach to high culture. For these people, there was nothing inherently wrong with the kinds of things which interested the *Sur* group; it was merely that Argentina's political and social system inhibited their diffusion to large numbers of ordinary people.

Waldo Frank, Ocampo's other guide in founding *Sur*, is not much read today, but he was perhaps the most overrated literary figure of his generation. Educated at Yale, a prolific poet, playwright, novelist, travel writer, and publicist, he was part of the "lost generation" which emigrated to Europe after the First World War. In Spain he met the Mexican poet Alfonso Reyes, who encouraged him to visit Argentina, which he did for the first time in 1929–30. Frank attracted huge crowds and scored an important success for American culture, which was then regarded as somewhat *infra dig* by the Argentine elite.

Why Frank made such an impact on the Argentines is not immediately apparent; years later local wits observed that he was important there because people thought he was important in the United States, and vice versa. Literary historians mention two factors which account for his reception—his apparent willingness to approach Argentines in the spirit of "inter-American" equality rather than condescension; and his rejection of "machine civilization," inspired by a conviction that emotional and atavistic impulses are more important than technology. Both sides of Frank's character were highly reassuring to Latin American audiences everywhere he went; it was a kind of pandering that was still new to them, and, when combined with good looks and considerable personal charm, must have been irresistible. Whatever the foolishness of his views on "machine civilization," he certainly did open a front in *Sur* for American culture—understood in its transcendentalist version. He also suggested the name of the magazine, which means "south" in Spanish.

In Argentina itself Ocampo gathered around her a coterie of talented young writers and poets—the most famous of which was subsequently to be Jorge Luis Borges, but which also included Eduardo Mallea, Adolfo Bioy Casares, Ezequiel Martínez Estrada, María Rosa Oliver, as well as two Latin American expatriates who settled for a time in Buenos Aires, the Mexican Alfonso Reyes and the Dominican Pedro Henríquez Ureña.

The importance of a new journal to Argentine literary life at a time like 1931 cannot be exaggerated, for in those years it was virtually impossible for any writer to make a living from his pen except through journalism. There were no Argentine book publishing houses; poets had to subsidize the printing of their own books, which they also had to distribute themselves; "culture" was European culture, something that one acquired at the Hachette or Garnier bookshop, or that was performed by a touring French or Italian company at the Colón Opera House. In spite of their pretensions, and even their patterns of consumption, the Argentine upper and upper-middle classes were philistine to the core.

Into such a world *Sur* brought a sophisticated, cosmopolitan literary taste and an unabashed regard for high culture. Between 1931 and 1970 the magazine published 350 issues, some of the special numbers dedicated to the literature of a particular country—Japan, Israel, Brazil, the United States. A typical issue featured cultural and philosophical essays, book and film reviews, and art criticism. *Sur* was particularly inclined toward translation, and many British, American, and French writers appeared there in Spanish for the first time, including William Faulkner (*The Wild Palms*, translated by Jorge Luis Borges), André Breton, Virginia Woolf, Graham Greene, and André Malraux. Over the years its roster of writers included François Mauriac, Jacques

Maritain, Alberto Moravia, Bertolt Brecht, Roger Callois, Thomas Mann, Rafael Alberti, Albert Camus, Jean-Paul Sartre, Simone de Beauvoir, Maurice Merleau-Ponty, and Antonio Gramsci.

Sur's contribution was not merely substantive—it opened whole new horizons to two generations of Latin American writers—but philosophical. It had no particular point of view, but it proclaimed certain values which could not easily be taken for granted—the importance of art for its own sake, of the highest standards of artistic quality, of freedom of expression. As the distinguished Mexican poet and anthropologist Octavio Paz later wrote, "What the *NRF* [*Nouvelle Revue Française*] was to the Europeans, *Sur* is for me: the world of letters conceived as complete—neither apart from, nor opposed to, other worlds—but also never subordinated to them."

It is perhaps inevitable that for many years *Sur* gave priority to European writers, and published Argentine and Latin American contributors in the back of the book. "The European ideal," Mr. King calls it, and with some justification. Nonetheless, he exaggerates the degree to which the journal neglected Latin America: by his own reckoning, *Sur* published Mario Vargas Llosa, Gabriel García Márquez, Guillermo Cabrera Infante, Carlos Fuentes, and Gabriela Mistral. With the exception of Mistral, at the time most of them had yet to achieve widespread recognition, so that *Sur* can rightly claim to have played a role in nurturing the new Latin American novel which later acquired so prominent a place in the cultural life of the North Atlantic area.

Victoria Ocampo's personal economic circumstances, like those of many Argentines, began to deteriorate in the 1950s; by the 1960s it was no longer easy to subsidize her literary review, even with occasional foundation grants and the introduction of advertising from American, British, French, and Argentine companies. By the end of the latter decade, *Sur* was appearing infrequently, and in 1971 Ocampo, advanced in years and increasingly frail, closed it down. It has no successor, and there are no potential candidates on the horizon. The reasons are not merely economic but definitional. Western Europe, and particularly Paris, has lost the viselike grip in which it once held Argentine culture, but after a decade of terrorism, counterterror, repression, and war, it is still difficult for Argentines to say today what are those distinctively "national" qualities which should inform intellectual and artistic life.

Ocampo and *Sur* became controversial precisely because they became enmeshed—even without meaning to—in a conflict between the liberal, cosmopolitan culture they espoused and the authoritarian populism that eventually overtook Argentina's public life. To understand how this happened requires a brief detour through Argentine political history.

Between 1880 and 1914, Argentina was transformed—culturally and economically—by European capital and immigration; but its political life was never fully reshaped to fit the mold of Western democracy. A suffrage reform made possible the victory of the country's first popularly elected chief executive in 1916, but the experiment in electoral democracy was brief. In 1930 the armed forces overthrew the government and up through the Second World War the country was ruled by a succession of conservative businessmen and military officers. In 1943, another military coup brought to the fore a new kind of leadership, personified by the labor minister, Colonel (later General) Juan Perón. In 1946, Perón was elected in his own right and for the next nine years he ruled as a quasi-dictator. When he quarreled with the Catholic Church, the military turned against him in September 1955, and forced him into exile.

Argentine historians still cannot quite decide how to evaluate the Peronist period; their ambivalence is justified. Mr. King claims that "Peronism was arguably one of the few truly democratic regimes in Argentine history," but it would be truer to say that it was one of the few regimes in which most Argentines felt they were represented—not quite the same thing.

Nonetheless, it would be wrong to underestimate the genuinely popular and reformist aspects of the period. Perón made the labor movement a major player in national politics. He closed the gap between the classes, particularly the working class and the white-collar class, and between the city of Buenos Aires and the rural provinces of the Interior. He opened up new opportunities to the sons of immigrants, many of whom became wealthy industrialists or successful professionals. He built roads, schools, and clinics in the neglected Interior. He broke down an unspoken "racial" code which separated the darker-skinned Argentines from descendants of European immigrants.

He also, however, showed minimal respect for freedom of the press and opinion; he persecuted independent trade unionists; he purged university faculties of non-Peronist professors; he exalted loyalty to his person (and that of his wife, Eva) above all other national qualities, and indeed insisted that Peronism was consubstantial with the Argentine nationality. He also mismanaged the economy to the point that by the end of his rule he was rationing some of the basic foodstuffs which Argentina had formerly produced in abundance.

After Perón's fall in 1955, his successors, military and civilian, could not agree on the nature of the new political order, save that it should somehow be both democratic and anti-Peronist, even if this meant excluding at least 35 percent of the electorate from full participation in politics. Some supporters of the "Liberating Revolution" hoped that in time Perón's followers would transfer their loyalties to other parties and forces; others simply hoped to suppress Peronism as long as necessary until it died a natural death. When this did not happen, they accepted military rule for an indefinite term as the least objectionable of all possible alternatives.

The birth and death of *Sur* thus brackets some extraordinarily dramatic moments in Argentine and Western cultural history. During the 1930s the fundamental controversy in Argentina (as in most of the countries of Western Europe) was the viability of liberal, democratic institutions, versus some form of right-wing authoritarian rule. In Argentina the debate was sharpened by the Spanish civil war, which was passionately debated in both Parliament and the press, and also provoked fistfights in streetcars and brawls in outdoor cafés. The coming of the Second World War divided Argentines still further, between those who favored the Allied cause and those who did not—though partisans of the Axis often claimed only to favor "neutrality."

The sudden advent of Perón was seen both at home and abroad as an unexpected transfer to the Western hemisphere of the same fascist forces just defeated by the Allied armies in Europe. The notion was exaggerated and in many ways wrongheaded, but it was at least understandable; many of the same people, including many of the same intellectuals, who supported the Axis in the Second World War, were now suddenly reborn as Peronists. These were also the same people who were put into university chairs

from which socialists, liberals, even conservatives were ejected
by the new Peronist university administrations. Conversely, everything which passed for secular and progressive in Argentina
was opposed to Perón. And this remained so in spite of the fact
that the new regime was also firmly opposed by those forces
traditionally associated with social and economic privilege.

In effect, the Perón period altered the fault lines of Argentine
culture, or perhaps merely made them more politically explicit.
Whereas Argentina (even under the fraudulent conservative governments of the 1930s) had been—however imperfectly—secular,
pluralist, cosmopolitan, and capitalist, in the Peronist period it
was clerical, doctrinaire, nationalist, populist, and statist. It produced no "strong cultural alternative," Mr. King writes, but rather
was "a ragbag of different ideological tendencies whose only
common denominator was their rejection of liberalism."

People associated with *Sur* made a convenient target, since
they were guilty on both cultural and political counts. Though
never active politically, Ocampo was a close personal friend of
Marcelo de Alvear (president, 1922-28), whose death in 1942
deprived Argentine liberalism of its only outstanding leader.
Borges, Bioy Casares, Mallea—practically all of the *Sur* writers—
were democratic centrists and cultural cosmopolites; they tended
to vote for the Radical party. They often taught or wrote side by
side with democratic socialists or even communists, though not
with Catholic nationalists.

During the Perón period the latter took their revenge. *Sur* was
never censored, but persons associated with it were harassed or
driven out of their jobs, particularly in the universities. Borges was
deprived of his livelihood at the Buenos Aires Public Library (and
peremptorily reassigned as "inspector-of-poultry in the public
markets"); Ocampo was briefly jailed on unspecified charges, and
incarcerated along with common criminals and prostitutes.

The terms of the Argentine political equation were reversed
after Perón's fall. The successor regimes, military and civilian,
were "liberal" only in the sense that they were opposed to
Peronism. The dictator's followers were exiled, jailed, or proscribed, but the cause did not die, largely because the country's
economic decline—which began in the early 1950s—continued
and deepened over the next two decades. Between 1955 and 1958,
Peronism was still the largest political force in the country, so

that no other party could capture the presidency without making a peace with it. By 1970 it was obvious that unless Perón died first, he would easily win the first genuinely free election the military chose to convoke, which in fact proved to be the case three years later. Thus, the choices became excruciatingly limited for persons of genuine democratic conviction, as Ocampo and the *Sur* group unquestionably were. To favor full expression of political opinion meant, in effect, a return of the dictator and all of his works; to fail to do so rendered the value of Argentine liberal currency almost worthless.

Meanwhile, in the 1960s various sectors of the Left who had opposed Perón during his presidency began to rethink the meaning of his regime. Disappointed that the Argentine working class continued to be loyal to the exiled dictator rather than to embrace one of the available Marxist alternatives, some intellectuals concluded that Peronism must not have been a South American variant of fascism at all, but a premature version of Third World socialism. In the service of this dubious claim, much recent Argentine history had to be rewritten, condemning decent democrats for their tactical convergences with the hated "oligarchy." The retrospective litmus test of political decency in the 1940s became in the 1970s one's "anti-imperialism," proven by neutrality during the Second World War and then by "non-alignment" in the cold war thereafter. Inevitably, *Sur* was bound to fail both tests.

To discuss these issues authoritatively requires a fairly nuanced understanding of some complex political and cultural issues. This John King has, along with a very firm grasp of Argentine history and the literary environment in which *Sur* writers operated. What he lacks is any apparent sympathy with liberal democracy, which in turn prevents him from being wholly fair to his subject. Those familiar with the British academic environment will recognize in his book some of its characteristic birthmarks: an extremely lengthy gestation period (work began on this study in 1973); a strong background in French studies; careful, well-wrought prose; a clear leftist bias; a leavening of obligatory anti-Americanism; and a romantic (and often inaccurate) perception of other Latin American countries, which he evidently knows far less well than Argentina. There is also, it must be said, a certain coyness to his argument. He attempts to defuse some of the criticisms to which his interpretation leaves him vulnerable by seeming to take them into account in advance; nonetheless, he persists in his point of view regardless of all the countervailing evidence.

Mr. King's brief against the *Sur* group is that its members eschewed Argentine nationalism, identification with Latin American culture, and political commitment. In an opening chapter he correctly identifies the great debate in Argentine cultural history—whether to be "European" or "American" (somewhat like the famous "Redskins" versus "Palefaces" argument in American literature). He also shows, again quite properly, that the position one took in this debate could (and often did) have political and economic referents. If one believes, for example, that the American environment (and the people who inhabit it) are essentially barbarous, as did Domingo Faustino Sarmiento (president, 1868–1874), then necessarily those who possess "culture" (defined as European culture) are the proper class to rule.

This is certainly the way that the Argentine upper class justified its privileged position during Ocampo's formative years. Mr. King fails to point out, however, that the very same group advanced policies—particularly foreign immigration, free public education, and foreign investment—that ultimately produced a large middle class to challenge its hold on political power. Moreover, almost all of the leaders of the first two democratic governments in Argentina (1916–28) were drawn from the very same elite; its most characteristic personality, President Marcelo T. de Alvear, had long served as ambassador in Paris and regarded himself as much at home there as in Buenos Aires. In addition, the Argentine "masses" (as King calls them) were themselves always divided in their cultural loyalties. Those who came from Italy and Spain—a quarter of the population in 1914, nearly a decisive majority in Buenos Aires, Rosario, Santa Fe, and other cities of the eastern littoral—continued to think of themselves as Europeans, and, if they could afford to, educated their children accordingly. Those who lived in the provinces of the Interior, particularly in the Andean states bordering on Chile, Peru, and Bolivia, were part of another world, light years behind (or at least, apart from) the bustling, sophisticated city-state of Buenos Aires.

Which was the "real" Argentina? Obviously, neither and both. To pretend as late as 1940 that the country was typically Latin

American, at least in the same cultural sense as Peru, Colombia, or Venezuela, would at best be a half-truth; a new wave of Spanish and Italian immigration following the Second World War would undermine the claim still further. The most important *political* fact of those years, however, was a change not in the mix of cultural components but in urban demography. During the war hundreds of thousands of darker-skinned Argentines emigrated from the Interior provinces to work in new industries in and around the capital, and by 1946 constituted a huge, unorganized political force to which Perón successfully appealed.

While there were strongly Argentine historical antecedents to Perón, he was never completely "American"; rather, he drew sustenance from a different "Europe" from that of Victoria Ocampo: instead of London or Paris, it was Mussolini's Rome or Franco's Spain. His particular genius, in fact, was his capacity to integrate both "American" and (his particular choice of) "European" currents into a single "Argentine" identity. It was a game so complicated, requiring such a careful, delicate balance, that many years would pass before anyone else could even attempt it. The point is that Argentine nationalism—of the kind that Mr. King faults *Sur* for having rejected—was not without its own European origins: Perón's personalism and authoritarianism were as much Spanish as Latin American, and in the end he was no more or less Argentine than Jorge Luis Borges.

Mr. King makes much of the fact that some writers who specialized in local color (Horacio Quiroga, for example) were less welcome in the pages of *Sur* than those who considered their work part of a larger European cultural horizon. Even so, it is remarkable how many Latin American writers eventually were published in its pages. The same is true of leftists like Gramsci, Sartre, and Brecht. Mr. King acknowledges as much, but then abruptly withdraws the concession by offering his own version of Marcuse's doctrine of "repressive tolerance":

> Gramsci...had warned against the seemingly liberal, all-embracing nature of such anthologies [issues devoted to the literature of a foreign country]; his work shows that hegemony is not maintained by imposing a uniform ideology, but by the way in which different ideological viewpoints are absorbed by the dominant discourse....
>
> In the case of Grarnsci, as in the case of Sartre, the universal moral significance of his writing displaced his particular political significance. Such

writers would have to escape the pages of *Sur* before their particular importance could be understood in Argentina.

In other words, *Sur* could only have met Mr. King's criteria for
ideological pluralism by publishing the most overtly political se-
lections of writers of whom he approves—writers on the Left,
needless to say—and only then by preceding and following their
work by other writers of like mind.

Perhaps the greatest injustice King commits against *Sur* is to
claim that it purposely avoided political commitment. Actually,
it would be nearer to the truth to say that Ocampo and her colleagues believed that some things were more important than
politics, and that a writer need not wear his politics on his sleeve.
Among other things, this explains their preference for the more
nonpolitical pieces of European Marxist writers. In general, however, the *Sur* group was suspicious of people who subordinated
art to ideology. Logically, then, the magazine was always hostile
to both fascism and communism. To say, however, that it was
apolitical, or deaf from confronting political responsibility when
the situation required it, is simply untrue, unless King's own ideological preferences are to be the sole criterion for who is committed and who is not.

It is perhaps worth recalling some of the positions taken by
Sur over the years. It supported the Republican side in the Spanish civil war, at a time when all "fashionable" Buenos Aires (including self-styled Argentine "nationalists") were pro-Franco. It
openly sympathized with the Allied cause (thus, inevitably, the
Soviet cause) during the Second World War. And it shared a
common attitude with the United States and Western Europe in
the cold war, and later with democratic (as opposed to leftist
revolutionary) forces in Latin America. This explains why, up to
the Cuban revolution, the *Sur* group sensed no particular antagonism from the Argentine Left. Indeed, between 1931 and
1948 they were part of the same broader "liberal" political community; because of the overwhelming need to marshal a common front against Perón, the relationship survived precariously
through the early years of the cold war.

Mr. King mostly disapproves of *Sur's* political preferences where
they were expressed—even to the point of taking issue with its support for the British cause during the Second World War. He points

out, somewhat archly, that the British government actually preferred that Argentina remain neutral, so that its merchant marine could safely deliver foodstuffs essential for the war effort. In the narrowest sense this may be true, but it fails to take into account the cultural environment in which *Sur*, the local British community, and the Argentine political class were operating at the time. In 1940 neutrality *as practiced* in Argentina was intended to be, and in fact was understood to be, an expression of pro-Axis sentiment, whatever the secret priorities of Whitehall. Forty years later, with Nazism a vague memory, it is easy to rewrite history from a *tiers-mondiste* point of view. What Mr. King appears to be doing is reading his repugnance for Thatcher and the rebirth of British patriotism back into history; for him, as presumably for many British academics of the Left, there can never have been a time when their country was on the "right side" of history.

Mr. King is correct to single out the Cuban revolution as the watershed event that dramatically altered *Sur's* position in Argentina's cultural life, and made it an object of controversy and ridicule. The way he puts it is this:

> *Sur* chose to turn its back on Cuba, and thus rejected much that was innovative in Latin American culture in the 1960s....

> To take an anti-Cuban line in a Latin American literary magazine at the time was virtually to condemn that magazine to the wilderness....

> Equally important, the anti-Cuba stance lost *Sur* the cooperation of many boom writers, the Cubans themselves, and a whole generation of Argentine intellectuals who were clearly identified with the Revolution....

> *Sur* had always read Latin American texts selectively, and could interpret Cuba only at the most literal level: as a communist, totalitarian regime.

For Mr. King, it would seem, it is more important to be in tune with the *Zeitgeist* than to adhere rigorously to one's own code of political decency. More remarkable still is the author's apparent presumption that as late as 1986 the jury was still out on the nature of the Cuban experiment. A more balanced appraisal would have emphasized the degree to which *Sur*, for all of its conventional "literary" tastes and its evident conservatism, was closer to understanding the nature of the situation on an island four thousand miles away—not to mention its threat to the freedom of its own writers and artists—than "many boom writers" and a whole host of Argentine intellectuals.[2]

We get a much clearer idea of Mr. King's objections to *Sur* when he finally reveals the kind of literary journal which he prefers—the Mexican quarterly *Cuadernos Americanos*. "It illustrated," he writes, "that an alternative attitude to that of *Sur* was possible and coherent, and its fortieth birthday has been recently celebrated with a large exhibition in Havana." To those who know both countries, the comparison would seem wholly out of hand: unlike Argentina, Mexico has a rich Indian heritage, and a strong Hispano-mestizo popular culture, which simplifies enormously problems of definition.[3] Still and all, one should not overrate the profundity or seriousness of *Cuadernos Americanos*: its *mejicanidad* is largely expressed through screeds against the United States, dime-store Marxism, and wholly unconvincing excursions into nativism. Mr. King seems not to know, by the way, that *Cuadernos Americanos* has long been subsidized by the Mexican government, as part of its ongoing campaign to domesticate its intellectual class and assure that national debate remains within certain restricted limits. Its "leftism" and "Americanism" are really nothing more than a fancy-dress swindle, as any Mexican intellectual—including any left-wing Mexican intellectual worth his salt—will tell you. A better example might be Octavio Paz's magazine *Vuelta*, but it too has "turned its back on the Cuban revolution," so perhaps its political commitment would fall short of Mr. King's requirements.

What kind of a literary review would have more nearly served the interests of Argentine national identity, cultural authenticity, and political commitment during the years 1931–1970? Even Mr. King admits that "[*Sur*'s] detractors provided no lasting alternative strategy." To be sure, Perón's government subsidized cultural activities of a sort, and rewarded complaisant writers and artists. But even Peronist critics, Mr. King writes, "admit that in cultural terms the pro-Peronist writers produced very little of value and that they represented a small section of the intelligentsia." A few costume films here; a few tangos there; one or two second-rate novels; the "cultural" supplement of Eva Perón's daily *Democracia*—all failed to outlast their immediate context.

The Perón period did, however, terminate once and for all the conditions under which "establishment" culture had been possible in the first place. It bankrupted the country and particularly the minor rentier class—the very group upon which serious culture had depended. It politicized the universities and provoked the first of many waves of emigration of Argentine intellectuals to Western Europe, other Latin American countries, and the United States. What was particularly deplorable about all of this was the celerity with which the old culture was destroyed without the slightest notion of what was to be put in its place, save for xenophobia and anti-intellectualism disguised as cultural nationalism. In that single sense Perón can rightly be said to have been the South American precursor of Third World socialism.

In the late 1960s and early 1970s, a vapid if harmless folkloricism was put into the service of a movement for "national and popular power"—that is to say, urban terrorism. (The guerrillas even called themselves *montoneros*, the name given to gaucho armies in the early nineteenth century.) In such an environment, *Sur* was necessarily irrelevant to the Argentine scene, not because of any deficiencies on its part, but because the best of European and international culture which it sought to bring to the country no longer evoked a local resonance. More was the pity, for the newer currents—both Left and Right—which dominated discourse in the 1970's left the country poorer, bloodied, greatly diminished. By the time Ocampo died in 1979, even the Cuban journal *Casa de las Americas* could not but refer to *Sur* as "the work of a woman who lived life on her own terms, and instead of expending her considerable resources on clothes, jewelry, and perfumes, directed part of them to make it possible for Argentina to have an up-to-date literary magazine." A grudging, modest tribute, whose very source confirms beyond all doubt its fundamental justice.

Notes

1. *Sur: A Study of the Argentine Literary Journal and Its Role in the Development of a Culture, 1931-1970* (Cambridge University Press, 1986).
2. As for "the Cubans," King passes over the fact that, with the exception of Edmundo Desnoes, not a single important writer identified with the early period of the revolution currently resides and writes in Cuba itself. Cultural bureaucrats disguised as writers—like Roberto Fernández Retamar—are quite another matter.
3. Even so, the Mexicans have not reached a consensus on the value of their Spanish heritage; in fact, it is the longest running controversy in that nation's history.

8

García Lorca and His Times

Imagine, if you will, a poet and playwright who died more than fifty years ago at the age of thirty-eight becoming the stuff of enduring legend—surviving decades of theatrical censorship in his own country and major aesthetic upheavals everywhere, including the death of poetry as a major art form. Imagine, too, that he wrote in a language that is not widely studied or read by the major literary intellectuals in Western Europe or the United States. And finally, picture such a figure commanding sufficient interest to justify a major biography by Ian Gibson, a world-class scholar, poet, and novelist, written over a ten-year period with the financial assistance of an improbable coalition of governments (Spain, Ireland, the United States, and Cuba), and published not by a university press but by Pantheon and Faber & Faber, two of the most prestigious commercial houses in the United States and Great Britain. That is the way—the only way—to give outsiders some sense of the abiding mystique of Federico García Lorca.[1]

García Lorca: A Life, is, inevitably, much more than the biography of a single individual. It is a detailed excursion through Spanish cultural life during the period between the First World War and the outbreak of the civil war in 1936, as seen from the vantage point of a literary-theatrical vanguard. The principal personalities of this group were Lorca, Luis Buñuel, Manuel de Falla, and Salvador Dalí, but it also included the Chileans Pablo Neruda and Vicente Huidobro, the Cuban Alejo Carpentier, and even the Russians Sergei Diaghilev and Igor Stravinsky. All of this is set against the background of a swelling social and political crisis, which finally erupted into a war that claimed a million victims, one of the very first of which was the poet him-

drama set at high pitch, brilliantly executed by a biographer who knows just what he is doing.

Though his career spanned a much longer period, Federico García Lorca was in many ways the archetypical literary figure—the poet laureate, if one will—of the Second Spanish Republic (1931-36). He was born in 1898 in the province of Granada to a landowning family of unusually liberal political inclinations and cultural tastes. The poet received a first-rate education and began writing at an early age, encouraged by teachers and established literary figures. At the same time he had a strong interest in music, and might even have become a distinguished pianist had not his parents refused to support a conservatory education in France. Instead, Federico went up to Madrid to obtain a law degree—"to have something to fall back upon"—although he lived entirely on subventions from his parents until he was well into his thirties. (In fact, much of the time as an adult he lived with them in a spacious apartment near the Prado in downtown Madrid.) His parents also subsidized the printing of his first book of poems in 1921.

Lorca came of age in Granada during the period immediately after the First World War, when the city possessed a vibrant cultural and literary life. Almost from the time he began writing he had excellent critics and colleagues with whom to discuss his work. And as a very young man he met and became friends with the composer Manuel de Falla, who commissioned him to write the libretto of an opera for puppets, *El retablo de Maestro Pedro* ("Master Peter's Puppet Show," 1923). When he moved to Madrid to enroll at the university, he almost immediately took up with Buñuel and Dalí. So in addition to abundant good looks, talent, and money, Lorca had immediate entree into the most talented circle of his contemporaries.

For most of the 1920s, however, Lorca was what Gibson calls a "private celebrity"—that is, he had not published much, and was not well known outside a small (if somewhat special) circle of friends and acquaintances. In fact, Lorca preferred to communicate his work orally to a live audience. Gibson attempts a description of those evenings at the Residencia de Estudiantes in Madrid, where the poet would recite his works to the accompaniment of his own piano music. The man's immense personal charisma on such occasions can only be suggested by Gibson's account; if only we had a recording, even a very bad one!

A personal crisis led Lorca to leave Spain in 1929 and spend a season in New York, in those days a somewhat more exotic destination for a Spanish literary figure than it would be today. The stay seems not to have been very successful, though it inspired a book *(A Poet in New York)* that remains one of the city's more remarkable literary testaments. Lorca arrived with no English and never bothered to pick up more than a few words while here. (Unusually for his class, he never acquired much French, either.) He made few American friends. He was not impressed with the United States, or rather what he saw of it, and returned to Spain via Havana (where he spent three happy months) full of silly, rather conventional European notions about this country—for example, he referred to New York as "Senegal with machines." Gibson tentatively suggests, I think wrongly, that Lorca's experience in New York moved him "toward a Marxist analysis of the human condition."

By the time he returned to Spain in 1931, the monarchy had been replaced overnight by a Republic of uncertain social and political content. After the fall of the monarchy, the fault line in Spanish politics shifted, and Republicans of the Left and Right found themselves at odds, while partisans of the old regime—the Church, the army, and the landed aristocracy—continued to dream of some kind of restoration. But in cultural policy, Republican Spain knew what it wanted: it followed the Soviet Union (or rather, what it naively imagined the Soviet Union still to be) by deploying artists, writers, and musicians across the country to bring culture to hundreds of remote and forgotten villages and towns. Initially Lorca was sent by the Ministry of Education to lecture and read poetry; subsequently he became part of a new university theater known as La Barraca, which travelled around presenting works of the Spanish classical stage.

Lorca's work with La Barraca encouraged him to begin writing plays of his own, the first of which, *Blood Wedding* (1933), was a modest success in Madrid and brought him for the first time to the attention of the wider Spanish public. The following year he took the play and members of the company to far-off Argentina, where it—and he—scored a huge success. Buenos Aires was then the richest and most important Spanish-speaking city in the world, the home of such distinguished literary figures as Jorge Luis Borges, Alfonso Reyes (serving there as Mexican ambassador), Leopoldo Lugones, the Uruguayan Horacio Quiroga, and the gifted Dominican critic Pedro Henríquez Ureña. Success in that demanding environment (and also in prosperous Montevideo, the capital of neighboring Uruguay) virtually guaranteed Lorca a market for his work elsewhere in Latin America and—for the first time—at home in Spain. The Argentine theater also afforded Lorca his first experience of independent financial success.

Upon his return to Madrid in late 1934, Lorca mounted a production of his new play, *Yerma*, a critique of the Spanish code of sexual honor, which opened at the same explosive moment that the Republican government was disestablishing the Roman Catholic Church. The following year, Lorca's play *Doña Rosita the Spinster* touched upon Granada's restrictive moral and spiritual environment—what Gibson paraphrases as "its resistance to change, its lack of vitality, and its intolerance." In normal times neither play would have been regarded as "political" in the strict sense, but in the context of a growing conflict among Spaniards about the meaning and value of the past, Lorca was seen as distinctly *parti pris*, which of course he was.

By early 1936 it was evident to Lorca's friends that the country was moving toward civil war, and they urged him to return to Argentina or travel to Mexico with the actress Margarita Xirgu, a friend who had created the principal character of *Blood Wedding* for delighted audiences in Buenos Aires. Instead Lorca remained in the capital until nearly the last hours of peace, taking the night train to Granada, somehow convinced that he would be safer there.

This turned out not to be the case, because the city and province fell into rebel hands almost immediately after the uprising against the constitutional government in Madrid. Though he had a wide circle of friends in his hometown, over the years Lorca had also acquired many enemies there. Among these were the romantic nationalists of the Falange, Spain's semi-fascist political movement, who defended the old order. Once the Republican authorities were deposed in Granada, militants of the new party in power—most of them semi-educated, distinguished only by the intensity of their *ressentiment*, went about the city settling old scores. Gibson retells here (somewhat more briefly) the authoritative account that appears in his first book, *The Death of Lorca*, published some fifteen years ago.[2] At first Lorca stayed at his parents' town house; when that became unsafe, he took refuge with the family of two young friends who were members of the local Falange. Even this did not protect the poet; a few days later he was plucked from his refuge by right-wing thugs and murdered at a remote spot in the country outside of town, then pushed into a common grave with other innocent victims of General Franco's *pronunciamiento* against the Republic.

Gibson remarks, rather dryly, that there was nothing remarkable about Lorca's execution. "The rebels," he explains, "were determined to liquidate all their left-wing opponents, and so far as they were concerned, Lorca was just one more 'Red,' albeit a particularly obnoxious one." Presumably Gibson is understating the case for dramatic effect. For his part, General Franco later admitted that Lorca's assassination was "a mistake," which for him was a remarkable concession. By executing without trial and without cause the brightest star of Republican Spain's literary firmament, the "Nationalists" destroyed whatever claim they might assert to represent all that was authentic in their culture. In all likelihood, before July 1936 the unpoetical Franco had never heard of García Lorca; for nearly forty years thereafter, he would never be allowed to forget him.

Any biographer of Lorca must address two rather complex issues—the relationship between the writer's personality and his work on the one hand, and between his work and Spanish literary tradition on the other. The first of these requires considerable delicacy, since Lorca is generally believed to have been a homosexual. Gibson approaches the subject gingerly by affirming that there is no conclusive evidence on this subject, and that much of the documentation (letters, diaries, manuscript memoirs) seems to have disappeared if indeed it ever existed in the first place. The Lorca family fully cooperated with Gibson; other families were less forthcoming, even though by that time most of the principals of the story had long since died.

Having prepared us, then, for negligible amounts of information, Gibson then blurts out everything he knows or suspects about the subject, which turns out to be quite a lot. From the very beginning, it seems, Lorca was uninhibited about his sexual needs, though he never overcame a deep sense of shame about them. At first he attempted rather crudely to seduce whichever young men attracted him, including the young Salvador Dalí (with whom he apparently had a brief affair before Dalí moved on to women). Eventually he became part of a discreet homosexual underground in Madrid and Granada, and later in New York and Havana. On one occasion Lorca met the American poet Hart Crane in New York at a decidedly extra-literary function—a party full of drunken sailors, where, in spite of serious language barriers, the Spaniard immediately made himself at home.

Lorca also seems to have had two sustained relationships, both with ostensibly heterosexual men—or, at any rate, men who subsequently married and fathered children—Emilio Aladrén and Rafael Rodríguez Rapun. It was Aladrén's decision to abandon Lorca for a woman that apparently precipitated the emotional crisis in 1929 that led to the poet's brief expatriation in the United States. Rodríguez Rapun, whom the poet met through the university theater, was his inseparable companion for the last four years of his life and, Gibson argues, may have provided the reason for Lorca's refusal to quit Spain even when in danger of his life. Rodríguez Rapun was killed in action on the Republican front in the Spanish civil war, and Aladrén died in 1944.

Gibson's brief is that as a poet and dramatist Lorca was strongly shaped by his status as a sexual outsider. On a first reading of the evidence, the case is not difficult to make. Much of Lorca's work deals with two recurrent themes, death and frustrated love; an important subtheme is the cruelty of Spain's puritanical sexual codes, and the damage they inflicted on the lives of women. (A perspicacious Argentine journalist once asked him why the leading characters in all of his plays were female.) In strictly Spanish terms, and bearing in mind that we are speaking of circumstances sixty or seventy years ago, Lorca could be regarded as something of a feminist. Perhaps feminism—a very old-fashioned kind of feminism, be it noted—was as close as he dared approach the subject of his own sexual marginality.[3] That was explosive enough, and may—as Gibson first suggested years ago in *The Death of Lorca*—have cost him his life, since in Granada homosexuality and feminism were assumed to be much the same thing, and both were despised in equal measure.

It is also possible that Lorca's sense of alienation from the sexual mainstream influenced his general view of society and shaped his politics, which were anticlerical, culturally pluralist, and broadly socialist. But as the son of a rich landowner Lorca might just as easily arrived at the same political notions through lofty idealism, guilt, snobbery, naïveté, or a combination of all

four. The phenomenon of the aristocratic leftist, of whom Lorca
is an example, has been extremely common in Spain and Latin
America during the twentieth century. But it is important to recognize a critical distinction: characteristically, such a person is
willing to make radical statements to the press, or even to sympa-
thize publicly with the Soviet Union, but is generally reluctant to
join the Communist party or its front organizations.

On the other hand, it is at least possible to entertain another
point of view. There need be no necessary and inevitable relationship between Lorca's politics and his personal psychology.
Indeed, the established social order in Spain that Lorca so often
vilified in flip remarks to journalists was the very same that provided him with a protected berth as a son of the *haute bourgeoisie*,
and insulated him to some extent from the humiliation of being
different from other men. From that (admittedly limited) perspective, under slightly different family circumstances and with
other cultural interests he might have turned out to be a fascist,
as did his contemporary José Antonio Primo de Rivera, founder
of the Falange Española, possible closet homosexual, and—inter-
estingly enough—the subject of another biography by Ian Gibson
which, unfortunately, has so far appeared only in Spain.[4] The
two men were not friends—though they knew each other—and
both came to the same end; Primo de Rivera was shot in the
Republican zone at about the same time that his followers were
dispatching Lorca in Granada.

Evidently, at times the poet was a frustrated and unhappy man,
though this does not seem to have prevented him from having a
warm relationship with his family and many satisfying platonic
friendships with a huge circle of talented and attractive men and
women. Nor did it prevent him from achieving high literary and
artistic distinction, both at home and abroad. The fact is that we
owe Lorca's work to his special circumstances; his achievement
cannot be separated from his private drama.

The matter of Lorca's special place in Spanish culture is even
more interesting. As in all countries situated on the immediate
periphery of Western culture, Spanish intellectuals have debated
since at least the eighteenth century the value of their vernacular
traditions in relation to the more sophisticated standards set by
a foreign metropolis. In the case of Spain, the model of civilization for the vanguard had always been France and specifically

Paris—indeed, during the reign of Charles III (1759–88) there was a serious attempt to reshape Spanish society, culture, and institutions along Bourbon lines, provoking much popular resistance. The subsequent war to expel Napoleon from the peninsula in 1812–14 was as much a *Kulturkampf* as a struggle for self-determination, and—if an inconvenient truth be told—it is not clear even now whether the Spanish people would not have done better to lose that war rather than win it.

In the same year Lorca was born, Spain lost both Cuba and the Philippines in a brief, humiliating contest with the United States. The defeat—"the disaster," as Spaniards always called it—provoked an extensive cultural soul-searching by the younger members of the literary establishment. Eventually, the Generation of 1898, as it became known, split in two. One faction attributed Spain's defeat to its refusal to come to terms with the modern world; the other insisted that the humiliation of 1898 was the consequence of Spain's abandonment of its vernacular tradition. This second group believed that Spain's problem was precisely its uncritical worship of the modern, what the traditionalist Right considered the false gods of materialism, secularism, and progress. Characteristically, the two most outstanding figures of the movement, José Ortega y Gasset and Ramiro de Maeztu, ended up on opposite sides of the barricade in the civil war nearly forty years later.

Lorca stands precisely at the point where these two diverging roads from 1898 finally loop around and cross. His work (and also his personal style) was firmly rooted in the vernacular traditions of his region, so much so that Jorge Luis Borges once referred to him rather disdainfully as "a professional Andalusian." But Borges missed a crucial point—namely, that Lorca was an Andalusian with a difference. Rather than cynically exploiting the folkloric aspects of his region for wide-eyed Argentines (or Spaniards from other parts of his own country), he approached them critically. If he was an Andalusian through and through, it was from a sharply "revisionist" perspective.

From the ninth to the fifteenth century, Granada was the place where Eastern and Western cultures converged. In 1492 the last of a long series of military campaigns had defeated the Muslim caliphate, compelling both the Moors and Granada's large Jewish community to convert to Roman Catholicism or to quit the country altogether. Paradoxically, what had made Granada a unique corner of Spanish culture was precisely its synthesis of Moorish and Jewish elements, but, in attempting to justify the Reconquest, four subsequent centuries of Spanish historiography denied or minimized the value of both.

Lorca was deeply troubled about this. As he said in a newspaper interview a few weeks before the outbreak of the civil war, the Reconquest—which, after all, can be legitimately regarded as the epoch of Spain's creation as a modern nation—was

> a disastrous event, even though they may say the opposite in the schools. An admirable civilization, and a poetry, astronomy, architecture, and sensitivity unique in the world—all were lost, to give way to an impoverished, cowed city, a "miser's paradise."

No doubt the remark romanticizes to a fault the Moorish kingdom, and cruelly shortchanges the achievements of Spanish Catholic culture, but it does at least go well beyond the calculated folkloricism, the cynical exploitation of "local color" which is all that most foreigners (and indeed, many Spaniards) ever saw of the region. Had Lorca been *that* kind of professional Andalusian there would be nothing to distinguish him from dozens of mediocre contemporaries. What the poet had in mind was what Gibson calls "a Granada that would preserve the best of the past but live firmly rooted in the modern age—what for Lorca was a universal Granadism." This concept is crucial to understanding Lorca's importance—he represents (along with Buñuel, Dali, and de Falla) an attempt to bridge traditional culture in Spain with the avant garde. His work, and theirs, seems to be saying, Yes, we are Spaniards, but we have found a way to reconjugate our national culture in modern, universal terms.

The issue is not a trivial one for writers in "underdeveloped" countries, which among other things may explain why Republican Madrid attracted an unusually large number of first-rate Latin American writers. Whether Lorca really accomplished an enduring synthesis of the traditional and the ultra-modern is, of course, another question. Some of the themes that he addressed in his plays, daring at the time, seem flat and dated today; for example, when *Yerma* was restaged in Madrid in the early 1980's for the first time since the civil war, the producers felt they could approximate its original shock value only by introducing extensive

male and female nudity. But at any rate, Lorca helped his own
and several subsequent literary generations to break out of ster-
ile, repetitive molds of expression and sensibility and to take Spain
beyond the ethos of Carmen, bullfights, and castanets.

Lorca also represents a social archetype: the artist as a public—as opposed to a political—figure. In Republican Spain the
line between the political classes and the community of letters,
broadly construed, was never very clear-cut; in fact, many ministers and government authorities, not to mention ambassadors,
were intellectuals (or pretended to be). But Lorca embodies something a bit different—the poet who attempts to shape political
discourse without involving himself in the day-to-day business of
government. The combination of lofty moral authority and freedom from political responsibility is, evidently, an irresistible cock-
tail for intellectuals the world over, so we can hardly be surprised
that even so likable a man as Lorca succumbed to the temptation. Some of his political statements, while often silly or embarrassing, were harmless enough—except to himself. His vaunted
challenges to traditional authority—particularly to the police and
the military, as exemplified by his "Ballad of the Civil Guard,"
which he was imprudent enough to read at a public recital a few
days before the outbreak of the civil war—helped to mark him as
an enemy to be liquidated when the opportunity presented itself.

One finishes Gibson's book wondering what might have happened to Lorca had he remained in Madrid in July 1936 instead
of taking the night train to Granada. Had he survived the war,
he would probably have been forced into exile after the defeat of
the Republic three years later, perhaps to Argentina or Mexico.
If he followed the pattern of so many other distinguished literary exiles, after lingering for a dozen or so years in mediocre
intellectual (and economic) circumstances, he might well have
been lured to the United States—to Austin, Albuquerque, or San
Diego, poor man!—to teach Spanish literature to dim American
college students who would have had no sense whatever of the
immense literary richness thrown in their path. In the late 1960s,
he might well have chosen to return to Spain for retirement; by
that time, the Franco government was relatively forgiving, and
demanded no *auto-da-fé* in exchange for restoring one's passport.

By then he would, of course, have been a shadow of the char-
ismatic personality that had departed some three decades be-

fore. Certainly there would have been no legend of Lorca and no legion of scholars and critics to tend it—no "Lorca International," as Gibson calls it. Perhaps there would have been new, qualitative advances in his drama, but it would have been difficult to find audiences for his plays, which in any case would have begun to acquire a certain artificiality as their author became increasingly detached from the culture and society from which he drew sustenance. As for his poetry—well, we all know what has happened to poetry.

There is something about Lorca's life and death that suggests a unified whole—a brief existence, intensely experienced, overpowering into supreme accomplishment in art, and then, suddenly, at its peak, literally snuffed out by the forces of darkness. Can this perfect circle hold the key to the enduring fascination exercised by the man and his work? Lorca's mystique may owe almost as much to his identification with the Second Republic, whose goal was to modernize a backward country without forfeiting its identity. The divisive issues of Lorca's Spain—secularization of education, separation of church and state, agrarian reform—seem inconceivably remote today, but this broader question—how to change while also remaining the same—continues to confront every society on the periphery of Western culture and, to some extent, those within it as well.

Notes

1. *Federico García Lorca: A Life* (New York: Pantheon, 1989); Pantheon. The book was originally written in Spanish and then translated into English by the author for its publication in England (by Faber & Faber) and the United States. It was published in Spanish by Grijalbo in two volumes, *García Lorca, I: De Fuente Vaqueros a Nueva York* (1985) and *García Lorca, II: De Nueva York a Fuente Grande* (1987).
2. *The Death of Lorca* was published in London by W.H. Allen, and in Chicago by J. Philip O'Hara (1973).
3. Apparently Lorca toyed periodically with addressing the subject of his own sexual concerns more directly, but none of the manuscripts were completed. Gibson makes reference to several; one assumes that in time these fragments will be published.
4. *En busca de José Antonio* (Barcelona Planeta, 1980).

9

Gerald Brenan

Although he died less than a decade ago at the ripe age of ninety-three, Gerald Brenan is already fast slipping into literary oblivion. Even in the field to which he made his greatest contribution—Spanish studies—today's graduate student would be hard pressed to identify the man, still less to have read his works. In some ways this is understandable: Brenan was not a university trained academic but a man of letters of the most old-fashioned type. He picked the subjects he wanted to write about; worked as long on them as he pleased. Because he did not need to worry about making a living, he could afford to wait until the public discovered him. Once it did, from the mid-1940s on, no figure in the English-speaking world was regarded as a better (or more readable) authority on Spain—its literature first of all, but its broader culture and life as well. Meanwhile, however, times (and intellectual fashions) have greatly changed.

The publication of a major biography of the man by Jonathan Gathorne-Hardy, first in Great Britain and now a year later in the United States, is a serious effort to rectify matters, though one approaches this weighty tome wondering whether it is really quite needed.[1] After all, Brenan himself was careful to provide us with an ample accounting of his life in two volumes of memoirs, *A Life of One's Own* (1962) and *A Personal Record* (1974). Those who knew the man only from his charming accounts of Spanish life in *The Face of Spain* (1950) or *South from Granada* (1957) were in for a shock when they finished the last of these two books, for in *A Personal Record* Brenan revealed himself to have been something of a monster—almost unimaginably selfish and self-centered, sexually predatory, and a sponger to boot. What could a biographer, particularly one who concedes he was personally close to the subject in his later years, add to the Picture of Dorian Gray?

The answer is—not very much and a great deal. Gathorne-Hardy had access to a huge cache of letters written by Brenan to various friends, as well as the opportunity to look into the papers of several of his closest contemporaries. Some of the people in the story were still alive when he began his research. He was also able to peruse a good part of what might be called the "Bloomsbury archives"—variously deposited now in King's College, Cambridge; the University of Texas Humanities Research Center; and McMaster and Sussex Universities. Many misstatements and exaggerations have been corrected; one-sided versions of events have been rounded out; some figures dealt with by Brenan only in passing (or not at all) have been given a full accounting. One stands in awe—let it be said straightaway—at the biographer's sheer industry and devotion. Unfortunately our view of Brenan, thus corrected and amplified, does not render him more appealing. One can only hope that *South from Granada*, not this biography, is the way that future readers discover the man and his work.

Gerald Brenan was born in Malta in 1894, where his father, a British army officer, was then posted. The family subsequently lived in Africa and India, until Hugh Brenan was forced into a premature retirement by encroaching deafness. Gerald's adolescence was a typical late-Edwardian idyll—public schools, long summers in fashionable watering places, holidays in France. Brenan's father expected his son to follow in his footsteps to Sandhurst, and to this end he saw to it that he was assigned to the leading games house at school. The young man already had other ideas, however, finding a world of his own in books and dreams of "abroad." When—despite his best efforts to fail it—Gerald passed the Sandhurst entrance examination, he sought to escape his fate by disappearing with one of his teachers, John Hope-Johnstone, on a long "walk." The excursion was originally intended to take the two as far as Turkestan but actually ended in Italy, by which time Hope-Johnstone had lost the relish for travel under rough circumstances, and young Brenan was totally broke.

Terrified at the prospect that his son might disappear forever, Hugh Brenan agreed to compromise. He sent the young man the funds to return to England, and relented on the demand that he go to Sandhurst. Instead, he allowed him to apply for a commission in the India Police, which for some unaccountable reason required competence in German. For this purpose Gerald went off to Germany, to study with a crammer, where he remained until June 1914. The following month he returned to Britain, just in time for the outbreak of war. Plans for the India Police were shelved; instead, his father was able to use old service connections to get him a commission in the Fifth Gloucesters, the unit with which he was to spend the next four years.

In spite of his rebellious temperament, Brenan had, by his own accounting, "a good war." This was probably because, with his firm knowledge of French, he was immediately picked out for liaison duties. This made it possible for him to move about much of the time with little or no supervision. He was even able to usefully employ the long periods of enforced idleness on the Western front by plunging into books. (He was already developing formidable powers of concentration—the kind that allowed him to go at a book as much as eleven hours at a stretch.) This is not to say that he was a slacker; at one time he was the artillery observer for an entire corps, one of a dozen along the entire Western front. He ended the war with both the Military Cross and the Croix de Guerre.

Sometime late in the war Brenan wrote a friend that his dream was "a cottage in Spain and the life on the roads and books and liberty." He was twenty-four years old at the time. For the next seventy years Brenan did exactly that—he went to Spain, he traveled, and he wrote. He never held a regular job of any kind. He was able to defy his parents on this score because of an elderly aunt, from whom he was able to extract a monthly allowance. (He subsequently inherited the whole of her estate.) This permitted him to take a house in Yegen, a remote village in the Alpujarras Mountains of Spain, the same place immortalized in his book *South from Granada*. There he read quite literally hundreds of books, sometimes as many as a dozen at a time.

Like the South African poet, translator, and critic Roy Campbell, whom he resembles in a number of ways, Gerald Brenan led a life which sounds more romantic in the telling than it was in reality. For one thing, he spent far less time in Spain than his books lead one to believe. (He was there on and off in 1921–24, and lived there again in 1935–37, but he did not return until well after the

Second World War.) Though in print he made much of Yegen's warmth and spontaneity, in letters home he often complained about the loneliness and boredom of the village (he was always begging friends to come out for a visit). He made few friends among Spaniards, and, at least in Gathorne-Hardy's telling, never advanced much beyond Andalusian-kitchen Spanish. (Unlike Roy Campbell, he neither sought out nor knew any of the major Spanish writers, at least until the very end of his life, by which time he had become a cult figure in post-Franco Spain.) Of the three million words of his correspondence which survive, not one letter is addressed to a Spanish recipient.

Indeed, for much of the 1920s the major focus of his life was not Spain at all, but "Bloomsbury"—that is to say, an effete group of self-indulgent bores and parasites recruited from the more affluent sectors of English bohemia. Here the draw was the painter Dora Carrington, a central figure in Bloomsbury circles, though it is difficult now to understand quite why. Certainly her artistic talents were vastly overrated; as for her feminine charms, those too elude our contemporary grasp. The best the gallant Gathorne-Hardy can do is to assure us that she "seduced men with her letters."

In the event, she drove Brenan to near distraction, and forced him into acute sexual rivalry with his best friend, Ralph Partridge, another writer whom he had met while serving on the Western front. Partridge eventually won the contest, but his victory was strangely Pyrrhic: apparently Carrington, who had strong lesbian tendencies, was really in love with the homosexual writer Lytton Strachey. She therefore forced her husband to accommodate a (necessarily inconclusive) *ménage à trois* at Ham Spray in Wiltshire. When Strachey died in early 1932 after an unsuccessful appendectomy, Carrington promptly committed suicide.

Brenan's loss of Carrington to Ralph Partridge led him to seek consolation in the arms of a succession of anonymous English shopgirls, and then back to Spain, where he fathered a daughter by his principal servant, Juliana. In 1931 he returned to England, where he met and married Gamel Woolsey. A striking woman from the American South, Woolsey had come over to England to pursue a dramatic career, eventually transferring her interests to literature. By the time Brenan met her, she was under the influence of the Welsh poet Llewelyn Powys, with whom she was liv-

ing in a *ménage à trois*. Brenan and Woolsey were married after a
whirlwind courtship—bigamously, as it turns out, since she had
not bothered to divorce the American husband from whom she
was separated.

In many ways Gamel was an ideal companion for Brenan. She
shared his love of travel and did not mind acute discomfort on
the road; she was good at foreign languages; she was equally
committed to the literary life. Another charm, presumably not a
small one, was her private income—the equivalent in 1990 prices
of about thirty-five hundred pounds a year. The Brenans lived in
East Lulworth, Wareham, for the first four years of their marriage, returning to Spain in 1935. The choice was dictated primarily by economics; Brenan preferred living in France, but it
was too expensive. Besides, Gathorne-Hardy writes, "Spain [of-
fered] just the right combination of monotonous calm to let him
write, with sufficient social junketing to keep him stimulated."
In some ways, he adds, the Brenans hardly lived in Spain at all;
most of their friends were either expatriates or friends visiting
from England. The fact that this time Brenan chose not a remote, impoverished village but Churriana, near Marbella (province of Málaga), underscored the preference for Britain Abroad,
rather than the Spain of most Spaniards. The Brenans' stay was
cut short by the outbreak of the civil war in the summer of 1936,
though they stayed on as long as they could, leaving Málaga—the
last British residents to do so—in 1937. They settled at Aldbourne
in Wiltshire, where Brenan plunged into the research that would
eventually produce *The Spanish Labyrinth*, the most extensive and
authoritative study on the origins of the Spanish civil war to appear in any language, which finally came out in 1943.

At the time Brenan was nearly fifty years old, and famously unknown. His output at that point consisted of one novel, published
under the name of George Beaton in 1934, which left no great
impression. The rest of his *oeuvre* was not only unpublished but
unfinished—six or seven novellas, a life of Saint Teresa of Avila (on
which he had already labored fourteen years), innumerable stories, plays, and verse narratives. Suddenly, and quite overnight, he
became the best-known interpreter of Spain to the English-speaking world, and over time, to much of the rest of the globe as well.

Even today it is difficult to overestimate the importance of
The Spanish Labyrinth. At the time Spanish studies hardly existed

as a discipline anywhere outside of Spain itself (and even there it was largely tethered to old-fashioned disciplines like philology). Because of the international impact of the Spanish civil war–the first ideological civil war of the twentieth century, and also the first civil war in a "backward" country which was viewed as a struggle by proxy between emerging great powers–hundreds of books and pamphlets on Spain had appeared in a dozen European languages between 1936 and 1939. Indeed, they would continue to appear long after Brenan's book was published. However, most of them were driven by the larger ideological issues, in which Spain–the real Spain–ended to get lost in the special pleading. There was also a tendency–particularly after the republican collapse–to indulge in revolutionary nostalgia. Even George Orwell's masterpiece, *Homage to Catalonia* (1937), does not fully escape the trap. Brenan thought of himself as "a conservative in the short range, a socialist in the long range," and was not easily carried away by utopian fantasies.

Brenan was not, to be sure, the first writer to question the pieties of left-liberal (or *marxisant*) historiography. A handful of Catholic writers in England and France had already labored to set forth the specifically Spanish issues in the war. But Brenan's book was the first to do so from a straightforwardly pro-republican point of view. He also greatly exceeded the Catholic apologists in balance and fairness, subtlety, and knowledge of where contemporary controversies belonged in the larger matrix of Spanish history. For the next two decades no book, certainly no book in English or French, provided outsiders with so rich and carefully textured a view of where Spain's past intersected with its present.[2] The amount of work which went into it can only be guessed by this sarcastic remark by Gamel, made in 1937 when he was already deep into the research: "Gerald's latest act is to read the entire history of ceramics before he ha[s] to write half a page about Spanish pottery." The painstaking craftsmanship, the patience, the willingness to slog through acres of intellectual underbrush is nowhere apparent in this or subsequent books; like an accomplished ballet dancer, Brenan made everything look easy.

These virtues also characterized the second great book produced at Aldbourne, *The Literature of the Spanish People*, published in 1950. It stood for many years as the most readable and enjoyable book on the subject, firm in its knowledge of materials and confident in its literary judgments. Of course, Brenan was building here on literally hundreds of thousands of hours of work spread over many decades; there was probably not a single work upon which he commented which he had not read several times. Moreover, unlike what passes for literary history today, it was a book not merely about literature but about the country itself.

Here are a few examples which illustrate the point. On the nineteenth-century novelist Benito Pérez Galdós: "Under [his] skin there was both a Christian who gave absolution and a Marxist who attributed the sins of the children to their fathers." On the work of Galician novelist Emilia Pardo Bazán: "Writing of a country proverbial for its wistfulness and charm, she never allows herself to idealize anything but the scenery." Or this remark about an early eighteenth-century novel: "We see in [these] early chapters what one is tempted to call the real Spain, the Spain of vast plateaux and earth-colored villages and bad communications, and the almost inconceivably monotonous life that goes on there."

Brenan also wrote from a critical point of view which, to put it mildly, would not be much in fashion nowadays. Just because of that it is worth quoting at some length:

> Works of art and literature are, in my opinion, to be valued by the depth and quality of the experience they convey, and by the immediacy and clarity with which the convey it, rather than by their moral and ideological rightness. Ethical considerations only come in when they affect that experience by extending it or diminishing it.

He felt constrained to make the point because of

> the tendency shown in recent years to look at literature through the glasses of an ideological preconception and to rate highest those authors whose attitude toward life is most in harmony with that of the critic. [This] seems to me to be regrettable...Literary criticism has its ethics, and it is the business of those who dislike the growth of the totalitarian mentality to resist the subjugation of art to dogma and to stand out for the free examination and enjoyment of the literary production of all races and ages. Art and literature are to be judged by broad humanist standards, or none at all.

It seems hardly possible that these words were written in the late 1940s, an era which—by contemporary standards—was a golden age of literary criticism. One can only hope Brenan would find the courage to write them again were he alive today.

The third great book Brenan wrote while in English exile (or perhaps began there and finished after his return to Spain in

1953) was *South from Granada*, an autobiographical account of his life in Yegen from 1919 to 1924. It is a kind of English travel book which tips its hat to the *costumbrista* tradition of Spanish narrative. Gathorne-Hardy puts it a bit differently, comparing it to Turgenev's *A Sportsman's Sketches*. "It does not describe the reality of his time in Yegen," the biographer explains, at least as compared to his letters or accounts by other people at the time. "The food is much pleasanter. He leaves out most of his loneliness and despair, and all of his struggles to write and his love for Carrington—say, seventy percent of his preoccupations."[3] But these are minor points. *South from Granada* established Brenan as "the finest writer on Spain this century." Or, as Puig de la Bellacasa, the Spanish ambassador to the Court of Saint James, put it, "He knows us better than we know ourselves."

Like many writers, Brenan is best met on the printed page. But since this is a full-dress biography, we are not allowed the comforts of discretion. So for those who haven't read *A Personal Record*, here he is with all his warts. We learn, for example, that Brenan greatly mistreated his wife—so badly, in fact, that she was given to extended fits of melancholy and thoughts of suicide. (As early as 1938 she told a friend she thought she had wasted her life.) Part of the problem was sheer exploitation—her own literary career was put aside so she could act as his cook-house-keeper-typist (she also translated many of the poems which appear in *The Literature of the Spanish People*). But most of it was Brenan's tireless philandering, particularly with young girls—a passion which dogged him into extreme old age. The fact that few of these romances were technically consummated—a point which Gathorne-Hardy pedantically reminds us of at every turn—does not seem very mitigating to the casual reader. How much less so must it have seemed to Gamel Woolsey herself!

Moreover, as Brenan got older the problem got worse, exacerbated by the decision to return to Churriana in 1953, where young women, both English and Spanish, were an ever-present temptation. There was, to start with, what can only be called an incestuous relationship with his daughter, Miranda (by the servant Juliana), who lived with Brenan and Gamel in England from about age ten onwards. There was Carrington's niece Joanna, whose visit to Churriana drove Gamel to drink and distraction. Then there was Hetty MacGee, an American girl of a type apparently quite common among expatriate communities on Spain's south-ern coast during these years, who occupied most of Brenan's attentions during 1958–60 and peripherally from 1961 to 1964. (Her photo in the illustrations reminds one of Somerset Maugham's remark about the sexually promiscuous: a man can feast to his heart's content every night if he is willing to confine his appetite to mutton chops and turnip tops.)

By now Gamel took to spending every summer in England, where she struck up a friendship with the Catholic novelist (and closet lesbian) Honor Tracy. It was Tracy who apparently gave her back some sense of her own worth; at any event, Gamel now began to stand up to her husband instead of simply swallowing his abuse. For example, when he told her that he was taking Hetty on a trip to Morocco, her response was this: "Gerald, you don't have to give me *so many* reasons for going. If I had money and a suitable companion, I'd set out tomorrow for the sources of the Amazon." As it was, the trip was no lark: Brenan, already sixty-five, forced Hetty to hitchhike with him across Morocco, under insalubrious—and often extremely dangerous—conditions.

After their return, Hetty—always ahead of the cultural curve—switched from being a proto-hippie to a feminist, logically aban-doning Brenan in the process. By now Gamel was a major alcoholic, consuming a bottle of spirits a day, plus a bottle of wine at each meal, and whiskey beforehand. Eventually her habit provoked hepatitis and a stroke, though in fact she was to die of cancer in 1968. While she suffered unspeakable agonies in the terminal phase, Brenan was busily putting in place her intended successor—a stunning young English poet by the name of Lynda Nicholson-Price.

According to Gathorne-Hardy, the sixteen years spent with Lynda were the happiest of Gerald's life. The two never mar-ried, and apparently never had sexual relations. Eventually he altered his will in her favor, in effect disinheriting his daughter. (To her credit, this was over the heated protests of Lynda her-self.) There was one more book, *A Personal Record*, published in 1972. In 1978 Lynda married Lars Pranger, a Swedish painter, with whom she had several children. It was an odd ménage, though the Prangers treated Brenan selflessly, nursing him through op-erations, breakages, and endless bouts of flu and fever. When they could no longer cope, they placed him in as congenial a nursing home in England as they could find.

Characteristically, the circumstances redounded to Brenan's benefit. The Spanish press was soon full of stories (inspired by what sources Gathorne-Hardy does not tell us) that the heartless Lynda had exploited a helpless old man and then turned him out of his house. Eventually two young Andalusians kidnapped Brenan from the nursing home outside London and brought him back to Spain, where the local government gave him the house in which he lived out his remaining years. This final episode, as tasteless as it is, perhaps tells us less about Brenan than about the elite that took over control of Spanish cultural institutions during the 1980s—full of fantasies inherited from the generation of their defeated republican parents, such as the supposed evils of the capitalist mentality, particularly as practiced by "heartless" Anglo-Saxons.

Gerald Brenan is about not merely a particular writer but an entire circle of people, both British and American, who were able to spend large amounts of time in Spain and elsewhere in the Mediterranean during the interwar and postwar periods, either because of family money, the relative strength of the dollar and pound sterling, or the grinding poverty of Spanish society, which made places like Churriana relatively inexpensive for foreigners. Brenan must have had an excellent time of it in the late 1950s and early 1960s, acting as host to Hugh Trevor-Roper, Betrand Russell, V.S. Pritchett, Augustus John, and Ernest Hemingway. These and others make interesting cameo appearances in the latter part of the book, and remind us that Brenan was appreciated by the best literary society in Britain and American even though he never became a "best-selling" writer.

With all due respect for the enormous work that went into this book, Brenan's place in literary history would have been better served instead by a collected edition of his writings, which would now include the journalism he did on Spain's transition to democracy for *The New York Review of Books*. The particular circumstances of his life seem less inspiring, at least in this telling, than the values that inspired his work. As he put it himself in the prologue to his history of Spanish literature, "the point of view from which I have written has been that of the person who reads literature for pleasure...All the efforts of critics are wasted unless they lead us back to an increased understanding and enjoyment of the originals." How revolutionary this sounds today, and how right! It moves one to hope that, one way or another, Gerald Brenan's voice has not been heard for the last time.

Notes

1. *Gerald Brenan: The Interior Castle. A Biography* (New York: W.W. Norton, 1993)
2. For some years the book was prohibited in Franco's Spain, though a pirated edition printed in Mexico in 1946 circulated clandestinely, as did a proper Spanish-language edition produced in Paris by the émigré publishing house Ruedo Ibérico in 1962. In 1985 it was finally published in Spain by the Barcelona house of Plaza y Janés. Meanwhile other editions had already appeared in Danish, Hebrew, Dutch, French, Serbo-Croat, and Italian.
3. Ralph Partridge was particularly incensed at the distortions. "What I really objected to" he later wrote Brenan, "was your picture of yourself as a selfless angelic character anxious to do everything for us, when what really you were after was seducing my wife."

10

Carlos Fuentes Discovers America

One of the more substantial cultural offerings to celebrate the quincentennial of Columbus's discovery of America was broadcast on the Discovery Channel on 19–23 April 1992. Entitled "The Buried Mirror: Reflections of Spain and the New World," it is a series of five one-hour programs on the history of Spain and Spanish America, written and narrated by the celebrated Mexican novelist Carlos Fuentes. The series embraces an extraordinarily wide range of materials, from the pre-Columbian Indian civilizations to Mexican immigrants in today's Los Angeles, from Spain's Gothic age to its current "consumer socialism." The underlying premises of the series are (1) that the events of 1492 did really inaugurate a New World, and (2) that the history of America (broadly constructed as the entire Western hemisphere) has been a long search for Utopia, a quest which has been vastly enriching to humanity as a whole.

A generation ago such notions would have been wholly unexceptionable. But today, when the Columbus quincentennial celebrations are being forced to assume some heavy political burdens, it is a positive relief to see and hear the story of the discovery and conquest of the Americas told with a sense of balance, discrimination, and wit. If the scholarship here is somewhat conventional, at lest it does not insist on judging the past purely in terms of the present. Although he is a man of passionate conviction, Fuentes the novelist is nonetheless capable of imagining perspectives other than his own, which is after all the first requirement of a successful historian.

The format of these programs is reminiscent of Sir Kenneth Clark's justly famous *Civilization* series. We are taken on a historical and geographical tour, with the same guide periodically popping out of the cloisters or pacing in front of the towers and tapestries. Fuentes's English is excellent, and although he is reciting a script, the delivery is more fluent and more reassuring than we might get from many native speakers. Moreover, the sites, both in Spain and in Latin America, are well selected, and the photography is excellent. Like *Civilization*, too, there is a book to accompany the series, though in this case the text goes far beyond the television script.[1] This allows Fuentes to develop some of the themes at greater length. Unfortunately, it also occasionally encourages him to abandon some of his courtesy and restraint.

The first program ("The Virgin and the Bull") covers Spanish history from its origins to 1492. Particular emphasis is given to the Gothic and Moorish periods, and (with the addition of Jewish settlement) to the emergence of what Fuentes calls a "tricultural" society. The second program ("The Conflict of the Gods") deals with the major Indian civilizations of the Americas—the Aztecs and the Incas—as well as with their conquest by a hardy, courageous band of Spanish soldiers. The third program ("Children of La Mancha") deftly summarizes the entire three centuries of Latin America's colonial period. The fourth ("The Price of Freedom") takes us from the wars of independence to the end of the nineteenth century. The fifth and final program ("Unfinished Business") brings the story up to date, but in many ways is as much about the United States as it is about Spain or Latin America.

Of the many observations one might make about this series, two in particular seem appropriate. In the first place, it demonstrates the degree to which the old historic grudge between Mexico and Spain has been attenuated. There was a time—and it was not so long ago—when no Mexican writer of any stature, and certainly none advertising himself as left of center, would have anything good at all to say about the Mother Country. True, the programs were partly underwritten by a group of Spanish banks and businesses. But that is not the point here. Now that Spain is socialist (at least in name) it has become politically respectable. And with the end of the cold war and the collapse of the Soviet Union, it remains the only alternative pole of attraction for Mexicans and other Latins who would wish to be freer of U.S. cultural influence.

In the second place, these films reveal just how much of a U.S.—as distinct from a Mexican—cultural icon Carlos Fuentes has become. Of course, he is, and deserves to be, a major figure of Mexican and Latin American letters. But throughout "The Buried Mirror," he reveals how intense his exposure has been not merely to our language and our way of life but also to our political and cultural sensibility—one might even say, to our political and cultural pieties. The text of his commentary is not merely written in an American version of English. Virtually all the metaphors he employs can have resonance only for an American audience. Even his cheap shots against the United States (most of which he saves for his book) are of the sort that would draw applause mostly from what might be called Jimmy Carter's America.

All in all, one would prefer to say nothing but good things about this series, since it is so much better than what normally passes for educational television in the country. And make no mistake about it, there is much good to say. The discussion of pre-Columbian civilization is serious—respectful but unsentimental—as is the coverage of classical Spanish civilization. The ambivalent nature of the conquest is emphasized, as is the fact that it was Spaniards who first raised the issue of the rights of the vanquished. At the same time, Fuentes shows how a genuinely syncretic "Latin America" culture emerged in the seventeenth century. Along the way he provides vivid sketches of some of the principal personalities in both Spain and Spanish-America: not just Cortés and Montezuma, but Las Casas, Sor Juana Inés de la Cruz, and also Goya, Velázquez, and Miguel de Cervantes. (When was the last time you heard *these* people seriously discussed on television?) The coverage of the Spanish American wars of independence and their aftermath is done with a sure grasp of the major themes. Fuentes conveys crisply and precisely how and why these countries were not ready for independence, and the way their development models in the late nineteenth century led to social explosions of 1910. (The latter, by the way, is illustrated by some remarkable archival footage.)

Somewhat less satisfactory, however, is the conclusion of the series ("Unfinished Business"), which advances a number of highly tendentious points about U.S.-Latin American relations. We are left unclear about exactly what Fuentes thinks is the obligation of the United States to these countries. Is it to pay their debts? To become a Latin American country in its own right? Or is it just to feel guilty and have a good long cry?

It is here that the project's principal deficiency is suddenly thrust into sharp relief. The films (and, even more, the book) suffer from a kind of double standard with respect to Spain and the United States. For Spain, we are offered history, which ultimately understands and absolves; for the United States we are offered sociology and economics, which judges and condemns. The double standard applies as well to both sides of the Rio Grande: for the Latins, the order of the day is sovereignty and dignity; for the gringos, it is openness and vulnerability.

Consider this: the final installment starts with Mexican illegals trying to cross the "cactus curtain" on the U.S. border while redneck immigration officers use helicopters, searchlight, and other paraphernalia to prevent their passage. The scenes are traumatic and at times even heart-wrenching. But they could hardly be regarded as seriously addressing the underlying issues. Fuentes airily dismisses the U.S. concern for secure borders, as he does a desire to maintain our own language and culture: the very same things he claims for Mexico and for Mexican-American in the United States. (At the same time, however, he proceeds to confirm our worst fears. The American Southwest was "always" Mexican, much in the way that the Alsace-Lorraine was "always" French; we might as well just open our borders and let it happen.[2]) Of course, this is not exactly what Fuentes says. But his presentation invites a casual viewer to infer it.

The text of the program itself more nearly emphasizes that we are all immigrants in the Americas, even the Indians (who came here from Asia across the Bering Strait); ergo, nobody has the right to exclude anybody, and the more polycultural a society, the stronger and more creative it is. Meanwhile, a number of important questions go begging. If as Fuentes says, the U.S. economy positively requires an unlimited supply of Latin migrant laborers, why, then, do we have an immigration service at all? If their culture is the most important thing that Latins possess, why is the same not true for the apprehensive "Anglos"? If not, why not? If so, then where does that leave the United States, or for that matter France or Germany, all of whom are now faced with increasing numbers of migrants from what used to be called the Third World?

Fuentes uses the illegal aliens as pawns in a game which the United States cannot win no matter what it does. If it admits them, it is exploiting them; if it does not, it is inhumane, condemning them to starvation. Just what obligations Mexico might have to its own people is something he does not dwell upon. (Nor does he consider the obligations of the Mexican governments he has supported in the past, one of which he was pleased to represent as ambassador to France.) Rather than being a society in its own right with responsibilities and difficult choices, "Mexico" (and by extension, "Latin America") is reified into the eternal victim from whom nothing need be asked. Perhaps this, not "trickle down" economics or Yankee imperialism, is the real cause of its comparative weakness and backwardness?

Much has happened in Latin America since these films went into production. Many of the anti-U.S. notions that inform the final installment are positively démodé—at least in Latin America, if not in certain venues in the United States. There must have been some furious reworking of the script toward the end, since there is a kind of muffled discussion of the new trends toward democracy and political participation, even though Fuentes himself prefers to finesse altogether the current move toward more open economic systems. These he is convinced do not and cannot work—at least in Latin America. ("Ha[ve] we not the tradition," he asks in the final passages of the book, the information, the organization, and the intellectual capacities to create our own models of development, truly consonant with what we ha[ve] been, what we were, and what we want to be?") Will there be a "Latin American" economics, much like "Arab" or "African" socialism? Is one even needed? A somewhat different reading of Fuentes's series might suggest another outcome. Bracketed between Spain in its past and the United States in its present, Latin America may be headed for a "Western" future—one far happier and more secure than any it has ever known. That has implications for the United States, and for the current conflict over "multicultural" education, though perhaps not exactly the implications that Fuentes and the makers of the series had in mind.

Notes

1. *The Buried Mirror: Reflections of Spain and the New World* (Boston: Houghton Mifflin, 1992)
2. One of the more fraudulent scenes in the series takes us to a class in some school in the Southwest. The teacher repeats the lesson, paragraph by

paragraph, in perfect English and perfect Spanish—à *la canadienne*. Possibly the scene is accurate and was not merely staged for cameras, but it is certainly not very typical of what passes for "bilingual education" in this country, which is usually nothing more than an excuse for schools to produce students illiterate in two languages instead of just one.

11

The Doleful Legacy of Carlton Beals

Prior to the Second World War, the role of the United States in world affairs was largely limited to Mexico, the Philippines, and the nations of the Caribbean Basin (Cuba, Haiti, and the Central American republics). Then, as now, Americans were not much interested in those places; most, in fact, were probably only vaguely aware of the influence that the United States exercised over them. The term "Third World" had not yet come into existence, replete with its heavy cultural and moral overtones, and apart from Protestant missionary organizations and a small number of American corporations, there were no domestic constituencies for "Latin American" or "Philippine" policy. Occasionally some sensational event—a civil war, a revolution—would push these countries briefly onto the front pages of American newspapers, but most of the time they received coverage only in the "little" magazines—particularly *The Nation* and *The New Republic*.

The situation prior to the Second World War sharply contrasts with that of the present day in other ways as well. Unlike today, in the interwar period few American journalists were college graduates; fewer still spoke foreign languages, and almost none could be described as politically or culturally left of center. On the other hand, those who wrote for the little magazines tended to be all three. In that sense, they were precursors of today's journalist-activist or journalist-as-participant, and their role in shaping elite opinion and even American foreign policy, especially in the late 1930s, was far from negligent. One such was Carlton Beals, who covered every major Latin American story from the Mexican Revolution in the 1920s to the Cuban revolution in the 1960s, and who is now the subject of a full-dress academic biography by John A. Britton.[1]

Though Beals himself does not emerge in these pages as a particularly interesting or sympathetic personality, his career does allow his biographer to explore a wide range of important subjects—most of them related to the "international" aspect of American cultural and political radicalism in the 1920s and 1930s. There are cameo appearances from many key figures of the period—Mike Gold, Ernest Gruening, Bertram Wolfe, Frank Tannenbaum, Waldo Frank, Joseph Freeman, Freda Kirchwey, as well as such foreign personalities as Diego Rivera, Aleksandra Kollontai, Julio Antonio Mella, Fernando Ortiz, M. N. Roy, and David Alfaro Siqueiros. The book lacks a certain intellectual weight and sureness of touch, and suffers from too close an identification with its subject; nonetheless, it brings to bear an impressive amount of research, not only from Beals's personal papers but from American and Mexican archives. On more than one count, it adds significantly to our understanding of the history of both countries, and above all to the wider phenomenon of Third Worldism past and present. The ghost of Beals stalks much of the news coverage that Americans have received about many countries in recent years, most notably El Salvador and Nicaragua.

Carlton Beals was born in Kansas in 1893, the first son of a lawyer-newspaperman and an English teacher, both of whom subsequently subscribed to the more radical version of American populism. Beals's father was something of a failure in both of his chosen professions; his prospects did not improve in California, where he resettled his family in 1900. But Carlton seems to have absorbed most of his father's basic values, above all his sense of moral superiority an his rejection of conventional American values. Upon his graduation from Berkeley in 1918 he fled to Mexico to avoid military service in the United States. He remained there more or less continuously for many years thereafter (with a brief interlude in Italy in 1922), learning the language and serving in various capacities—as an English instructor to the staff of revolutionary chieftain Venustiano Carranza, as a teacher at the American School in Mexico City, and then, for almost a decade, as a correspondent for the *New Republic*.

During the 1930s, Beals expanded his interests to Cuba and Peru, to each of which he devoted full-length books. His obsessive and wrongheaded campaign of character assassination against U.S. Ambassador Harry Guggenheim in Havana—even his admiring biographer comes close to calling it that—played an important role in preparing the way for the Cuban revolution of 1933. Concretely, by representing U.S. policy as being more favorable to dictator Gerardo Machado than it in fact was, Beals helped to undermine the ambassador's attempts to ease Machado out quietly, in the process polarizing the conflict among Cubans. Beals was also the first American journalist to interview Nicaraguan General Augusto Sandino, who had become a Latin American legend through his leadership of a guerrilla campaign against a small expeditionary force of U.S. Marines. In 1937 he participated briefly in the efforts of Leon Trotsky, by then an exile in Mexico, to clear his name against Stalin's accusations at the Moscow Trials and by the early 1940s he had become a frequent contributor to mainstream American magazines. In the late 1940s and 1950s, however, the American national mood was distinctly uncongenial to radicalism or people who wrote about it; Beals thus holed up on a farm in Connecticut owned by his fourth wife, writing on a wide range of nonpolitical topics for minor magazines and book publishers. He returned to public view briefly in the early 1960s to write for the Cuban news agency Prensa Latina, as well as to produce one last major book, *Latin America: World in Revolution* (1967). He died in 1979.

Britton reports that one of Beals's professors at Berkeley told him that he had "the knack of writing"—to which he added, "Don't let your pen be idle." The gentleman had greatly overstated the case, though his advice was sound. Beals was blessed less with talent than with sheer industry—over the years he wrote thirty-four books and more than two hundred magazine articles. At his best, as in *Banana Gold* (1932), his work resembled that of the more talented travel writers of the day. Most of the time, however, his prose was deeply purple—tasteless, hyperbolic, undignified. His *Porfirio Díaz, Dictator of Mexico* (1932), for example, is pockmarked by expressions like "corral and kosher" or "know his onions." When one American academic expert on Peru took issue with his book *Fire on the Andes* (1934), he accused the man of being "a rancid Bourbon, a kisser of the toes of aristocracy, a sacred institution chest-pounder." As he grew older his style simply became more acerbic, as he substituted vituperation for argument; *Latin America: World in Revolution* seems to have been written with his liver. Presumably he owed his preeminence to the fact that then, as now, journalists were notoriously shiftless, and the few who—like Beals—were not became disproportionately influential.

Between 1910 and 1930 Mexico was torn by a series of civil wars which subsequent historians call the Revolution. At one level, the conflict was about issues which had been smoldering since the late colonial period—land tenancy, the prerogatives of the Roman Catholic Church, and racial distinctions. At another, it turned on relations between Mexico and the United States, which had become in the late nineteenth century the country's largest source of foreign capital and investment. And finally, it represented a struggle for power among leaders of an ascendant class of revolutionary generals, most of whom subsequently became businessmen-politicians and eventually founded a new order not significantly different from the one the Revolution replaced.

During the 1920s Mexico was a favored place of pilgrimage for American radicals, largely because (to them) its regime represented the antithesis of Coolidge prosperity and what Beals called "the American herd gospel: success, college friends, a conventional engagement...a job in the shipping office." According to Britton, Beals was particularly attracted to "the humble lifestyle of the Indian and mestizo peasants, convinced that they were morally superior to the middle-class, materialistic money-grubbers of the United States." At no point in the book, it should be mentioned, does Britton question whether this characterization is adequate to the period; indeed, he repeats the notion periodically as if it is above all scholarly discussion.

Actually, the romantic phase of the Revolution ended early, as did its quarrel with the United States, with whom a treaty settling outstanding claims for expropriation was signed in 1923. By the mid-1920s, General Plutarco Elías Calles had become a virtual dictator, assisted by thuggish labor and peasant leaders whose principal task was to suppress all of the rebellious tendencies out of which they themselves had emerged. As Britton points out, Beals was somewhat late in recognizing this.

During the 1920s, in fact, Beals was something of an unpaid press agent for the Mexican government, which carefully monitored his articles in *The New Republic* and hastened to massage his ego when he seemed to be veering from the official line. In most cases, however, Beals needed no disciplining. When José

Vasconcelos, former minister of education, challenged Calles's stand-in for the presidency in 1929, in an election marked by fraud and violence, Beals assured readers of *The New Republic* that the defeated candidate had no support; when Vasconcelos's followers questioned the veracity of his reports, Beals conceded that they might have a point, but that "the matter is not worth going into now."

Likewise, when he visited war-torn Jalisco in 1927, he discovered that the Catholic guerrilla movement there was largely a response to government provocations, but he hesitated to publish his findings—for fear, he confided to friends, of giving aid and comfort to advocates of U.S. military intervention! By the end of the decade, when his disillusionment with Calles was complete, instead of setting the record straight and admitting his errors, he moved on to Machado's Cuba, where he could offer uncritical support for a revolutionary cause which had not yet triumphed.

Britton puts at the center of Beals's attraction to Mexico his "anti-imperialism," not merely his opposition to U.S. military intervention in the affairs of other, weaker peoples but his opposition to U.S. economic influence through investment and the export of technology. "His qualified advocacy of modernization by revolution and his unqualified condemnation of imperialism," he writes, helped to establish "the basis for a new framework of understanding and explaining the complex process of change that was underway not only in Mexico but elsewhere in Latin America, Africa and Asia." He even credits Beals's views with being a kind of primitive precursor of what is known today as "dependency theory," a shorthand term for the notion that some countries are poor because others are rich, and that all foreign influences in pre-industrial countries necessarily lead to poverty, not progress.

In some ways this characterization of Beals is apt, to the extent that dependency theory seeks to have it both ways. That is, it tends to idealize primitive cultures in isolation at the same time that it purports to favor the *fruits* of modernization (health, literacy, rising living standards), using the quasi-religious concept of "revolution" to avoid explaining how to get from one state to the other. Thus, almost alone of American radicals, Beals opposed not merely the "Dollar Diplomacy" of various Republican administrations but Franklin Roosevelt's "Good Neighbor Policy," the centerpiece of which was a series of reciprocal trade agreements which opened U.S. markets to Latin American experts.

For Beals, this policy was a device for siphoning off valuable raw materials and currency from Latin America, as if the act of entering into ordinary commercial transactions amounted to a looting of the southern nations. He never explained where he expected these countries to get the resources to improve the lot of their peoples if they could not sell their products abroad. All he knew was that U.S. influence was bad, in whatever form it took. In fact, in his view, Roosevelt's abandonment of military intervention was actually the more insidious, since it paved the way for "the subtle, but even more debilitating policies of economic exploitation." "Like most economic nationalists in Latin America," Britton writes approvingly, "Beals saw government action, not private initiative, as the most practical means to guide national economic development. That *Latin American* nationalists might reason thus is one thing; why Beals—a foreigner—felt obligated to subscribe uncritically to their views is quite another. Moreover, that his biographer could write as if Beals's ideas have never been tried—whereas, in fact, for more than fifty years they have been the conventional wisdom in Latin America and now stand revealed as the first cause of its widespread economic and social decay—speaks volumes about the ideological blindness which afflicts important sectors of the American academy, particularly that which specializes in "Third World" studies.

Throughout Britton's book there are frequent references to communism and communists, as well as to efforts by American government agencies to link Beals to the Soviet Union. The author was able to obtain Beals's file from the FBI under the Freedom of Information Act and quotes from it profusely; like most documents of this kind, it makes for piquant reading. Beals moved in radical circles in Mexico and the United States, and obviously knew many people on the Left in both countries, including communists. The fact is, however, that he was never a communist, or for that matter even attracted to communism, particularly in its Soviet incarnation. He quarreled with Michael Borodin, the Comintern's representative in Mexico in the 1920s, as he did with assorted other Russian agents or their sympathizers. It would appear, actually, that he quarreled with almost everybody.

Beals's stance as an independent radical recommended him to Max Schachtman, leader of the American Socialist Workers Party, who invited him to participate in the Dewey Commission, convoked in Mexico City in 1937 at the request of Leon Trotsky. The commission, it will be recalled, was a response to the show trials staged by Stalin in Moscow the year before whose purpose was to "prove" that his defeated rival in the struggle for power had all along been secretly in the pay of the German Kaiser, Imperial Japan, and the British Empire. (It is perhaps worth noting that contemporary liberal and leftist opinion appeared to require such extraordinary responses in order to vindicate Trotsky's revolutionary honor.)

Beals arrived late from the United States and in a bad humor; took umbrage at the fact that several crucial sessions had been held without him; and exacted revenge by acting as the devil's advocate in the proceedings. He eventually resigned in a huff, refused to sign the commission's final report, and in fact took up the cudgel against it in the American liberal press. This chapter shows Beals's biographer at his worst: Britton makes a lame and unconvincing case for his subject's role in the matter ("Beals was coldly objective [while] Trotsky apparently saw the hearings as a chance for personal vindication"), but he does at least succeed in convincing us that—contrary to the later allegations of Trotskyists in the Unites States—Beals harbored no Stalinist sympathies. Evidently, his vanity and outsized sense of self-importance were far larger than any particular political commitment.

During the late 1950s friends advised Beals that a new revolution was brewing Cuba, which led him to revisit the island for the first time in many years. He did not meet Castro on this occasion, but what he learned did not impress him favorably. Ironically, for once his tendency to shoot from the hip led to a bull's eye: he described the incipient Cuban dictator as a "quick-tempered, impatient, imperious, violence-prone adventurer, whose father built a landed empire on theft and corruption, and left his son the legacy of a youth shattered by his father's vaunted infidelity." Once the revolution triumphed, however, Beals cast caution to the winds and became a member of the Fair Play for Cuba Committee, a group of American pro-Castro apologists. Revisiting the island in 1960, he was reminded of Mexico in the 1920s; "I feel much younger," he wrote. "I feel rejuvenated. It

seems that everything around me is filled with youthful energy."
Britton adds, "His writing...was full of an ebullience that, at times,
bordered on naïveté. He failed to detect, or perhaps refused to
allow himself to see, that Castro was headed ever closer to Russia."

Shortly after seizing power Castro took up an old suggestion
which Beals had made long ago—that the Latin Americans should
have their own news organization, interpreting world events from
their own point of view. Thus was born Prensa Latina, for whom
he became an occasional writer. The agency sent him on a lecture
tour of Mexico and South America, with the understanding that it
would distribute his travelogues and commentaries. Midway in the
journey, however, director Fermín Revueltas was replaced by Jorge
Massetti, an Argentine friend of Che Guevara, and Beals found
his articles subject to censorship and heavy rewriting. He wrote
privately to a friend that Prensa Latina had become "Communist
lock stock and barrel, and has degenerated into a combination
censorship bureau [for Cubans] and a propaganda bureau abroad."
In the same letter, he warned that if the Cuban Communists did
not moderate their actions, "the whole revolution is going to be
wrecked." He quietly terminated his relationship with the news
agency, but never criticized Castro openly.

"Beals was a secular prophet who challenged middle-class comfort and conformity with the disturbing reminder that most of
the people in the Western hemisphere did not fit into the bourgeois mold. His singular advocacy of the legitimacy of revolution and the illegitimacy of imperialism constituted a personal
campaign against the expansionist, business-oriented, materialistic and individualistic society that he rejected." Thus Britton's
epitaph for his hero. Certainly it is the way the Beals himself
would have wished to be remembered.

Without doubt, Beals rejected American society as he found
it, but his radicalism sought a larger theater for its fullest expression. For him, anti-Americanism was a kind of organizing philosophy, against which all other institutions, nations, and
movements were judged. This explains why he was attracted to
Latin America in the first place, since it was the one region of
the colonial or semi-colonial world during the interwar period
where hatred of the United States (as opposed to Britain, France,
or Holland) was something of a fixation by intellectuals and politicians. It also helps to account for his love affair with the Mexi-

can Revolution, which waxed and waned not according to its own peculiar rhythms but according to the way it was perceived as an anti-paradigm to the American way of life. Once Calles made his peace with Washington, his government lost its appeal for Beals, who simply moved on to Peru, and then Cuba, always in quest, as one critic wrote, "of the tumult and chaos his soul loves." Thus, Beals's interest in Castro was tepid during the latter's "moderate" (pre-1959) political phase, and reached fever pitch only when the Cuban dictator sought and obtained a direct confrontation with the United States.

Beals's career established the basic parameters of "engaged" or "committed" journalism as it would subsequently emerge in the 1960s—a commitment not to Marxist ideology but to a vague notion of undifferentiated "revolutionism"; the snobbish manipulation of claims to expertise in exotic cultures; a contempt for the purported "materialism" of Western societies without offering an alternative to the poor of the pre-industrial world; a rigid, reflexive anti-Americanism; the creation of false dichotomies—particularly between economic development and political independence; above all, the notion that a symbiotic relationship exists between the Unites States and less developed countries, in which the interests of one cannot be advanced without detriment to the interests of the other.

Above all, it prefigures the way in which journalism has come to shape so much of our perceptions of the world, and, by indirection, the views which our own elites hold about our country and our culture. Beals's biographer is right to make strong claims for his subject's importance; his doleful legacy continues to be felt wherever American society finds itself in conflict with others who choose to side with our enemies, regardless of the cost to us, to them, or to their own, long-suffering peoples.

Note

1. *Carlton Beals: A Radical Journalist in Latin America* (Albuqueque, NM: University of New Mexico Press, 1987).

Part III

Cubans, Americans, and Cuban-Americans

12

U.S.-Cuban Relations: Back to the Beginning

The publication—after the usual thirty-year delay—of the U.S. diplomatic documents relating to the collapse of the Batista regime in Cuba and the emergence of Fidel Castro comes at a particularly propitious moment.[1] For the first time in decades, Washington is faced with the prospect of serious political change on the island and, with it, the need to redefine a relationship heavily fraught with historical baggage.

Obviously, nobody can say when that change will occur or what form it will take. But it certainly will be no less traumatic for Cubans than the upheavals of 1898, 1933, or 1959—events that in one way or another redefined the very nature of the Cuban nationality and, therefore, also the country's relationship with its most important neighbor. At the same time, because Cuba's problems have had a way of becoming our own, this volume of *Foreign Relations of the United States* helps us to understand how we got where we are today.

Under review are some six hundred documents, including cable traffic between the U.S. embassy in Havana and the State Department; minutes of meetings of the National Security Council, the Cabinet, and interagency working groups; memoranda of conversations with President Eisenhower and Secretary of State John Foster Dulles (later, Christian Herter); and special National Intelligence Estimates (NIEs) on Cuba produced by the CIA at the request of the executive branch.

It will probably surprise no one that there is little in this volume likely to revise the conventional historiography of U.S.-Cuban relations. That is, those who believe that the blame for the current state of affairs lies entirely with the United States—either for supporting Batista or for pushing an idealistic Castro into the arms of the Soviet Union or, more likely, both—will have to continue their search for the "smoking gun"; it certainly will not be found here.

Nor is there much new in the way of hard information on this crucial period. The main lines of the story related in the documents—the agony and collapse of the Batista regime, the accession of Fidel Castro, the growing confrontation with the United States, and, finally, the break in diplomatic relations and the imposition of economic sanctions—is already well known. However, these documents do add a crucial sense of texture and some new and unexpected wrinkles to the story.

The most important of these is the sense of widespread confusion and disagreement among the various parties involved in Cuban policy during these crucial thirty-six months—Departments of State, Treasury, Agriculture, and Defense; the U.S. business community in Cuba; the White House and Congress; and last but not least, the American press. (We are continually reminded that in those unimaginably remote pre-Vietnam days, both Congress and press were often inclined to be nationalistic and even bellicose.)

These documents lay bare the fact that until quite late in the day there was no single, crisp response to the events in Cuba, nor—given the complexity of American interests there—could there easily have been. For much of the time, Washington was engaged in a complicated balancing act—between those who wanted to allow the government in Cuba greater latitude for self-correction and those who wanted to land on it full-force; between those who favored economic weapons to discipline the Castro regime and those who feared the loss of an important market; above all, between those who wanted to deal with Cuban events in isolation, and those who preferred to see them in their wider global (that is, cold war) context. Only toward the end of the period covered in these documents did the Eisenhower administration definitively shift from the former to the latter, and that only when the Soviet Union's involvement in the island (and Cuba's voluntary alignment with Moscow) made any other response impossible.

Getting Batista Out

General Fulgencio Batista had come to power in Cuba through a coup d'état in March 1952, so that at the time the volume opens, he was about to complete his (self-designated) six-year presidential term. Though he ruled as a dictator, Batista was no ordinary Latin American martinet; he had been freely elected to the presidency in 1940, and presided over a remarkably progressive government during the Second World War, with the support and even for a time the participation of the Communist party. His return to power in 1952, after eight years of highly corrupt and grossly ineffective administration by civilian politicians, had been greeted with frank relief by some Cubans and by massive indifference on the part of others.

By early 1958, however, Batista had exhausted his political credit with the Cuban public, including important sectors of the business community. He was now facing growing civic opposition consisting of not only unemployed politicians, but jurists, academics, professionals, students, and labor leaders. Though Fidel Castro's 26th of July movement was already active in the Sierra Maestra mountains in the easternmost province of Santiago, it was the civic opposition—which most nearly represented the major forces of opinion—that dominated the political scene in 1956 and 1957.

Batista's refusal to come to terms with this relatively moderate political force was based on the cynical calculation that by simply digging in, he would force open the potential divisions within its ranks, eventually rendering it irrelevant. In this he was correct: by early 1958, the civic opposition was beginning to fall apart. What Batista failed to see was that under such circumstances Cubans would not necessarily turn back to him, but would recur to whatever alternative remained. As 1958 wore on, *faute de mieux* Fidel Castro became the logical and inevitable focus of opposition sentiment.

Batista regarded the United States embassy as an important pawn in this game, since—like most Cubans—he held fast to the notion that Washington possessed the power to make and unmake governments on the island. This was evidently untrue, but its widespread acceptance throughout Cuba meant that all actions taken by the United States, including ones of mere symbolic value, acquired the potential of becoming major political facts. This point was driven home to Washington continually by the serving American ambassador, Earl E. T. Smith.

In the years since our Cuban debacle, Smith—a Florida investment banker and major contributor to the Republican party—has not enjoyed good press. At the time of his retirement, he was regarded as the very antimodel of an American ambassador in Latin America, someone who—through his lack of academic preparation (he did not speak or understand Spanish), ignorance of the country to which he was accredited, and uncritical support of an unpopular dictator—managed to permanently damage his country's interests.

The cables in this volume suggest a rather different picture. They reveal Smith to be remarkably well-informed on Cuban events and tragically prophetic as to that nation's future. Rather than specifically pro-Batista, he might be described as rigidly (and, as it turned out, prematurely) anti-Castro. But his purpose is clear: not so much to sustain Batista's dictatorship as to prevent it from collapsing until it could be replaced by free and fair elections, which were promised for June 1958 (and subsequently postponed to November).

This proved a far from easy task. By early 1958, Batista was playing a cat-and-mouse game with the State Department over restoration of constitutional guarantees. Washington's view was that both these and an atmosphere conducive to free and fair elections were necessary antecedents to further shipment of arms to the Cuban government; Havana, on the other hand, regarded the latter as a necessary precondition to reestablish its credibility and "negotiate from strength" with its opponents.

Meanwhile, some members of Congress and one or two democratic Latin American governments were beginning to complain that—in violation of existing treaties—U.S. military equipment sold to Cuba for "hemispheric defense" was being used for internal purposes, including, it was (incorrectly) alleged, napalm for the bombing of civilian populations. Washington demanded assurances from Batista that this was not the case. Smith argued that such a demand was both unrealistic and improper. ("If we feel that such use of MAP equipment is improper, [the] only way to be sure of avoiding it is to refuse to supply [it] in the first place.)"[2]

The Department obliged him on 14 March 1958 by promptly putting a permanent hold on the shipment of both armored cars and M-1 rifles, the "psychological effect" of which, the ambassador cabled, "may bring about [the] overthrow of Batista."[3] While its effect was less devastating than that, Smith was right to note a drastic shift in the political landscape; by embargoing arms shipments, the United States had not—as it thought—taken itself out of Cuba's civil strife, but rather placed rebels and government on a plane of equality.

The change in mood was obvious not only in Havana but in Washington. Acting Secretary Christian Herter wrote Smith that "from here it appears that [the] Batista regime has utterly failed to convince [the] Cuban people and certainly [the] U.S. public of its intention to carry out free elections." It asked for an immediate estimate of "its ability to survive [the] present crisis and for how long." The same cable called for an analysis of alternatives, including an evaluation of Fidel Castro.[4]

Between March and November, the cable traffic is dominated by two issues. The first is a tug-of-war between Ambassador Smith and the State Department over the resumption of arms shipments. The embassy in Havana outlined with considerably cogency the methodological impossibility of isolating U.S. equipment and personnel trained to use it from the main fighting forces of the Cuban army, which were by now engaged in fighting Castro's rebels. The Department, however, was beginning to worry that bombing and strafing rebel areas might lead to "reprisals against Americans." One visiting official even suggested that the U.S. government "should consider the evacuation of our people from the area and perhaps from other areas in Cuba [as well]."[5]

The other issue had to do with elections. Batista knew that, all things being equal, his hand-picked candidate, Andres Rivero Agüero, stood little chance of succeeding him. Therefore, he balked at restoring constitutional guarantees until the last possible minute, effectively preventing the opposition from organizing a campaign of its own. By late July, the State Department was despairing that there was little prospect of "anything resembling an acceptable election in Cuba." This could only redound to the benefit of Castro's 26th of July Movement, which the Department regarded "so far [as having] given no indication of political or moral responsibility. "

The same document admitted that the arms embargo had not convinced Batista to lift his state of siege and allow normal political life, putting the Department in the uncomfortable position of having to weigh "an expiring unpopular regime" against "an incoherent cluster of revolutionary groups whose total uncoordinated efforts add up to nothing but a vacuum."[6] For his part,

Ambassador Smith responded that "instead of winning friends in Cuba, the [net] result of our neutral position is to please no one."[7] It was a situation that the United States would face many times in the future, in Latin America and elsewhere.

The elections were scheduled for 3 November. By mid-August, Foreign Minister Gonzalo Güell was informing Ambassador Smith that promised plans to restore civic rights some forty-five days prior to the event were no longer feasible—this time because military progress against Castro's rebels had not gone as well as expected. This state of affairs, the minister archly added, was "due to the failure of the G[overnment] O[f] C[uba] to receive the necessary arms from the United States."[8] Though Smith was disappointed, he cabled Washington that he still hoped that the government's overthrow could be avoided until it had the opportunity to transfer power to its successor, and in the meanwhile begged Washington not to discourage "other nations" (Belgium, Canada, and Great Britain) from selling arms to Batista if the need arose.[9]

The elections went off on 3 November as anticipated—that is, with Batista's candidate winning by default. Ambassador Smith tried to blunt the effect by arguing to Washington that the elections, though far from perfect (!), were still better than none at all. Ironically, President-elect Rivero Agüero seemed to hold a more modest view of his own prospects, since he told Smith over lunch a few days after his victory of his intention of abbreviating his presidential term to two years and calling a constituent assembly to allow Cubans to iron out their political differences. [10]

Other Cubans, including members of the high command of the Cuban army, had even less confidence in the new president's prospects; a civilian sent to Washington by the generals urged the State Department on 18 November to support a preemptive coup (with civilian support) to forestall Rivero Agüero's inauguration on 24 February 1959. When a senior American diplomat expressed considerable skepticism, the intermediary insisted that "any indication by us of a desire for change would 'solve Cuba's problems in seven minutes.'"[11]

Between Batista and Castro: The Pawley Plan

In late November, Ambassador Smith returned to Washington to argue for support for the new government, including a token shipment of arms. Secretary Dulles told Smith that neither were possible "unless and until there is evidence that [Rivero Agüero's] program has the support of major segments of the population."[12]

Meanwhile, without Smith's knowledge, the State Department and the CIA had delegated William D. Pawley, former ambassador to Peru and Brazil, to visit Batista privately and offer him the opportunity to live with his family in Florida if he agreed to name a caretaker govermment—a civil-military junta composed of five of his political opponents. This would provide the United States with an acceptable government to which to ship arms, and would forestall the victory of Fidel Castro. Since Pawley's mission was unofficial, however, he could not offer Batista the ironclad assurances he demanded. The dictator, therefore, showed him to the door.[13] Two weeks later, on 14 December, Ambassador Smith received instructions to "pull the plug" on Batista—that is, to inform the Cuban government that the United States would not support, even *in ovo*, the government of Rivero Agüero.

This amounted to a death warrant for the regime. Some of its highest functionaries—civilian and military—either headed for exile in the United States or sought to make their peace with Castro's rebels. Castro himself grew to mythic proportions in a matter of days, as he rushed forward to fill the political vacuum. So much was this the case, that when Batista finally agreed to resign on 31 December 1958, the State Department was forced to concede that they could not deny Castro a place on the junta that Ambassador Smith was hastily trying to cobble together.[14] As this information was being received in Washington, Batista, his family, and his closest collaborators were fleeing Cuba in private planes for the Dominican Republic.

Who Was Castro?

From the very beginning, the Batista government tried to represent Castro and his movement as Communist to the embassy and the State Department. These charges were viewed with considerable skepticism, but, as 1958 wore on, Washington demanded increasing amounts of information about the rising revolutionary leader.

The confusion was understandable. In the first place, Castro denied being a Communist, but what is even more to the point, so did his Argentine associate Ernesto ("Che") Guevara when directly questioned by Homer Bigart of the *New York Times*.[15] Moreover, the chief appeal of Castro and his movement was its calculated ideological ambiguity. As the U.S. consul in Santiago explained to Washington, the revolutionaries represented "anything and everything to anyone and everyone.... The Castro movement has an unusual appeal to all sectors of Cuban society, either legitimate or convenient."[16]

In the second place, the relevant agencies of the U.S. government were unable to uncover any concrete evidence of Communist connections, possibly because there were none to be found until very late in the year, when (we now know) the Cuban party made its first demarches to the Castro movement. The result was a kind of vague discomfort that was not very helpful in making difficult policy choices. A good example is the report of the Bureau of Intelligence and Research (I&R) at the Department of State in April that there is "little about [the] top leadership [of the 26th of July] to inspire confidence.... Although the evidence available to the Department does not confirm the Cuban government's charge that Castro is a Communist, it does suggest that he is immature and irresponsible."[17]

By late September, when Castro's prospects had perceptibly improved, there was a call for fresh information. The Division for Research and Analysis for the American Republics explained that "the best information which we have at hand supports the belief that Fidel Castro is not a Communist and that Communists do not play a dominant role in the leadership of the 26th of July Movement." But it hedged its bets by adding that "our information is not as conclusive as we would like."[18]

At a meeting of the National Security Council on 23 December—that is, little more than a week before Batista's collapse—CIA director Allen Dulles suddenly argued that "the Communists appear to have penetrated the Castro movement, despite some effort by Fidel to keep them out. If Castro takes over in Cuba, Communist elements can be expected to participate in the government."[19] This assessment caused President Eisenhower to sit up and demand to know why an issue of this importance was being brought up only now—with Batista evidently *in extremis*. The ensuing minute makes fascinating reading:

> The Vice President [Nixon] said...we could not support Batista in order to defeat Castro. [1 sentence (1 1/2 lines) not declassifed].

Mr. Allen [USIA director] wondered why the United States should attempt to prevent a Castro victory. Mr. Dulles said there was a feeling Castro was backed by extremely radical elements. The Vice President [Nixon] pointed out it would be undesirable to take a chance on Communist domination of Cuba, which had one of the largest Communist parties in the hemisphere in proportion to population....

The President believed the U.S. should take a position progressives could support. Mr. Quarles [Deputy Secretary of Defense] thought there was no "third force"...to support. The President saw hope of a "third force" growing in strength and influence if it were organized around an able man and provided with money and arms. Secretary Herter felt a contingency paper was needed.[20]

Within hours of Castro's victory, Secretary Herter was reporting that the best intelligence on the subject is that "[Communist] infiltration has taken place but [its] extent and degree of influence [are] not yet determined from the evidence available." To which he added, "It is... clear that [the] 26th of July Movement has shown little sense of responsibility or ability to govern Cuba satisfactorily, and that its nationalistic line is [a] horse which Communists know well how to ride."[21]

Of course, to Cubans—if not to Americans—Castro himself was far from an unknown, having been active in politics since his university days. Indeed, he was even a candidate for the Cuban Congress in the 1952 elections that were never held. In 1956, he and a group of companions attempted to seize the Moncada fortress in Santiago de Cuba, the island's second largest city, a foolhardy venture that led to his trial and imprisonment. Amnestied in 1955, he had moved to Mexico, from where he launched another revolutionary expedition the following year, establishing his base in the Sierra Maestra mountains of Eastern Cuba.

When they were not trying to tar Castro with the communist brush, Batista's people were often quite accurate in their evaluations, or at least prescient. For example, President-elect Rivero Agüero told Ambassador Smith that there was really no point in attempting to reach a settlement with Castro, whose basic interest was in preventing a negotiated outcome rather than promoting it. He characterized the rising rebel leader as "a sick man...consumed by an overwhelming ambition to overthrow the Government by force."[22] Foreign Minister Güell told the U.S. envoy that "if Castro succeeds, Cuba will have a real dictatorship. With Castro's communistic projected program, [the] situa-

tion in Cuba will be worse than in [any] Latin American country—and that includes Guatemala."[23] While Smith seems not to
have bought the communist charges, he did feel that the United
States could not do business with Fidel Castro.[24]

The United States Faces the Revolution

Roughly two-thirds of the cables in this volume deal with the
period between Castro's assumption of power on New Year's Day
1959, and the decision of the United States to break with the
regime in the final days of 1960. Between January and April of
1959, the United States attempted to come to terms with the new
government, naming a new ambassador and establishing contact
with its authorities, many of whom turned out to be moderates
or even conservatives well known to the embassy and the U.S.
business community. The high point of this period was Fidel
Castro's visit to the United States in April.

The second period, from May to October, is dominated by the
promulgation of an agrarian reform law that struck frontally at
an important segment of the U.S. agribusiness community. In
the third, from October 1959 to January 1960, the last moderates had left the government, leading Washington to pin its hopes
on the emergence of a respectable anti-Castro opposition. The
fourth runs from January to April 1960, when the U.S. ambassador was recalled and the Eisenhower administration began to
formulate a plan of covert action against the regime.

The fifth, from April to July 1960, is characterized by a new
policy intended to weaken the Cuban economy, undermine support for Castro, and lead to political change. The sixth, from July
to September, deals with the response by the United States (and
to some degree the Organization of American States [OAS]) to
increased Soviet support for the Cuban government. The sev-
enth and last (September–December 1960) deals with the considerations that led up to severance of diplomatic relations.

Much of the controversy surrounding the current nonre-
lationship between the United States and Cuba swirls about different interpretations or uses of chronology. Was Castro "pushed"
into the arms of the Soviet Union, or did he "jump" of his own
accord? Was he reacting against an arrogant, insensitive United
States, or was he pursuing a course of action upon which he had

decided in advance? What do the documents in this volume contribute to this controversy?

*There was really no "honeymoon" with the Castro regime, but neither
was the United States rigidly and unalterably opposed to working with
the new government.* While the U.S. government and business community were unenthusiastic about Castro's victory, both favored
immediate recognition of the new regime. Ambassador Smith was
immediately replaced by Philip Bonsal, a career diplomat with
extensive Latin American experience, who was regarded as—and
in fact, was—"softer" than his predecessor. Batista, languishing in
the Dominican Republic, was repeatedly refused a visa to enter
the United States. The embassy in Havana recognized that the
new government was a coalition of several tendencies, with the
Communists by no means the most powerful. Chargé Daniel
Braddock, who thought Castro had an ambivalent attitude towards
the United States, urged "a cautious and restrained policy."[25]

Almost from the very beginning, however, the new government gratuitously engaged in fiery anti-American rhetoric, supposedly inspired by the role the United States had played in
supporting Batista. Old charges of napalm were revived to stir
up popular emotions, even though, as Washington now discovered, during the previous six months it was Castro, not Batista,
who had been the principal recipient of U.S. arms, albeit clandestinely.[26] Within two weeks of his victory, Castro was accusing
the U.S. military mission in Havana of "spying," and demanding
its recall. Castro and Guevara began to support rebel expedi-
tions in neighboring countries—the Dominican Republic, Nicaragua, even Panama.

At the same time, sensational show trials of former Batistiano
officials and collaborators—followed by drumhead executions—
were taking place at various places around the island. The speed
and, above all, the lack of concern for judicial niceties with which
these took place led to considerable criticism in the U.S. press,
which Castro himself took as a personal affront. (After Hiroshima,
he declared in one speech, the United States had no moral right
to call others to account.) In another speech, on 5 February, Castro
attributed his country's perennial economic troubles to "dicta-
tion by U.S. ambassadors."[27]

During this same period, moderate and conservative members of Castro's government were trying to set up a visit for him

to the United States. This, they hoped, would smooth out some of the problems in bilateral relations, and at the same time influence him in a sensible direction at home. Before the White House and State Department had an opportunity to reach a decision, Castro had gone ahead and accepted an invitation to address the American Society of Newspaper Editors in Washington.

This put the Eisenhower administration in an extremely embarrassing position. At a meeting of the National Security Council on 26 March 1959, the president and his closest advisors actually contemplated refusing Castro a visa, but were finally persuaded to stand down by Allen Dulles, who said that "there was a slow-growing movement against Castro in Cuba [and] we must be careful not to do anything which would tend to discourage its growth." The cancellation of the Castro speech, he suggested, "might be such an action."[28] The Department therefore set into motion the mechanisms for what protocol refers to as a "Working Visit."

Much criticism in retrospect has been leveled at President Eisenhower for failing to receive Castro when he came to Washington, particularly since the Cuban prime minister (as he was from February 14) was fobbed off on Vice President Richard Nixon. In fact, however, Eisenhower's decision to be away from the capital predated knowledge of the visit. Indeed, the president told Herter on 31 March that if for some reason his plans changed, "disagreeable as it might be, he would, if here, see [Castro] at his office."[29] Moreover, Castro accepted "with pleasure" the prospect of meeting Vice President Nixon in Eisenhower's place.[30]

Contrary to what Nixon has later said in his memoirs and elsewhere, his meeting with the new Cuban leader was almost cordial. According to the vice president's own memorandum of the meeting, they argued at length about Castro's decision to postpone elections for four years; his opposition to private capital in the development of Cuba; and his treatment by the American press. Nixon seems to have liked Castro, or at least admired his evident leadership abilities, though, as minuted for the record, "he is either incredibly naïve about communism or under communist discipline—guess is the former."[31] For his part, Castro later put it out that Nixon had spent much of his time defending the Somoza dictatorship in Nicaragua.[32]

There was no "lost opportunity" to buy Castro off with offers of economic aid. It has been known for some time that Castro had instructed his financial advisors who accompanied him to Washington not to ask for U.S. aid.[33] The documentation here goes even further, revealing that moderate elements "in or near the government" were urging the embassy in Havana to postpone aid even in the event that it were requested, at least until Castro (1) ceased his anti-American rhetoric, (2) curbed growing Communist infiltration of the government, and (3) modified his radical socioeconomic measures, such as a highly unrealistic rent control law. "They express [the belief]," Braddock cabled, that "U.S. assistance now would postpone [the] date for [a] showdown on [the] economic situation."[34]

Indeed, the embassy reported, a number of people within the government were confiding to it the "hope that [the] United States will be firm in handling Castro, and either force him to reverse his present trends of irresponsibility and radicalism internally and neutrality internationally or break with him."[35] In Washington with Castro, Cuban Central Bank president Felipe Pazos confided to officials at State and Treasury that he felt himself helpless in the face of other, closer and more important advisers. Having been ordered not to request economic assistance, Pazos confined himself to asking for an increase in the Cuban sugar quota.

This evident division between Castro and his senior economic advisors apparently persuaded the Eisenhower administration that the new regime was a shaky affair that might not last. This impression was certainly underpinned by cables from Havana explaining that "Cubans opposed to communism, both in and out of the government, are beginning to take firm and outspoken stands."[36] Castro's economic policies, such as they were, were so unrealistic that it was difficult to imagine how—in the absence of massive Soviet aid of a type that was then considered unlikely—the government could satisfy the country's basic needs.

Land reform was a serious irritant, but it was overruled by other U.S. interests and concerns. On 17 May 1959, a new agrarian reform law was promulgated that, in effect, confiscated the properties of large American land and mill owners in Cuba. This provoked a more complicated response from Washington than Castro himself has subsequently claimed.[37] In the first place, the

State Department accepted immediately Cuba's right to expropriate; its objection arose from the provisions for compensation, which did not pretend to take U.S. properties on the island at anything like their true value. However, even this was not viewed as an insuperable difficulty; the Department instructed Bonsal to urge the Cuban government to enter into negotiations leading to a satisfactory settlement.[38]

In the second place, although agribusiness was an important part of the $774 million in U.S. investment in Cuba, it was by no means the only economic interest there. Indeed, the sugar quota, which reserved for Cuba about 25 percent of the U.S. domestic market, flooded the island with hard currency, creating a huge market for American products, from insurance to wholesale groceries, from the sale of movie tickets to electrical appliances and automobiles. Thus, even as late as December 1959, when the American business community as a whole was beginning to see in Castro's cavalier treatment of U.S. property a dangerous example that might spread elsewhere in Latin America, the U.S. Chamber of Commerce in Havana was still opposing punitive suspension of the sugar quota.[39]

Third, Cuba's prearranged position in the U.S. domestic sugar market meant that it was not possible to abolish its quota overnight without causing serious shortages and disruptions at home. At one point, the Eisenhower administration even thought that it might be necessary to ration sugar until several growing seasons had elapsed and the import quota could be reallocated.[40] Moreover, decisions about the domestic sugar market were made on a four-year basis by the Agriculture Department, the next quadrennium of which was supposed to begin in mid-1960. Given the uncertainties created by the new situation on the island, Washington was understandably reluctant to act precipitously.

Fourth, there was a genuine fear in Washington that punitive use of the sugar quota—quite apart from contravening General Agreement on Tariffs and Trade (GATT) rules, and also the norms of the OAS—would have counterproductive political effects in Cuba itself. As Secretary Rubottom noted in early December 1959, such an act would strengthen, not weaken, Castro domestically, and would disarm the growing opposition on the island. Another consideration, presumably not a small one, was the need to keep the Cuban economy sufficiently viable to eventually compensate American companies for their losses.[41]

Finally, the Eisenhower administration's hand was stayed by a sense that perhaps a more friendly Cuban government might be in place twelve to fifteen months hence. This was, as it turned out, a radical misreading of the local reality. But the Cubans, including apparently their embassy in Washington, were likewise guilty of self-deception: they thought Washington's reluctance to abolish the quota overnight *meant that the United States could not live without Cuban sugar*, thus encouraging Havana to become more unyielding on the subject of compensation for expropriated properties, and on other matters as well. Indeed, Castro had taken to claiming that the sugar quota, which assured a market for half of Cuba's crop and provided the country with two-thirds of its foreign exchange, was somehow a colonial burden from which he proposed to liberate his country.[42]

With respect to the sugar quota, then, the Eisenhower administration can hardly be accused of a lack of restraint. As late as April 1960, when the first shipment of Russian crude oil to the regime was already en route and envoys from Havana were in Moscow discussing military commitments, Washington was still reluctant to suspend it altogether; instead, it ordered the Agriculture Department to make its import allocations on an annual rather than quadrennial basis.[43] It pulled the Cuban quota only in July, when a Cuban-Soviet mutual security treaty was under active discussion in Havana and Moscow.

Despite its distaste for unfolding events in Cuba, throughout 1959 the Eisenhower administration made serious efforts to crack down on exile overflights and other exile-based counterrevolutionary activities. Almost immediately after Batista's fall, various right-wing military and civilian elements that had managed to escape to the United States began to operate against the island from bases in Florida. Typically, these involved anything from the airborne distribution of leaflets to the dropping of incendiary bombs on Cuban cane fields or sugar mills.

As early as October 1959, Rubottom warned Undersecretary Herter that unless "concerted effort is made to halt such activities...the impression will undoubtedly be gained in Cuba and other quarters that they have the tacit approval of the U.S. government."[44] The proper course of action, he added, was to encourage a "suitable opposition" within Cuba.[45]

Moreover, Rubottom explained, such activities were counterproductive from the point of view of U.S. policy. They were grist for Castro's propaganda mill; they encouraged him in his efforts to obtain arms from the Soviet bloc; justified his posture before hemispheric opinion; tended to consolidate support for the regime at home; and endangered the lives of Americans resident in Cuba.[46]

There can be no doubt that serious efforts were made by the U.S. government to end these overflights. They were outlined in detail at a cabinet meeting on 25 March 1960.[47] At the same time, there was a genuine reluctance to become involved politically with the kinds of people who perpetrated them. For example, in June, Secretary Herter told President Eisenhower that Ambassador Pawley was working with a group of right-wing Cubans, including former Batista police officials. "The President asked Mr. Herter to call up Mr. Pawley and tell him to get out of this operation [less than one line not declassifed]."[48]

The State Department struggled as long as possible to insert the Castro revolution into the known taxonomy of Latin American nationalist regimes. This was not always easy, because from almost the first days of the new Cuban government, Communists played a role wildly disproportionate to their domestic political following or their role in the overthrow of Batista. Moreover, as Ambassador Bonsal put it in July 1959, "of as much concern to the Embassy as avowed Communists are revolutionary leaders who, while denying they are Communists, follow a course which we believe favors communist objectives and stimulates anti-Americanism."[49]

Nonetheless, Castro's rhetoric often simply restated the stock themes of Cuban nationalism, which after all much predated the existence of communism on the island (and elsewhere). This encouraged efforts on the part of the State Department to compare the new Cuban government with others in recent Latin American history that, though initially brandishing the banner of anti-Americanism and nationalism, had moderated over time. As late as January 1960, Secretary Rubottom made reference to the Perón regime, which had been overthrown in Argentina five years before.[50] The following month, the Department's policy-planning staff argued that, with luck, the United States might get something like the Bolivian revolution of 1952.[51] This line of analysis had concrete policy implications: if Castro was an "indigenous Latin American nationalist," the United States could afford to wait out the natural course of events. If, on the other hand, Cuba was (or was becoming) part of the Soviet family of revolutions, immediate plans had to be made to neutralize or overthrow it.

By late March 1960, the Central Intelligence Agency (CIA) was beginning to get a firmer conceptual grip on Castroism. A special NIE the following month reported that

> Fidel Castro remains the dominant element in the regime and we believe he is not disposed to accept actual direction from any foreign source. His susceptibility to communist influence and suggestion, and his willing adoption of communist patterns of action, spring from the parallelism of his revolutionary views with the current communist line in Latin America, from his conviction that communism offers no threat to his regime, and from his need for external support.[52]

While the Agency did not believe that Castro and his government were "demonstrably under the domination or control of the international communist movement," both were likely to continue to accept communist advice and pursue policies advantageous thereto. This was so less because of a devotion to Marxist ideology as such than because of a felt need to confront the United States. That in turn was pushing him

> to look to the Bloc for support, including provision of military equipment, [and] should the Castro regime be threatened [by the United States], the U.S.S.R. would probably do what it could to support it.

In other words, it was only quite late in the day that Washington stumbled on the fact that Castroism was something utterly *sui generis*–an authentic, indigenous Latin American revolution that for reasons of its own (size, weakness, proximity to the United States, economic vulnerability, culture, and mind-set) chose to align itself with the Soviet bloc. The same week the Agency produced this estimate, the 5412 Committee that oversaw covert operations began to plan what later became known as the Bay of Pigs operation.[53]

There was considerable confusion, uncertainty, and ambivalence in Washington's assessment of the growing Soviet threat in Cuba. This was wholly understandable, since in 1959 the Soviet Union's interests in the Latin American region were confined to a few trading companies and a score of local Communist parties, most of which were small and uninfluential (though not, as it happened, in Cuba). Soviet geostrategic doctrine had long written off much of Latin America, and certainly the circum-Caribbean, to the historic U.S. sphere of influence—a practice that Premier Khrushchev later referred to pejoratively as "geographical fatalism." His decision to reverse this policy, leading to the Cuban-Soviet alliance, was therefore wholly unpredictable.

From the beginning, the Eisenhower administration was uncertain whether the Soviet bloc might guarantee Castro's survival by replacing the United States as the principal market for Cuban sugar. This eventuality seems to have bothered it far less than the possibility of a Cuban-Soviet mutual security treaty, which would not only place a major Latin American country firmly in Moscow's camp, but also shift the geopolitical balance in the region. On the other hand—here a major paradox—the possibility of an overt Cuban-Soviet military relationship was almost welcomed by Washington as a way of "defining" matters and presumably making it easier to force the OAS to deal with Cuba on the basis of the Caracas resolution.[54]

The two issues—sugar and security—converged in a highly illuminating fashion at an interagency meeting on the Cuban question held at the State Department on 27 June 1960. When the subject of renewal of the sugar quota came up, Treasury Secretary Anderson argued against half-measures: "The time has come to say to the President that we should cut off all economic support to Cuba."[55] Rubottom, representing the regionalist's point of view, opposed dramatic actions ("tearing...up [trade treaties] as if they were scraps of paper"), which would not only undercut the Cuban opposition but many friends in Latin America as well.[56] When Anderson taunted Rubottom about taking Cuban abuse "lying down," the latter responded that "the Department had worked for over a year to setup Castro for a knock-out and would regret very much being stampeded at this time."[57] His voice dripping with sarcasm, Anderson went on to ask Rubottom

if in his opinion Castro is, indeed, in the process of falling on his face. He added that his guess is that time is completely on Castro's side. If the United States lets Castro announce U.S.S.R. support, will this not give him important strength both domestically and in the hemisphere?

The Treasury Secretary added that "should Castro do this it might rather aid us in making a good case with the rest of the countries of the hemisphere."

Defense Secretary Thomas Gates asked Rubottom "what his reaction would be if Castro comes back from the U.S.S.R. and announces a mutual security agreement or some form of agreement permitting Russian bases in Cuba." Rubottom replied that the announcement of an upcoming visit to Cuba by Khrushchev and Castro's (then current) visit to Moscow might well

> tear the mask from Castro's face and show him for the commie stooge that he is. If this clear communist course which Castro has set does not unite the hemisphere and the Cuban opposition, if we are not successful in our efforts to educate and persuade hemispheric opinion, then we may very probably have to do the job ourselves, but at great cost.[58]

There was another reason why a Cuban-Soviet mutual security treaty might well serve U.S. purposes: while isolating Cuba from its neighbors and providing Washington with a powerful ideological weapon, it would probably be militarily worthless to Havana. That is, in the event of a showdown, Moscow was unlikely to come to Cuba's aid. This was the view of Secretary Herter,[59] who added with remarkable sensitivity:

> it is [my] feeling that the Soviets would not like to see a complete takeover of Cuba by the Communists, but desire rather to create the most possible devilment for the United States while leaving the burden on us to provide Communist domination.[60]

What Secretary Herter could not foresee was that the Soviets might opt for the more costly course, or be pushed into it by Castro himself. In retrospect, it appears that the optimal scenario for Moscow (Cuba as a cost-free irritant to the United States) was simply unattainable, given Cuba's extreme geographic and economic vulnerability. The Soviets were, therefore, caught in a trap of their own making—either to abandon their new ally altogether, or take on the burden of subsidizing it indefinitely, as well as risk a military confrontation with the United States.

On 10 September 1960, the first shipments of Soviet arms arrived in Cuba. Two weeks later, CIA director Dulles told the National Security Council that "Cuba was now virtually a member of the Communist Bloc." For his part, Secretary Dillon explained that the United States "was now beginning to implement certain actions with respect to Cuba and was clearing the deck...certain other actions"[61]—that is, to prepare an exile force to invade the island and overthrow the Castro government.

The argument between "letting Castro hang himself with his own rope" and applying economic sanctions became irrelevant throughout the course of 1960 as both policies proved ineffective. From the very beginning, the State Department assumed a "soft" line with respect to dealing with the Cuban government, partly because of sensitivity to Latin American opinion, partly because it recognized that Castro continued to enjoy broad support within Cuba and that attacking him frontally would prove counterproductive. The most eloquent spokesman for this point of view was Ambassador Bonsal himself, who repeatedly argued that it was vitally important that "if the revolution fails it should be for exclusively Cuban reasons."[62]

In practice, this policy proved extremely difficult to pursue because the Cuban government itself persisted in provocative actions whose evident purpose was to goad the United States into retaliatory action. Bonsal's self-effacing personal style and the Eisenhower administration's determination not to be stampeded by Congress, the press, or others into precipitous cancellation of the sugar quota only encouraged Castro and Guevara to go further. At the same time, U.S. patience and restraint discouraged and demoralized the growing domestic opposition on the island, upon which Washington was eventually counting to improve the situation on the ground. Rubottom put it this way:

> We have to walk a tightrope—while trying to keep up a semblance of good relations with the present regime we must, at the same time, try to keep alive any spark of opposition and to let the opposition know we are aware of its existence and not committed to Castro.[63]

Economic pressures on the Castro regime, begun in March 1960 and culminating with the suspension of the sugar quota in July, did not seriously shake its hold on power. Indeed, from a political point of view, such actions probably worked to Castro's favor. As Rubottom put it in a letter to Secretary Herter:

> We must remember that a Cuban thrown out of a job because of U.S. reprisals is likely to become anti-U.S. and pro-Castro while one out of work because of Castro's own mistakes is likely to become anti-Castro and pro-U.S.[64]

In other words, the United States could not fail to react in some way to Cuban confiscation of American property for fear of encouraging similar actions elsewhere in the hemisphere (and the world). But neither could it punish the Cuban government without undermining its (Washington's) larger political agenda on the island, which was to encourage acceptable anti-Castro elements to replace the new regime. It was the Soviet Union that stepped in to break this vicious circle, by agreeing both to replace the United States as the principal market for Cuban sugar, and to sell arms to Castro. Moscow thus singlehandedly imposed an entirely new logic to U.S. policy, placing Cuba within the larger framework of cold war priorities. This, in turn, finally made it possible for Washington to cleanly define its paramount interests on the island, and sacrifice other, more traditional economic, political, and regional considerations.

Concluding Observations

Insofar as these documents shed any light on the current U.S.-Cuban imbroglio, they depict from the very start two planets set in utterly different solar systems. One official of the Policy Planning Staff, speaking of the Castro regime, put it this way: "We have never in our national history experienced anything quite like it in the magnitudes of anti-U.S. venom, claims for expropriation, or Soviet threats to the hemisphere.... I think we fail to realize that Castro does not speak our language and does not want to listen to it.[65] For his part, President Eisenhower confided to the National Security Council that "it was difficult to figure out what Castro was trying to do...nothing seemed to have an effect on" him.[66]

For the United States, the Cuban revolution was both unexpected and incomprehensible. The Castro regime bore little or no resemblance to anything it had yet seen in Latin America. If it were merely nationalist-populist rather than communist, why did it not respond to the kinds of initiatives that had been successful with such governments elsewhere in the region? Barring a transformation to totalitarian dictatorship, how did it propose to make its bizarre economic measures work? And if it was a regime of communist inspiration, when would it finally declare its true colors?

There was, of course, no "bourgeois" logic to Castro's revolution. Cuba's welfare had long been linked to the United States, and could not be separated from it without paying a ruinous price. When President Eisenhower asked Ambassador Bonsal how Cuba "could make a living if it was unable to sell its sugar," the latter replied that "the present government had not thought that problem out."[67] This was true as far as it went, but fell far short of the political imagination required. In effect, Washington failed to go beyond the calculations of double-entry bookkeeping; to grasp that what for it was sheer madness represented for many Cubans a long-awaited, orgiastic release. Or that Castro would succeed in fashioning a political system capable of repressing whatever second thoughts his fellow countrymen might have by the time they got around to having them.

Most of all, the Eisenhower administration took no note of the long- and even middle-term political implications of a massive migration of Cuban professionals and members of the middle class that began sometime in mid-1959 and greatly accelerated throughout 1960. In effect, with each day there were fewer people in the country of the type that Washington expected to lead a post-Castro government, and fewer potential members of its constituency. It was not even certain what could or would replace Castro in the happy eventuality of his disappearance. "There is not a clear enough realization among our own people," the official at the Policy Planning Staff wrote, "that pre-Castro Cuba will not return, or that, if we are to reestablish influence within Cuba, it must be in a context different from that which obtained in the past."[68] In many ways, this problem persists thirty-five years later.

For its part, from the very beginning, the Castro regime went off in directions that had little or nothing to do with the United States. Indeed, one is struck in these documents by the degree to which U.S. policy was basically irrelevant to the course of revolutionary events. At no point did the new regime even deign to engage the Eisenhower administration on the major issues of the bilateral relationship. Ambassador Bonsal—who urged upon Washington a policy of patience and restraint almost to his last day on the island—was shunted aside and repeatedly refused appointments with Castro, the foreign minister, or other high officials. When he managed to see these personalities, they invariably lied to him or offered disingenuous responses to his appeals.[69]

There were important contradictions within the U.S. business community in Cuba, and between it and the government in Washington, but the Cuban government took no note of these and made no effort whatsoever to exploit them to its own advantage. This was so because there was no apparent Cuban design of co-existence with the United States in any form, merely a desire to punish, to humiliate, to confront—a posture that caused all elements of the American side to eventually close ranks and advocate a full-dress economic and political embargo.

With the best will in the world, then, it is difficult to see what policy would have purchased a good relationship with Castro's Cuba, since such a relationship was never even offered as a theoretical object for sale. The regime defined itself (and, indeed, the very Cuban nationality) entirely in terms of its opposition to the United States and all its works. The decision of the Soviet Union to subsidize the Cuban economy made this posture easier to assume and sustained it over three decades, but one cannot be certain that it would not have survived even so—a point now being brought home by events since 1989. Cuba seems to have proven that a small country living in the shadow of the United States can purposely pick a fight with it and live to tell the tale; but how much beyond that still remains to be seen.

Notes

1. John P. Glennon, Editor-in-Chief, *Foreign Relations of the United States, 1958–60: Cuba* (Washington, DC: GPO, 1991)
2. Doc. 11, 20.
3. Doc. 38, 62
4. Doc. 33, 56.
5. Doc. 111, 166.
6. Doc. 112, 170, 172.
7. Doc. 117, 188.
8. Doc. 123, 196.
9. Doc. 133, 215.
10. Doc. 154, 253–54.
11. Doc. 158, 260.
12. Doc. 263, 270.
13. Ambassador Smith eventually learned of the mission from Cuban sources.
14. Doc. 201, 328.
15. Doc. 25, 47. Castro issued a similar denial to U.S. consul Wollam in Santiago in July, Doc. 81, 128.
16. Doc. 18, 34.
17. Doc. 47, 77.
18. Doc. 135, 216. The same analyst added that it "would indeed be serious if our Government assumed that the movement was not Communist and later proved to be so," but, he added, the inverse was also true.
19. Doc. 188, 302
20. Doc. 188, 303.

21. Doc. 203, 331.
22. Doc. 154, 253.
23. Doc. 46, 75.
24. Editorial note, 12.
25. Doc. 254, 406.
26. As I&R pointed out in mid-January, "if we had received additional information over the last six months on the amount of military equipment Castro was receiving from the United States, we might have had a somewhat different appreciation of his strength." Doc. 226, 363.
27. Doc. 248, 395.
28. Doc. 266, 442.
29. Doc. 269, 446.
30. Doc. 269, *supra*; Doc. 271, 449.
31. Doc. 287 (editorial note), 478. For the full text see Jeffrey J. Safford, "The Nixon-Castro Meeting of 19 April 1959," *Diplomatic History*, 4 (1980): 425–431.
32. Doc. 288, 477.
33. Rufo López Fresquet, *My Fourteen Months with Castro* (Cleveland and New York: World Publishing Company, 1966), 100–12. López Fresquet was minister of the treasury from 8 January 1959 to 17 March 1960.
34. Doc. 274, 454.
35. Doc. 279, 467.
36. Doc. 302, 504.
37. Interview with Castro in Lee Lockwood, *Castro's Cuba, Cuba's Fidel* (New York: Vintage Books, 1969) 159–60. See also the erroneous version of López.
38. Doc. 311, 515–16.
39. Doc. 412, 709–11.
40. Doc. 536, 959–60.
41. Doc. 406, 693–96.
42. Doc. 310, 512–15, which summarizes a remarkable conversation in this regard between Cuban Ambassador Ernesto Dihigo and Assistant Secretary Roy Rubottom. After the quota was finally abolished, Foreign Minister Raul Roa's sister-in-law confided to Ambassador Bonsal that such action was "anticipated and desired by Castro"; the fact that "it cuts deep...meant that he could charge economic aggression all the more effectively." Doc. 548, 995.
43. Doc. 501, 887–89.
44. Doc. 375, 633.
45. Doc. 376, 638.
46. Doc. 462, 808–09
47. Doc. 493–874.
48. Doc. 529, 945.
49. Doc. 330, 554.
50. Doc. 419, 733.
51. Doc. 458, 796.
52. Doc. 491, 870.
53. Doc. 481, 850–51.
54. This was the consensus reached (under heavy U.S. pressure) by the OAS foreign ministers at their 1954 meeting in the Venezuelan capital, by which countries that opted for alliances with extra-hemispheric powers were subject to collective sanctions. It provided a sort of juridical umbrella under

which the United States intervened to depose the Arbenz regime in Guatemala, which was in the process of acquiring arms from the Eastern bloc.
55. Doc. 536, 960.
56. Ibid., 961.
57. Ibid., 962.
58. Ibid., 962.
59. Reflected also in a Special NIE prepared by the CIA (22 March 1960). See Doc. 491, 871.
60. Ibid., 965.
61. Doc. 583, 1074–75.
62. Doc. 362, 604.
63. Doc. 365, 620.
64. Doc. 473, 832.
65. Doc. 458, 795–6.
66. Doc. 474, 833.
67. Doc. 436, 833.
68. Doc. 458, loc. cit.
69. Doc. 342, 570. Foreign Minister Raúl Roa told Bonsal on 23 July 1959 that "he personally was strongly opposed to communism and that he believed there were no Communists in important government positions."

13

America's Culture Wars and
the Cuban Revolution

The capacity of the Castro regime to survive more than half a decade beyond the collapse of its Soviet patron has once again raised fundamental questions about the Cuban revolution, and what amounts to the same thing, its relationship to the United States. Is Cuba the one country in the world where communism, discredited as a system everywhere else, finally has found a place where it "works"? What does "working" mean, beyond assuring that U.S. economic, political, and cultural influence in the country are held to a bare minimum? Has the U.S. economic embargo actually helped Castro retain power by providing him with an excuse for his country's parlous state? If so, then why is the near-totality of Cuban foreign policy presently organized around getting the embargo lifted?

These enduring questions, and the elusiveness of their answers, are symptoms of a uniquely antagonistic relationship between the Cuban Revolution and the United States. To be sure, all of Latin America's revolutionary or semi-revolutionary regimes this century have provoked some sort of negative American response. But in no case has the antirelationship approached the same level of intensity, nor endured so many changes of historical and geopolitical context. Nor has any Latin American revolution proven so impervious to compromise over basic points of principle.

The reason is disarmingly simple. In its essence, the Castro regime represents a challenge not merely—or even particularly—to American hegemony in the Caribbean, or American investment in Latin America, or American military influence in the region, but what has often been referred to as "the American Way of Life." Precisely because Cuba was the most Americanized Latin American nation prior to 1959, its abrupt and unexpected departure for the Soviet bloc was a stunning blow to American self-esteem. As the *Economist* put it recently (6 April 1995), "The Cubans are [America's] contemptuous cousins who have walked away with the family oil fields and factories...America is hurt and offended by Cuba as only a close relation can be."

Indeed, more than any other event since the Second World War, the Cuban revolution has succeeded in illuminating the unique nature of America's "post-colonial" crisis. Unlike Great Britain, France, Holland, or Italy, the United States is not an "old" country whose culture and national identity are the product of centuries of gradual accretion, something above and beyond constitutions, parliaments, or indeed political regimes. Nor is it a middle-level power like Canada, which can quietly enjoy a high standard of living without arousing antagonism, envy, or resentment. Rather, the United States is a "proposition country"— a fictitious construct based on certain ideas and ideals; it is these and only these which hold together a nation which otherwise has little by which to define itself.

Consider, by way of contrast, the case of France. Though it fought long and hard to retain its overseas territories after the Second World War, once it finally accepted defeat, French society experienced a vast surge of optimism and self-confidence which carries it forward to this day. Even the most intransigent could mitigate their anguish at the loss of empire with the thought that the Indochinese and the Algerians—having proven unworthy (as they would put it) of French culture and civilization—would end up with the worst part of the bargain, an argument that, however self-serving, has been largely validated by subsequent events.

Given its anomalous nature as a proposition country, however, such consolations are unavailable to the United States; in effect, it has no choice but to consider its institutions of universal value and applicability. Their successful rejection by others casts troubling doubts on their quality and even their legitimacy. Accidents of geography and history have led Cuba to play an important role in the U.S. dialogue with itself.

An Implicit Confrontation

At the beginning, of course, this aspect of the Cuban Revolution was the least evident of all—which explains why Castro himself was something of a popular hero in the United States before and immediately after his assumption of power. True, the Cuban dictator Fulgencio Batista had his apologists and supporters in the American press, Congress, and business community, but for the Eisenhower administration he was something of an embarrassment, and for the U.S. public, or at least that part of it which was aware of events in Cuba, Batista was a tyrant and a monster. As our penultimate ambassador in Havana, the late Earl E. T. Smith, recalls ruefully in his memoirs, *everyone* in his embassy except himself was on the side of the rebels—even the local representatives of the CIA![1]

Castro's victory, if anything, greatly enhanced his popularity in the United States, if for no other reason than that Americans love a winner. In fact, his "private" visit here in early 1959, shortly after taking power, had all the characteristics of a triumphal procession. Though President Eisenhower escaped meeting with the new Cuban prime minister (Castro was shunted off to spend a charmless hour with Vice President Richard Nixon), huge and friendly crowds greeted him wherever he went; he spoke to respectful audiences at both Harvard and Princeton universities; far more importantly, he was favorably introduced to more than fifty million American viewers on Ed Sullivan's Sunday night television program. Nor was this friendly reception without its effects; Carlos Franqui, editor at the time of the official daily *Revolución*, has since recalled seeing the Cuban leader crouched by the long-distance telephone in his New York hotel suite, emotionally fending off the attacks of his brother Raúl (who had remained behind in Havana to manage the store), who accused him of "selling out to the Yanquis."

Even the show trials of Batistiano collaborators—real or imagined—followed by hastily-organized executions ("paredón!") or the expropriation of American properties, though both excited critical comment in the U.S. Congress and media, were not sufficient to turn the tide of American public opinion. Ambassador Philip Bonsal took up his post as Smith's successor in early 1959 determined to make the new relationship work, but as he recalls in his memoirs, as time went on it was apparent that Castro and his people were not interested in discussing details which were amenable to diplomatic negotiation—specific laws expropriating specific properties—but rather were obsessed with shifting the entire direction of Cuban history.

Inevitably, this meant a radical change in the relationship with the United States; within this context, nothing the United States did or failed to do would divert Castro from his chosen course, though some of the things which it nonetheless did do—particularly the arming of and training of exiles, or pressuring the American oil companies in Cuba to refuse to process Soviet crude—did make it look as if Havana was reacting to U.S. provocations, rather than pursuing its own agenda. Of course, once Castro announced that he was a Marxist-Leninist (and hinted, also, that he always had been one), literally overnight he lost the support and sympathy of the broad American public.

The cold war was the proximate cause of the estrangement, or perhaps better said, the pretext, but relations between the two governments would have deteriorated even in its absence. This was so because the Cuban revolutionary ideal of "normal" relations with the United States was, at a minimum, one in which both countries would treat one another as if they were approximately equal in importance, size, and power. Now, since this was clearly not the case, Castro's agenda could be satisfied only if Washington was willing to indulge in a bit of play-acting, and some rather self-effacing play-acting at that. But even this would not have been enough. For the only way for the small country to "prove" it was the equal of the big one was to continually test the latter's tolerance and capacity to absorb frontal attacks—not merely on its economic or geopolitical interests, but its *amour-propre*, its prestige and self-respect.

The confrontation with the United States was implicit, then, from the very beginning; as a matter of fact, Castro has subsequently said as much. The alliance with the Soviet Union was purely conjunctural; some other great power, with a wholly different ideology, might well have played the same role had it existed. The fact that the nationalistic strands of Castro's revolution became almost immediately entangled with cold war politics obscured this fact for decades; only today is it possible to adequately perceive the quarrel in its true and original dimensions.

This is not to say that the United States had no reason to be concerned with the Cuban alliance with the Soviet Union. Quite the contrary: it was a uniquely provocative geopolitical threat. But it was also something more—a firm *cultural* rejection of everything American society represented at home and abroad—the bourgeois values of order, property, and individualism, a rejection couched in terms particularly meaningful to every country in Latin America, and possibly also to most of those in what used to be called the Third World.

The Cuban rejection was also a critique (sometimes implicit, sometimes explicit) of the failings of American society—its tendency towards the impersonal in human relations, its ready acceptance of wide disparities of wealth and poverty, its problematic race relations. Indeed, even before Castro marched his country into the Soviet camp, Cuban government media specialized in documenting what might be called the dark underside of the American Dream. One might even venture to say that it is this, rather than socialism, which constitutes the core ideology of the Cuban revolution. In this perspective, to be Cuban—a real, red-blooded Cuban—is not only *not* to be North American, but even more, not to *want* to be North American. This attitude puts a deeply personal coloration on what should be ordinary relations between states, and explains why the antagonism between Cuba and the United States remains so qualitatively different from those with other Communist (and other Latin) adversaries.

Cuba as a Mirror to Americas

If the Castro regime has always represented something of an antimodel to the American Way of Life, the response to it has been strongly conditioned by the way Americans feel about their own country, its institutions, and their society in general. Periods of self-confidence at home have encouraged negative feelings towards the Cuban experiment, and vice-versa. The Cuban revolution occurred at something of a high point in American postwar self-confidence, so it is not surprising that a dislike of Castro and all his works was widely shared across the political spectrum between about 1960 and 1968. These were years which not only coincided with an unprecedented burst of American prosperity, but the steady outflow of refugees from the island, most to the United States. This flight was seen as a kind of silent plebiscite on which way of life most Cubans would have preferred had they had the opportunity to freely choose. They also coincided with the Cuban missile crisis and its aftermath, which convinced many Americans that only American strength, combined with Khrushchev's commendable realism, had prevented a tropical maniac from blowing up the world.

In the center of this period we have the Civil Rights Act of 1964, which removed all legal disabilities to which Americans of African origin were subjected in Southern states. At the same time, President Lyndon Johnson was launching an extensive social welfare and jobs program in the United States known collectively as the Great Society—which proposed to bring the United States somewhat closer structurally to some of the social-democratic countries of North Europe.

By the end of the decade, however, American society was in crisis. A war begun in Southeast Asia was going badly; the civil rights movement in the United States was giving way to the quest for Black Power; a refusal to raise taxes to finance both war and social programs produced a predictable spurt of inflation; and the sense that the American elite had lost its nerve generated a youth rebellion which took apolitical forms—drugs, sex, rock music, opting out of normal patterns of education and career development—which nonetheless had strong political implications.

What American journalists and politicians call "the sixties" was really the first half of the 1970s. Probably the low-point of American self-confidence was reached in 1976, at the very end of the Ford administration. By that time the United States had sustained the first oil shock, which caused a sharp drop in employment and living standards, as well as a number of domestic political scandals—some of which had international implications. Not just Watergate but revelations of U.S. involvement in covert activities in Vietnam, Chile, the Dominican Republic, and Cuba itself, provoked a climate of shame and regret, particularly in elite cultural circles and the media.

A strongly "revisionist" mood was in the air, which finally found embodiment in the Carter administration which took office in 1977. Its view of the United States and its role in the world was very nearly a photographic negative of that of the Eisenhower administration a generation before. In place of pride and self-confidence, the prevailing tone was one of repentance and self-reproach. Overnight enemies became friends, and vice versa. The purpose of foreign policy was to get the United States on the side of "history," defined in this case as the supposedly inevitable expansion of anti-Western (when not explicitly anti-American) regimes, trends, and currents around the globe.

Cuba was a marked beneficiary of this new mood. A poll taken in 1977 showed that fully 30 percent of Americans held a "somewhat favorable" view of the Castro regime, with an additional 3 percent expressing "very favorable" views."[2] This still left the overwhelming majority of Americans with negative views—31 percent "somewhat unfavorable" and another 21 percent "very unfavorable" (15 percent "don't know")—but the poll suggested a widening *tranche* of tolerance for Castro which, if continued, might eventually expand to encompass outright sympathy. Some American politicians, notably Senators George McGovern (D-SD) and Claiborne Pell (D-RI) began to visit Cuba and engage in extensive talks with Castro; McGovern seemed troubled by the problem of political prisoners, but assured readers of the *New York Times* that "Castro has the support and outright affection of his people," which, he emphasized, he had earned through accomplishments in housing, health care, and education, themes to which he and other Americans both liberal and left would often return. McGovern's views, which once would have been regarded as daringly advanced, were becoming almost conventional.

One indication that this was in fact the case was a perceptible shift in U.S. government policy. The Ford administration opened diplomatic discussions with Havana in 1975, culminating in the establishment of interest sections in each other's capitals. Washington also reversed its position with respect to relations between Cuba and other Latin American countries, removing its formal objection within the OAS to other nations in the hemisphere reestablishing diplomatic relations with Havana.

It appeared that the United States itself was about to follow this course, and the Carter administration came into office in 1977 resolved to do just that. Before that could happen, however, Castro intervened massively in Angola, transporting an entire army halfway around the world (in Soviet aircraft) to fight there under a Soviet general for evident Soviet purposes, and began conniving with the Sandinistas in Nicaragua and the Farabundo Martí guerrillas in El Salvador. The Carter administration was pained by these moves, to the extent at least of adjourning further discussions with the Cubans *sine die*.

Hardly had the negotiations collapsed than more than 120,000 Cubans seized the opportunity to leave the island for the United States through the port of Mariel in 1980. Many of these were black and poor, in no way resembling earlier Cuban refugees, who had been somewhat carelessly written off by elite Americans as relatively privileged beneficiaries of an old and unjust regime. The Mariel affair suddenly cast the revolution in a new and even less flattering light. It also coincided with a general decline in the fortunes of the Carter administration and the discrediting of its overall worldview. This was particularly bad news for Castro, since Carter's replacement was fiercely anti-Communist, and was inspired by a kind of pugnacious optimism about the United States which did not suggest any particular vulnerability to traditional Cuban forms of reproach.

Attitudes towards Cuba: Elite and Non-Elite

President Reagan clearly despised Fidel Castro, and the latter returned the compliment, referring to him more than once as the Hitler of our time. For Reagan, bad relations (or rather, no relations) with Cuba were good domestic politics—and not just in the Cuban-American community. By the mid-1980s, U.S. self-confidence was on the mend, and most Americans saw no reason to accept instruction on their obligations to mankind by Third World dictators or their representatives at the United Nations.

Attitudes towards Castro and Cuba suffered a corresponding decline. A poll commissioned in 1988 revealed, for example, that only 9 percent of Americans now had a "somewhat favorable" opinion of his regime (1 percent favorable), while 37 percent declared themselves "somewhat unfavorable," and fully 44 percent "very unfavorable." (The "don't knows" had slipped to 9 percent.)

The 1988 poll is particularly interesting because it separated for the first time elite and broad public responses to its questions. Thus 31 percent of elite respondents ("opinion leaders") registered a "somewhat favorable" or "very favorable" view of Cuba; 35 percent considered Castro to have been good for the island (compared to 9 percent of the general public), and fully 65 percent considered Cuba "not a particularly serious" or "not at all serious" security threat to the United States (compared to 26 percent for the general public). Opinion leaders shared broader public doubts on the human rights situation in Cuba, though with slightly fewer registering "very unfavorable" responses (39 versus 48 percent for the general public).

The 1988 poll also revealed sharp differences in policy pre-scriptions. A slight majority of the general public (15 percent "very strongly," 36 percent "fairly strongly") favored resumption of diplomatic relations with Castro, compared with 94 percent of the elites. Even more interesting, while 58 percent of the general public believed that the existing trade embargo should be maintained "until relations improve," fully 57 percent of elites believed it should be lifted unconditionally. An overwhelming majority of elites—90 percent—favored negotiations with Cuba on key problems, which might or might not lead to either diplomatic relations or the resumption of commercial exchange (the same question, unfortunately, was not asked of the general public).

A more recent poll conducted by the Chicago Council on Foreign Relations (1995) underscores the division between the two tiers of American opinion, while at the same time revealing that U.S. popular attitudes towards Cuba and Castro have not been much affected by the end of the cold war. The Cuban dictator himself remains one of the least popular foreign leaders, located on a barometer of public esteem midway between Yassir Arafat and Saddam Hussein. As a country Cuba ranks in popularity well below China, Saudi Arabia, or India, and only barely edges out North Korea.

More surprising, perhaps, is the fact that when queried about the proper U.S. response to a popular uprising in Cuba, nearly half those ordinary Americans polled (44 percent) favored military intervention there, bested only by the percentages which would favor a similar response if Russia invaded Western Europe or Iraq invaded Saudi Arabia. The gap here between popular and elite opinion is particularly striking, since only 19 percent of the people defined as "leaders" would favor a similar course. The spread between popular and elite levels on this one issue is wider than on almost any other hypothetical situation which might call for the use of force.

Insofar as attitudes towards Cuba may reflect the way Americans feel about their country, the 1988 and 1995 polls suggest two things—one, that the general public has largely recovered from the crisis of self-confidence which characterized the mid-1970s, and two, that the elite public has not. This of course is telling us on a specific issue what we already know generally—namely, that educated, more affluent, and more influential Americans tend to view their own society more skeptically and self-critically than the ordinary citizen. It also underscores the degree to which the "cultural revolution" which the United States has experienced since 1968 has become institutionalized through higher education, the quality press, and certain social expectations which associate adversarial views with urbanity and sophistication.

Of course, the fact that elite Americans tend more strongly to favor "negotiations" with Cuba than their less-educated co-nationals does not say very much about their negotiating objectives, or what outcomes they would find minimally satisfactory. Their basic policy prescription is limited to greater flexibility in U.S. Cuban policy, an attitude which could only be productive to the degree to which it were reciprocated in such areas as human rights and greater political democracy on the island. So far there is not much evidence that Castro has a response of this kind in mind. Therefore the differences between elite American attitudes and those of the broader public, while marked, are at this point somewhat theoretical.

The Revolution and the American Left

So far we have been discussing mainstream American opinion. But what of the radicals, the left, the blacks, or others who regard themselves as on the margins of American politics, or even outside of it? This is an enormous subject which deserves careful discussion and the establishment of some crucial distinctions. First of all, when we speak of the "left" in the United States we must recognize at least three different groups—one which might be broadly characterized as "humanist," that is, pacifist and humanitarian, with some commitment to redress of minority grievances and often greater economic empowerment of the poor, though not in any rigorous or doctrinal way; "New Left," which is to say radical, militant, socialist in economic doctrine but libertarian or even iconoclastic in personal and cultural values; and finally, Marxist-Leninist, that is to say, those people who are or were close to or affiliated with the U.S. Communist Party (CPUSA).

Cuba has appealed to all three of these groups, though not at the same time. The earliest admirers of Castro and Castroism were American humanists, who regarded themselves as post-Marxist and certainly post-Stalinist socialists; what they thought they had found on the island was a revolution made not by workers and soldiers, but intellectuals and students—people just like themselves!

It was this quality in particular which so appealed to sociologist C. Wright Mills, whose book *Listen Yankee!* (1960) extracted from Cuba the lesson that it was time for American radicals to abandon the "labor metaphysic"—instead of waiting for the American working class to become revolutionary, the argument went, they should take matters into their own hands. In this way Mills, though he actually predates the New Left, is also one of its important precursors, and the Cuban example, or what was supposed to be the Cuban example, one of its seminal inspirations.

Some humanists were artists strongly inclined towards existentialism, and in that sense almost antipolitical; their Cuba was revolutionary in a very different way—full of "bearded soldiers, sensual and armed women, and a general Mardi Gras atmosphere." (Paul Lyons) This phase was very brief, evidently, but extremely intense; its most important legacy was to resume the dialogue between politics and culture in the United States that had been blunted by both Stalinism and the era of the Popular Front.

It should be added here that the humanists and existentialists lost their enthusiasm for the revolution fairly early on, though quietly so; until the Padilla case in 1971 none felt moved to express any particular disagreement with the Castro regime, and even today the artistic community in the United States feels vaguely uncomfortable with attacks upon Cuban communism, even when they do not come from the right—as exemplified by the equivocal response to Nestor Almendros's film *Conducta Impropria* (1983). On the other hand, few of these people are inclined to spend any political capital defending Castro either.

The next phase coincides with the development of the "New Left" in the United States—from about 1963 to 1968. (These years also bracketed growing American military involvement in Vietnam, a rising protest movement against military conscription, and among younger educated Americans, a growing current of sympathy for Third World revolutions and revolutionaries, including, obviously, Castro and the legendary Che Guevara.) What distinguished the New Left from its humanist and pacifist predecessors was its willingness to work with Communists, in spite of abiding tactical and doctrinal differences. In fact, Cuba was quite important in breaking down the wall between Old (e.g., communistoid) Left and New in the United States, since Castro's revolution demonstrated that even if the party was sometimes a bit late in its rendezvous with "history," it still had an important role to play in the reconstruction of society. And then of course the fact that Castro himself assimilated Marxism-Leninism—however tardily—forced those who sympathized with his revolution to at least rethink their attitudes towards Stalinist conceptions, particularly as regards democratic centralism, the role of the state and authority in general, and cultural policy.

The New Left period also saw an increase in American radical travel to Cuba. Of course, such revolutionary tourism had existed since the very beginning of the Castro regime, but it greatly accelerated after 1966, and reached a new phase in 1969, with the creation of the Venceremos Brigades, American teams who went to Cuba during the cane-cutting season to assist in the harvest and also undergo serious political education. To the extent that this experience had any impact on the visitors, in the short run at least, it was to encourage a greater ideological specificity—many young Americans for the first time consciously and militantly defined themselves as revolutionary socialists rather than merely antiwar resisters or cultural rebels. Unfortunately, the situations in prerevolutionary Cuba and Nixon's America were radically different; therefore much of this new commitment found expression not in conventional political organizing but in violence which was highly counterproductive—Weatherman's "Days of Rage" in Chicago, various bank robberies and bombings, etc.

The New Left itself collapsed sometime after 1970, splitting into sectarian factions more at war with each other than society. During the same period, Cuba began to lose much of its appeal to American radicals, partly in fact because so many of them had visited the island, and found themselves troubled by certain aspects of "mature" Cuban socialism—the militarization of labor, the emergence of a new class of party bureaucrats and military officers, the persecution of artists, homosexuals, and other cultural nonconformists (the Padilla case, 1971), the dogmatism and censorship of the government media, the evident failure not only of the ten-million-ton harvest in 1970 but widespread scarcities and rationing.

By the mid-1970s, in fact, the most enthusiastic American visitors to the island were those associated with the American Communist party, who loudly declared everything to their liking; others either had to keep their doubts to themselves or—as Frances Fitzgerald observed—perform "a kind of surgery on their critical faculties...reduc[ing] their conversation to a form of baby talk, in which everything is wonderful, including the elevator that doesn't work and the rows of Soviet tanks on military parade that are 'in the hands of the people.'"

Evidently, the varied responses of the American left to the Cuban experiment have been shaped largely by the shifts and turns of government policy there. During the early "humanist" phase, Castro was at pains to avoid ideological definitions, and even after declaring his allegiance to Marxism-Leninism, there were still idiosyncratic aspects to the regime (particularly in the cultural realm) which distinguished it from the Soviet model. As late as the mid-1960s, Castro was still trying to avoid identifying too closely with Moscow, to the extent of creating organizations like the Organization of Latin American Solidarity (OLAS) which were intended to open a new, Third World front of support.

After 1968, however, Soviet influence in the island increased, repression grew apace, and whatever idealistic or revolutionary features of the regime which had once appealed to independent leftists—moral (as opposed to material) incentives, people's militias (as opposed to the regular army), and so forth—were phased out. At each step of the way the Cuban government demanded a higher degree of uncritical assent from its American admirers. This led to a complete reversal of constituencies—since the mid-1970s, Cuba has appealed principally to those Americans who positively celebrate the replication there of the Soviet model, as opposed to those who were originally attracted to the revolution precisely because they were searching for alternatives to the Stalinist paradigm.

Meanwhile, moves towards normalization of relations between the United States and Cuba in the late-1970s introduced new kinds of American tourists—politicians, journalists, businessmen, a few liberal (as opposed to radical) activists. By then the Cuban government had plainly lost interest in the American left; it could promise nothing and deliver nothing—not even uncritical support. Indeed, at this point mainstream politicians like Jimmy

Carter or George McGovern or former government officials like Robert McNamara were far more to Castro's taste than disappointed American radicals; precisely because this has never been their revolution, they do not feel particularly cheated by its outcome.

Of course, there have been differences all along between the way American radicals and liberals have viewed the Castro regime. American liberals have never appreciated or apologized for its repressive aspects, nor felt that its particular vision of social reconstruction was appropriate for the United States (though some have thought it was perfectly alright for Cuba). They have invariably been critical of its human rights record. In contrast, historically the American left has tended either to deny or justify the embarrassing facts of the Cuban revolution.

Quite recently, however, the views of the American liberal community and the American left on the Cuban question have begun to converge. First, both concede that the human rights situation is deplorable, and not improving. Second, both think that Cuba's educational and health policies (or as they are more often called, its "achievements") must be balanced out against political repression. Just how this balancing should occur we are never told; nobody seems willing to say that they think Castro's educational and health policies *justify* repression, but between the lines one reads a certain concern over whether these revolutionary gains could be expected to survive the collapse of authoritarian structures on the island. (This in itself contains an interesting political subtext well worth exploring.)

Third, all agree that some sort of democratic opening is desirable in Cuba, though they often speak of the Cuban-American community in Florida as if it were at least as big an obstacle to this consummation as Fidel Castro himself. Finally, almost all liberals and radicals agree that at this point the lack of political forward movement in Cuba is due to the U.S. economic embargo, which is another way of saying that—in their view—the survival of Stalinist political forms there have less to do with Castro's personality, his perceived (and real) political interests, the outlook of his associates, or the structure of his regime than its inability to trade with the United States. In that sense, for Americans left of center, the tendency to blame their own country for the follies and misfortunes of others has remained the most important ingredient in shaping attitudes towards Castro and his revolution, surviving other hopes and other illusions abandoned along the way.

Blacks and Hispanics

A word here about American blacks and "Hispanics." Almost from the beginning Castro has reached out to the more radical sectors of American black leadership, and his gestures have often evoked favorable response. At his 1961 visit to New York to attend the General Assembly of the United Nations, Castro purposely decamped to Harlem, where he received Khrushchev outside Hotel Teresa to the general acclaim of area residents and black political activists. Robert Williams, a fugitive from Southern justice, established himself in Cuba in the early 1960s and for some years broadcast in English to the American black community on something called Radio Free Dixie. Stokley Carmichael, former civil rights activist turned Pan-African revolutionary, was an important participant in the 1967 OLAS meeting, where he delighted thousands of revolutionaries from all over the Third World by predicting "the United States is going to fall...I just hope I live to see the day." Ex-convict and author Eldridge Cleaver (Soul on Ice) passed through Cuba on his flight from bail in 1968, before settling in Algeria.

Paradoxically, as American blacks have attained greater rights and wider participation in the political process, not just black revolutionaries but mainstream black leaders have tended increasingly to identify with and defend Castro and his regime. Most members of the Congressional Black Caucus and their staffs have been conspicuously sympathetic visitors to Cuba, and four black members of the House of Representatives (Ron Dellums, George Crockett, Charles Rangel, and the late Mickey Leland) have been vehement critics of U.S. Cuban policy, particularly with regard to the economic embargo. The Rev. Jesse Jackson, self-styled president of Black America and frequent candidate for the Democratic nomination for the presidency, visited Cuba in 1984, and virtually endorsed the regime at a church service in Havana in the presence of Castro himself.

Clearly, in his role as the maximum enemy of the United States and all its works, Castro cannot but exercise a certain fascination on the most alienated and angry members of this minority. However, his appeal has been rather more limited than one might expect. First of all, other international causes, particularly South Africa, and more recently Haiti, have been far more compelling to the black community, and have absorbed the near-totality of its attention and political energies. Second, although most black intellectuals share Castro's anti-Americanism, most black Americans do not; the majority are, in fact, notably patriotic. They reproach the United States for not living up to its promise; they do not seek other promises in other countries. Third, there is a sharp discrepancy between the evident blackness of large segments of the Cuban population, and the equally evident "whiteness" of its leadership—a discrepancy which is too apparent to be avoided when one is actually on the island itself.

Finally, even those American blacks most predisposed to believe the best about Cuba—political intellectuals, writers, poets, dancers, filmmakers—are ambivalent about the Cuban government's tendency to discourage black pride and Afro-Cuban cultural awareness. To generalize very broadly, these people define themselves first and foremost as black—politically and culturally— they are Americans only by geographical accident and (as they would say) historic tragedy. Therefore, it is difficult for them to accept the notion that racial identity should be submerged in a broader national framework—not just in the United States but in any multiracial society. (They are often stunned to learn, for example, that the Cuban national census does not even break the population down by racial categories.)

As a result, black intellectuals in the United States are divided over the Cuban experiment—while all think it is good for Cuba, they are not clear on exactly what lessons it might hold for their own country. This reflects a far older division between Marxists and Black Nationalists—between those who think that the problem is one of economic exploitation, to be altered by radical measures of an economic type (expropriations, "reparations," "freedom budgets," or what have you), and those who believe in what might be called "vertical liberation"—sorting the society into racial cohorts, each of which should be free to determine its own destiny, but giving priority to national forms over socioeconomic content.

A somewhat similar problem attends the so-called Hispanics in the United States, complicated by the fact that this group is far too diverse to have a common viewpoint on something as abstract as Cuban Marxism-Leninism. The basic divisions within this group derive first from their societies of origin—Mexico, Cuba, Puerto Rico, Central America, Colombia, and other South American countries; then, class and educational level; then, degree of integration in the mainstream "Anglo" society; finally, political awareness and political orientation. Differences are therefore both horizontal and vertical.

Moreover, of all these groups only three—the Mexicans, the Puerto Ricans, and obviously, the Cubans—are sufficiently numerous, organized, and articulate to have any pronounced views on Cuba and Castro. Even so, most Mexicans and Puerto Ricans in the United States are apolitical, or interested principally in issues which directly affect their lives, such as welfare, job and immigration policies, housing, educational opportunities, and so forth.

The growth of Chicano studies in universities in the Western and Southwestern United States, and Puerto Rican studies in New York, has engendered an academic intelligentsia which has a somewhat more intense interest in the subject, to judge at least by their journals and public pronouncements. Even so, Chicano and Puerto Rican intellectuals could be said to be "pro-Castro" only in a very limited intellectual and emotional sense; they derive inspiration from the spectacle of a small "Hispanic" leader successfully confronting the "Anglo"— and in the corner of the Hispanic world where no one dared to challenge his authority. But how to apply that inspiration to practical politics within the United States is a more elusive problem.

In Puerto Rico itself, of course, the Cuban prescription would seem to be self-evident: political revolution followed by economic expropriation followed by socioeconomic transformation. But for Puerto Ricans who prefer to remain in the United States, or wish to settle there, it is difficult to see what relevance the Cuban model might have, particularly since almost all of the political and economic demands of the continental Puerto Rican diaspora would seem to require greater integration rather than efforts to cast their cultural distinctiveness into yet sharper relief (The same is true, *pari passu*, for those Mexican-Americans who have no particular interest in resettling in Mexico.)

A Continuing Fascination

With the end of the cold war, the Cuban revolution has lost much of its ideological specificity, but the country itself continues to exercise a unique fascination for America's media and cultural elites. For some, Cuba feeds a growing nostalgia for an ever more distant youth—a nostalgia which poses no threat to the present version of themselves, and nicely blurs the compromises and betrayals they have been forced to make to arrive at their current level of affluence and power in American society.

For others born too late to have experienced the 1960s (or in some cases, even much of the 1970s), Cuba and Castro are among the last surviving icons of the party they missed. Many of these people are nonpolitical, or their politics are limited to demands for greater personal rights and human liberation; surely nothing could be farther from the ethos and spirit of the Cuban Revolution. For them Castro is simply another celebrity they've seen on television, like Madonna or Michael Jackson—with the added appeal that Senator Helms doesn't like him. (How bad, then, can he be?)

At somewhat less exalted levels of American society, Castro's revolution remains anathema. Castro himself seems not to fully grasp this point, which explains his periodic (and often costly) miscalculations. He imagines that his only serious enemies in the United States are the Cuban-Americans (and not all of them). Flattered and gratified by the reception he receives from members of the American Establishment, including now important members of the business community, he fails entirely to see the country that stands behind them. There, his revolution, his regime, and his person are taken at full face value, and provoke a very different response.

Notes

1. See my review of the diplomatic documentation finally published after a thirty-year lapse in "Cuba and the United States: Back to the Beginnings," in *World Affairs Quarterly*, Vol. 156, No. 3 (Winter, 1994).
2. While we have no comparable data on attitudes towards Cuba for the period prior to 1968, everything we know about U.S. public opinion for this period suggests that the mid-1970s survey must have been an abrupt departure.

14

The Cuba in Our Mind

When the Soviet empire imploded some six years ago, most observers—East and West—assumed that the disappearance of the Castro regime in Cuba was but a matter of time. After all, no member of the socialist family of nations had received such generous economic subsidies from Moscow; none was more culturally vulnerable to outside influences or more geographically exposed; none had made so heavy an ideological investment in Lenin's vision of the future. Having bet on the wrong horse, Castro's Cuba was therefore destined—to borrow Trotsky's durable phrase—for the dustbin of history.

So far, at least, those predictions seem to have proven excessively deterministic. True, in the absence of Soviet oil, machinery, foodstuffs and other consumer products, Cuban living standards have fallen catastrophically, and may not yet have touched bottom. True as well, ordinary Cubans, particularly young people, are deeply alienated from the regime. (Cuban walls now bear such pungent inscriptions as "Down with You-Know-Who!") Finally, until the recent immigration agreement, unprecedented numbers of Cubans were attempting to leave the island on makeshift boats.

Nonetheless, Castro has never seemed more firmly ensconced in power. Those who have been bold enough over the years to declare themselves his enemies are now dead, in exile, in jail, or cowering in fear of arrest. While everything else in Cuba seems to be breaking down, the repressive apparatus is more effective than ever. The small dissident movement, hounded by the police and government mobs, offers an example of high courage—but no apparent alternative for ordinary Cubans. The very fact of Castro's survival in the face of multiple predictions of his demise seems to have braced up the Cuban dictator psychologically. It has also strengthened the interpretive hand of those of his apologists, supporters, or sympathizers abroad, who would have us believe that, whatever has happened elsewhere in the world, in Cuba—a country once known for rum, cigars, beaches, gambling, and the rhumba—communism has finally found a place where it really "works."

This view is not wholly confined to the far left. Not long ago a right-wing Chilean congressman of my acquaintance urged me to consider the possibility that "in some countries, socialism, that is, Marxist socialism, can become a national project." When I objected that this particular national project seemed destined to starve an entire people to death, he agreed. It was an unpleasant project, he averred, certainly not one he would wish for Chile, but an authentic expression of that particular country's national quest nonetheless. Or consider an excerpt from a cover story of the international edition of *Time* magazine (6 December 1993). "Through a combination of charisma and pride," wrote senior editor Johanna McGeary, Castro "still holds the island's fate in his hand...Cubans [regard] their revolutionary heroes as Americans do...Che Guevara is their Lafayette, Fidel their George Washington." If this is so, one cannot help wondering why, thirty years on, we are still awaiting the appearance of Cuba's version of Thomas Jefferson, John Adams, and James Monroe. Or is it rather that Cuba—unlike the United States, France, or for that matter Russia—is somehow capable of surviving indefinitely on the myth of a single cathartic revolutionary moment?

If Cuba turns out, after all, to be the one place in the world where communism really "works," Ernest Preeg has shown us just what "working" really means.[1] In the old days (that is, before 1989), 85 percent of Cuba's trade was with the Soviet Union, 90 percent of which was restricted to five primary products. Because it was based not on comparative advantage but purely circumstantial political alignments, this relationship introduced radical distortions into the island's economy. For example, in 1986 Cuba received eight times the world price of sugar for its harvest. This naturally led Castro's planners to increase the acreage devoted to sugar by one-third, while reducing that devoted to food products like corn by in some cases as much as 50 percent.

The sudden loss of the Soviet market is therefore a triple blow. There is no ready-made outlet for what Cuba is geared to produce (sugar); the prices it can now command for sugar are a fraction of what it formerly received; and there is no apparent alternative source of foreign exchange. This means not only that there are no resources with which to buy what cannot be produced at home (e.g., foodstuffs), but that new investment to restructure the economy must be postponed indefinitely. Meanwhile, lack of fuel, fertilizer, and spare parts has undercut even the sugar harvest, which did not quite reach four million tons in 1994 (slightly less than half what it was in the heyday of the Cuban-Soviet relationship). It is expected to be even less in 1995.

But Cuba's decline is not merely quantitative, but qualitative as well. As Preeg observes:

> Cuba has become an undeveloping country. Bicycles are replacing automobiles. Horsedrawn carts are replacing delivery trucks. Oxen are replacing tractors. Factories are shut down and urban industrial workers resettled in rural areas to engage in labor-intensive agriculture. Food consumption is shifting from meat and processed products to potatoes, bananas, and other staples.

Cuba is not, of course, the first country in (what used to be called) the Third World to pursue a strategy of autarky leading to de-development. But—given its demonstrated superiority in political repression—it is one of the few countries capable of carrying such policies forward over the longer term. There are precious few loopholes in the system, which means that dogmatism and rigidity will not be as extensively tempered in Cuba (as in, say, Franco's Spain) by inefficiency, corruption, and administrative oversight.

The one area where Cuba can expect to move forward is in tourism, where some European and Canadian concerns have started to make new investments. But in spite of the fulsome claims made, Cuba cannot replicate the past success of Mexico or Spain in this regard, since the effects on the economy as a whole are limited by the small space reserved for market logic by the large, still nearly universal nonmarket economy. More to the point, an increase of tourist revenues to $250 million by 1995— which seems already to have been achieved—pales into insignificance when compared to the loss of *$6 billion* in Soviet resources since 1989.[2]

There is also much talk of new investments in nickel, sugar, telephones, and such basic industries by Mexican, Canadian,

British, and other European consortia. There are, in fact, some three hundred foreign firms now operating in Cuba, but most of these have yet to make a new investment commitment; rather they are positioning themselves in the eventuality that the U.S. trade embargo is lifted and the government shifts to a full-scale market rationale. (Presumably they are also betting that no successor-state will penalize them for collusion with the Castro dictatorship, a wager they may just lose.) So far the needed changes have not occurred—not, at least, on a scale sufficient to encourage the investors to move beyond the realm of speculation and marginality.

Stated succinctly, without drastic economic and political reform there is no way out. But of course, to change the system too drastically would render it unrecognizable, and altogether beg the question of whether Cuba has really proven Marx right after all.

Guilt Management as Art Form

Over the last five years there has been a subtle but perceptible shift in Cuban studies in the United States to take these new realities into account. Whereas formerly much of the emphasis was on the alleged economic and social "successes" of the revolution, particularly in the areas of education and health, today the viability of the regime is located in its historicity, in its deep roots with the Cuban past, and its continuing capacity to validate certain pre-Castro trends and tendencies in Cuban politics—a need which, to follow the logic of the argument, even now is best served by hunger, rationing, repression, and cultural isolation. If one accepts—but only if one accepts—the notion that Cuban history is "about" the need for independence from the United States to the exclusion of just about everything else, then the Castro regime's demonstrated capacity to liberate the island from American influence can be represented as a towering achievement which requires little or no other justification. It is a case of heads-I-win (things are better because of socialism), or, alternatively, tails-you-lose (things are better even if they are not).

This intellectual shell game is the subject of Irving Louis Horowitz's *The Conscience of Worms and the Cowardice of Lions*.[3] In a few brief but telling pages, it retraces the crooked path—twisted in both the geometric and moral sense—taken by what we might call "Castrology" in the United States these past three decades. Horowitz is particularly qualified to undertake this task, since he is a distinguished sociologist in his own right, and for nearly twenty-five years the editor of *Cuban Communism*, long established in its many editions as the reader of record.

Horowitz reminds us that in its early days (1959–62), the appeal of the Castro regime for the intellectual left in the United States was precisely its utopian, existential characteristics (at last, a non-Stalinist version of revolutionary change!), and those who, *per contra*, pointed to its incipient authoritarian features were dismissed as philistines and cold war provincials (C. Wright Mills, *Listen, Yankee!*, 1960). Oddly enough, however, these same people expressed no disappointment whatsoever when Castro shortly thereafter dropped all pretense to "humanism," and adopted the Soviet model, right down to the doorknobs and light switches.

Rather than reexamine their original premises, they simply took refuge in the argument that whatever had gone wrong in Cuba was entirely the fault of the United States. The classic exposition of this argument—guilt-mongering raised to a high art form—is William Appleman Williams' s *The United States, Cuba, and Castro* (1962), and its point of view survives in many quarters of our political culture today, in spite of the many disclaimers the Cuban dictator himself has made on the subject. (Unlike his foreign apologists, Castro fully grasps the contradiction between deploring a policy and celebrating its outcome.)

By 1968 it was clear that the Cuban regime had not made much progress towards economic development, so it was necessary to emphasize its "moral" achievements—such as the elimination of material incentives to productivity. (During this period, which lasted roughly into 1973, Che Guevara rather than Castro was the operative icon.) Castro's periodic quarrels with the Soviets gave the claim a superficial gloss of credibility. Sophisticated European ideologues like K.S. Karol (*Guerrillas in Power*), even argued that Cuba in its revolutionary purity had as its destiny "to reveal to the rest of the world [not merely] the real nature of America's foreign policy," but also to "la[y] bare the true nature of the Soviet bloc." "In this revisionist scenario," Horowitz dryly observes, "it was Trotsky, not Stalin, who would provide the blueprint for Cuban happiness."

By the mid-1970s such romantic *jeux d'esprit* were forgotten; Castro had fully dispensed with moral incentives and composed his differences with the Soviets. (Plans to publish a Cuban edition of the complete works of Trotsky were likewise shelved.) Now, in fact, the Maximum Leader was spending much of his time (and a huge percentage of his limited resources) advancing Soviet interests in the Third World through the export of weapons, advice, and soldiers. At that point, many of his American admirers transferred their admiration from literacy campaigns or figures on milk production, to Cuba's putatively selfless "proletarian internationalism" (e.g., the Cuban military adventurism in approved locales like Angola, the Horn of Africa, and later Central America). Strange to say, these were the very same people who were quick to denounce other Latin American military institutions, the "bureaucratic-authoritarian" state in places like Argentina, Brazil, and Chile, and the U.S. relationship to both. In other words, and to paraphrase Molotov, Cuban militarism (like European fascism in 1940) turned out to be "a matter of taste." This methodological double standard, Horowitz writes, amounts to nothing less than "a subversion of social science in favor of covert political support for a dictatorship."

These are strong words, but if anything they understate the case. Well into the mid-1980s—that is, before the collapse of the Soviet Union—many researchers (notably Andrew Zimbalist and Claes Brundenius) persisted in arguing (in Horowitz's paraphrase) that "unqualified dependence on sugar as a crop [was] overestimated, that Soviet aid ha[d] been greatly exaggerated, and that the rectification process ha[d] been a great success." Only an unforeseen catastrophe—the end of the Socialist Commonwealth of Nations—brought Castrologists up short. Now many of them argue that all of the problems of the island, from the shortage of fuels to the lack of political liberalization, can be directly traced to the continuing U.S. trade embargo.

At the end of the day, then, it appears that we are supposed to judge the Cuban Revolution—an epochal event putatively representing one of the culminating moments in mankind's struggle for liberation and dignity—not on the basis of its production indices, contributions to human welfare, or improvement in the quality of the country's civic and cultural life, but on Castro's success in defying a *trade embargo*. Yet at the same time we are assured that whatever deficiencies persist after thirty-five years of socialism would somehow be corrected—if only American tour-

ists could join with Canadians, Europeans and Latin Americans
to gamble and whore once again at Havana's beachfront hotels!

Such logic-defying exercises make sense only if one accepts a
monistic interpretation of the island's history, one which con-
fuses the Castro regime with the country, and casts Cuba into
the role of eternal victim, exempting it (and its leadership) from
any responsibility for its follies or errors. Post-Gorbachev
Castrology in the United States thus takes up its position at the
point where Cuban nationalism and anti-Americanism (domestic or foreign) intersect.

The centrality of Cuban nationalism to Cuban historiography
hardly requires emphasis. Indeed, the two are virtually inseparable. The official canon—which presented the country's struggle
for nationhood as a story with a happy ending—was barely established in Cuban school textbooks at the beginning of this century before it was broadly repudiated. Disillusioned by the results
of the first two decades of independence (1901–21), successive
waves of "revisionists" rummaged through the past to explain
their country's lingering deficiencies. These they variously attributed to the island's Spanish heritage, to its emergence as a
nation-state three-quarters of a century later than other Latin
American countries, to the untimely death in 1895 of the great
"apostol" of Cubanidad José Martí, and above all to the United
States, whose tardy but decisive intervention in the war of independence (1895–98) all but assured that the new republic would
be forced into a quasi-protectorate with its powerful neighbor to
the north.

The bill of indictment against the United States was long and
detailed, intemperate in tone and relentlessly unforgiving: from
the Platt Amendment, by which Washington arrogated to itself
the right to intervene in the island (revoked only in 1934), through
the two U.S. occupations (1906–09; 1917–22) and the heavy-
handed involvement of Ambassador Sumner Welles in the revolution of 1933; to the creation of the "sugar quota" which reserved
to Cuba a quarter of the U.S. domestic market (forcing it into a
monoculture from which there was no easy escape.)

Some of the historians who raked these coals back and forth
during the 1930s and 1940s, like Emilio Roig de Leuchenring,
were communists or at least close to the Cuban party, and they

remained on the island after the advent of Castro to enjoy privileged berths in the new state apparatus. But many were not. The most eminent "revisionist" of all was Herminio Portell-Vilá, who from his chair at the University of Havana trained several generations of Cuban students (one of them was in fact, Fidel Castro) to attribute all of their country's problems to the United States. Such histrionics did not prevent Professor Portell-Vilá from marrying an American, from periodically teaching at American colleges, even from accepting a Guggenheim Foundation grant to finish his multivolume screed *Historia de Cuba en sus relaciones con Estados Unidos y España* (1938).

Nonetheless, once Castro began expropriating American companies and goading the United States into suspending the Cuban sugar quota—which is to say, once he began to put his old professor's preachings into practice—Portell-Vilá took the first available ship to Miami. (He later established himself in Washington as an expert on Cuban affairs at one of the more right-wing lobbying groups.) An even more interesting case is that of Carlos Márquez-Sterling, whose *Historia de Cuba*, still available as far as I know from an émigré publishing house in Miami, rants against the United States in virtually every chapter except the last—the one which, after all, explains why Señor Márquez-Sterling was signing the prologue in Miami rather than Havana.

Revisionist Theories

The ideological fit between revisionism and Castroism is too evident to require comment. Rather more interesting, however, is the way that revisionist themes have resurfaced in the work of Cuban-American historians working in the United States, many of them born here or brought to this country as small children. Three particular cases present themselves for our attention. Two are chapters by Louis A. Pérez, Jr. and Jorge Domínguez in Leslie Bethell's portmanteau volume, *Cuba: A Short History*.[4] The other is Marifeli Pérez-Stable's *The Cuban Revolution: Origins, Course and Legacy*.[5]

For some time now Louis Pérez, Jr. has been the principal exponent of Cuban revisionism in the United States, utilizing the latest social science concepts and techniques to make some of the same points, with the rather different twist that, unlike

Portell-Vilá or Márquez-Sterling, he has no vested interest in separating the traditional agendas of Cuban nationalism from the Castro regime. Quite the contrary: he sees a significant continuity between the two (which has an interesting political subtext of its own). The particular period with which he deals in this volume is 1930–1959, that is to say, the run-up to Castro's seizure of power, but he ranges rather more widely over time to get there.

For example, he dusts off the hoary myth that by 1898 the Cuban insurgents had virtually defeated the Spanish army, and would indeed have obtained independence on their own, had not the United States intervened at the last minute to assure itself control of the new state. This is simply untrue. (We should be grateful, however, that he forbears from claiming—as many Spanish and Cuban historians still maintain—that the United States purposely exploded its own battleship *Maine* to provide an excuse for intervention.) He dredges up the old arguments against trade reciprocity with the United States (as if there was really much of an alternative for a small country which was shattered by nearly a decade of civil war, and whose colonial elites fled after the collapse of the metropolitan power with what capital they could take with them). "Within a decade of the war of independence," Pérez writes, "the United States had become a pervasive presence in Cuba, totally dominating the economy, thoroughly penetrating the social fabric, and fully controlling the political process." (Of the three assertions only the first is at all defensible; the second is true only for the urban elites, and not always them; the third would come as an acute surprise to a succession of hapless American ambassadors who struggled for more than two decades to get a handle on Cuban politics.)

It is certainly true that Cuba in the 1920s and 1930s could hardly be called an independent country in the same sense as was Argentina, Colombia, or even Mexico. American investment and American markets occupied too central a role, and the failure of Cubans to generate a political class with its own sense of self meant that the U.S. embassy in Havana was expected to play a proconsular role, whether it actually did so or not. The situation was anomalous and left the door open for many misunderstandings. Pérez, however, has no feel for ambiguity. Instead, he writes that

Cuba participated in and depended entirely on the United States economic system in much the same way as U.S. citizens, but without access to U.S. social service programs and at employment and wage levels substantially lower than their North American counterparts.

This amounts to saying that Cuba was a slave-labor colony for American capital, and that the relationship with the United States was entirely one sided. Now, evidently, wage and employment levels in pre-Castro Cuba were substantially lower than in the United States, but so were living costs. More to the point, thanks to a privileged position in the U.S. sugar market, Cuban living standards were significantly higher than most other countries in the region, (and taken as a whole) indeed higher than any Latin American country except for Argentina and Uruguay. True, the gap between urban and rural Cuba was abysmal, as was the lack of adequate social services outside Havana and a few other cities (which by the 1950s nonetheless accounted for nearly half the island's population).

But there was nothing about the relationship with the United States that necessarily dictated that the economic benefits of reciprocity had to be distributed in this particular fashion; how successive Cuban governments utilized the island's earnings from sugar, tobacco, and rum was a matter of near-total indifference to the U.S. government or private business. What is true is that, like all other primary producing countries, Cuba was highly dependent economically on forces beyond its control—the world price of sugar, the cost of borrowing money, the ups and downs of the U.S. economic cycle. The wonder of it all is that Cuba benefited so hugely from its "dependency." If Castro and his followers missed this point (as Pérez seems to miss it now), it was not lost on the dozens of other countries that lobbied the Senate Agriculture Committee to take Cuba's place when the Eisenhower administration suspended the island's sugar quota in 1960.

Not that all Cuban governments before 1958 were completely insensitive to landlessness, illiteracy, and social injustice. As a matter of fact, at the time of Castro's seizure of power it was one of the more advanced Latin American countries in both social services and labor rights. However, it also suffered from a succession of governments (mostly civilian) who outdid themselves in cynicism, nepotism, and corruption. Pérez is aware of this problem, but apparently regards it as vestigial; instead, he defines the central issue as alleged U.S. pressure to keep Cuba from diversifying its production and trade.

No doubt many Cubans believed that this was the dominant purpose of American policy; it is even possible to find dispatches from American diplomats who thought so as well. On the evidence, American reciprocity did not promote a satisfactory level of Cuban diversification and development. But let the record show as well that its absence has not done so either: the island today is far more dependent on sugar exports than it was at the time the United States suspended the quota in 1960.

Relative to What?

What happened after Castro came to power is summarized in fifty-some brisk pages of *Cuba: A Short History* by Jorge Domínguez. A professor of government at Harvard and author of numerous books and articles on Cuba, Domínguez manages to remain faithful to the spirit of revisionism without falling into some of its obvious factual pitfalls. For example, he freely admits that Castro did not request U.S. aid during his first visit to this country as Cuban supremo in 1959, but manages to load the blame onto American shoulders nonetheless. "Had such aid been requested and granted, it would have tied Cuba's future closely to the world capitalist economy and to the United States." The revolutionary leaders, he adds, understood this, and also grasped that "it was impossible to conduct a revolution in Cuba without a major confrontation with the United States." Thus Castro and his associates are exonerated in advance from failing to even try to reach an understanding with Washington, while the United States (in its incarnation as a "world capitalist economy") stands condemned for existing at all!

Domínguez's evaluation of the performance of the Castro regime is even more casuistic. He freely admits that there has been a signal inability to increase production or diversify exports and markets—which is to say, Cuban living standards overall have dropped these last thirty-some years. He even concedes that this situation has been greatly aggravated by Castro's penchant for military adventures abroad, which consistently diverted managerial talents and enormous resources into nonproductive outlets. Nonetheless, since the country's economic burdens have been more equitably distributed than before, we can regard the revolution as a "relative success." Relative to what? If the socialization of poverty is a "relative success," one has to wonder whether "relative failure" is even conceptually possible.

Marifeli Pérez-Stable's *The Cuban Revolution: Origins, Course and Legacy* seems to promise a good deal more. In the first place, she is sensitive to the full complexities of Cuban politics in the 1950s, and does not fall into the trap of assuming that all roads necessarily lead to Fidel Castro's accession to power. Quite the contrary, she begins by insisting that "social revolution and the ensuing radical transformation of Cuban society were neither inevitable nor aberrational." The old Cuba, she writes, "sheltered these options as well as others that were never or only partially realized."

In two brilliant opening chapters she identifies a persistent structural problem: by the 1950s, sugar had ceased to be the motor of economic growth in Cuba, yet it still outweighed all the other alternatives. Moreover, Cuban politics being what they were, advocates of import-substitution industrialization were isolated and ineffective. (Paradoxically, part of the problem was the relative strength of the labor movement, itself a product of Cuba's unusually advanced version of agro-industry.) Thus, Pérez-Stable writes, Cuba was prevented from generating its own version of "dependent capitalist development," such as occurred in other Latin American countries in the 1950s and 1960s.

These observations are provocative and interesting, inasmuch as they allow us to imagine what might have happened in Cuban history. But they do nothing at all to help us understand the events that actually occurred. Castro's victory over Fulgencio Batista was the product of the dictator's unpopularity, not the need (real or imagined) for some sort of social transformation. Castro understood this better at the time than Pérez-Stable seems to understand it now, since his program before taking power was confined to the restoration of the Constitution of 1940, which was a perfectly bourgeois document to which no one on the island (or for that matter, in the United States) could have taken exception.

Unfortunately, once Castro achieves power, Pérez-Stable's considerable powers of analysis sharply decline. The dividing line between the official version of Cuban events and the author's own account becomes confused and uncertain. The role of the United States is often distorted, sometimes downright wrong.[6] Also, she seems not to fully grasp the difference between Leninist and pluralist approaches to labor history. Clichés like "sovereignty, equality, inclusive development" act as self-justifying props, even though they often describe phenomena quite the opposite of their normally accepted meanings. Cuban society in all of its complexity is suddenly compressed into a one dimension, subsumed under the incantation "Fidel-Revolution-Fatherland."

In these middle chapters, Pérez-Stable veers back and forth between pinpointing the hard facts of Cuban political sociology and attempting to soften their ideological implications. Perhaps the best example is her account of "proletarian power" in socialist Cuba:

> The working class bore the burden of legitimating socialism, but workers did not have the power to make national policies. Their charge was to work hard. The Communist party exercised power on their behalf, and Fidel Castro was the premier expositor of their welfare. The correct proletarian *conciencia* was to abide by party directives and charismatic authority. In that sense, Cuban socialism was like the other contemporary socialist experiences: the working class wielded power vicariously.

What is perhaps most remarkable about this and other similar passages is the peculiar tone in which they are written—as if the revolution were still a promise yet to be tested, rather than something about which there is now a wealth of data based on actual performance. When it comes time to face the bottom line, she has no choice, then, but to let the readers down without much advance warning. After a dizzying ride through thickets of utopian rhetoric and S-curves of socialist triumphalism, Pérez-Stable suddenly announces:

> Two decades after the revolution there was still no room for dissent: *Con Cuba o contra Cuba* continued to define Cuban politics. Ninety miles away from the United States and the prosperous Cuban-American communities, the Cuban government surely had to contend with unreasonable comparisons and inordinate expectations. Still, the challenge for Cuban leaders lay in satisfying basic needs—especially in the supply, diversity, and quality of food and other consumer nondurables—more efficiently, and they had barely met it.

This is a bitter pill indeed. To sweeten it, she reverts to a "revisionist" mode by blaming the United States for "undermining the future prospects for political stability in Cuba." After carefully documenting the regime's failures in almost every area of economic and political life, she concludes:

By giving Fidel Castro cause to appeal to the patriotism of millions of Cubans, the United States was continuing to fuel radical nationalism. Because of U.S. hostility, the Cuban leadership had a credible pretext for refusing to implement meaningful changes, and consequently the probabilities for peaceful transformation were diminishing.

"A credible pretext?" Credible to whom? Perhaps credible to Professor Pérez-Stable, but not necessarily to the millions of Cubans for whom physical survival has suddenly become a daunting challenge. Nor can Castro himself—with his almost unlimited appetite to power—be so easily dismissed. It is not "hostility from the United States" which is preventing him from embracing "meaningful changes," but a disposition towards absolute rule which by now has calcified ideologically. Indeed, "bourgeois" logic alone would suggest that, on the contrary, such "meaningful changes," if carefully contained, might actually bolster Castro's rule for as long as he requires (which is to say, for the rest of his life).

The Most Efficient Jailor

In the past, writers broadly sympathetic to the revolution tended to deny the regime's political deficiencies altogether. They also emphasized the Cuban dictator's success in attaining a truly independent role in world affairs. Today the same people (or the same kind of people) have shifted into cognitive reverse. Now the order of the day is to depict Castro and his regime as basically shaped by the vectors of American policy. This allows them to squarely and unsentimentally face the deteriorating economic, political, and human rights situation while at the same time exempting Castro from any major responsibility for it.

In this category the *pièce de résistance* is Gillian Gunn's *Cuba in Transition: Options for U.S. Policy*,[7] which has had some modest success in left-liberal foreign policy circles. Its author, who directs the Cuba Project at Georgetown University, is a frequent visitor to Cuba, and chairs a study group which makes it possible for the Washington policy community to meet upper-middle level Cuban officials. Her public posture is one of objectivity and dispassion; how convincing it is depends wholly upon the disposition, sophistication, and specialized knowledge of her readers.

Although she pretends to strike a certain equidistance between the two countries, in *Cuba in Transition*, at least, Gunn embraces a curious double standard. On one hand, there is Cuban nation-alism, in whose name all manner of sins can be forgiven. On the other, we have U.S. responses to Cuban misdeeds, which even when strictly limited to verbal reprimands, merit a firm rap on the wrist. The analysis moves back and forth between positing a connection between economics and politics, and conceding that none exists. The arguments are often circular and repetitious; at times they are also extremely disingenuous.

Let it be said straightaway that Gunn is clearly in favor of some sort of *economic* reform in Cuba. She has evidently spent time with people on the island of like mind. On the other hand, she, like they, fears that swift political change "could jeopardize not only the current regime, but, far more importantly, Cuban sover-eignty." She characterizes the current political scene as

> polarized and tense...Fear of U.S. intervention or domination, fear of rac-ism, fear of losing the social safety net, fear of chaos, and the retribution it might occasion—all these deeply ingrained, historically rooted aspects of Cuban political culture [have been] manipulated by the propaganda ma-chine to justify political stagnation.

In this mix, Washington's posture, she writes, "has made it easy for those opposing political reform to create a false bond between intransigence and nationalism." (At other points in the text she insists that the bond is far from false.) Surprisingly, however, Gunn's principal target is not the U.S. economic embargo, but rather Washington's failure to understand the centrality of Castro's role, without whom no change in Cuba is possible. Indeed, we are coun-seled to be grateful to him for the tiny measure of economic liber-alization the country has already experienced:

> Had the party been in power absent Castro [she writes] it would have been far more difficult to obtain...acquiescence. With Castro at the helm, the Cuban political machine is like a large ship with one captain. Though it turns slowly, the ship of state moves as a cohesive unit.

> Without Castro, Cuba could resemble a flotilla of small ships, each with its own captain and a different idea of what direction to take. Such a chaotic atmosphere is conducive to violence.

This statement fairly takes one's breath away, since it revives (in different ideological guise) justification for personalistic dic-tatorship previously employed in places like Franco's Spain, Pinochet's Chile, even Trujillo's Dominican Republic: namely that, however regrettable, a suffocating authoritarianism is the only conceivable form of government for a given country, since the alternative is not democracy but "chaos" and "violence." Even more disingenuous is Gunn's argument that there is a "rough correlation" between the Cuban government's "sense of vulnerability and its willingness to tolerate dissent." *Q.E.D.*, those of us who wish to see more space for independent political thought and action in Cuba should do everything we can to reassure the Cuban *government* that it has nothing to fear from us. This we can do by moderating the embargo, cooling our rhetoric, and engaging in "negotiations." We are also enjoined to address the "anxiety of the poor." According to Gunn, the Cuban poor fear

> that change will result in the destruction of the social safety net and return of white exiles perceived to have outdated racial attitudes, and the security network's preoccupation that upheaval will let loose both internal and external revenge seekers.

Now, to believe that the lack of political liberalism in Cuba is the product of external threats is to reveal a political illiteracy of the most startling kind. Evidently, there is a relationship between the two on the ideological and rhetorical level, but to go much farther than that amounts to regarding Castro as a helpless victim of larger forces, rather than—like all dictators—an actor who has consciously chosen his role. The fact that his country must face the consequences along with him is tragic, but in no way alters the basic facts of the matter.

As for the Cuban poor, the United States is ill-placed, to put it mildly, to reassure it that what remains of its social safety net will survive the Castro regime, since we seem congenitally unable to agree on the size and cost of our own. The point is becoming increasingly moot anyway, since those services are rapidly unraveling from lack of resources (the absence of a Soviet subsidy). One cannot conclude discussion of this point, by the way, without taking issue with Gunn's arch comment that Cuban concern with social justice "is not a Castro invention...[and] therefore...will not disappear as a source of friction with the United States," as if our problems with Cuban governments past and present have somehow been driven by a repugnance for school lunch programs and free medical care!

Towards the end of her book, Gunn seems herself to have lost confidence in some of her arguments, since she suddenly reverts to the panic mode. If the United States fails to change its policies, it could produce street protests, leading to violence, civil war, and U.S. military intervention ("not at all conducive to building a democratic system and a liberal economy"). She also threatens us with a huge bill for peacemaking and reconstruction costs (entirely overlooking congressional parsimony in the cases of Nicaragua, Panama, and now Haiti). She does not anticipate what happened last year—not civil war, but a spurt of outmigration, explicitly provoked by Castro. This was inconvenient for the United States, but hardly apocalyptic (and with the additional benefit to the Cuban dictator of relieving him of yet more opponents to his regime).

Unquestionably the crisis of the Cuban economy and society affects the United States, if for no other reason than geographical proximity. But such is the curious relationship between the two societies that it is often difficult to decide who has won each successive round. For example, the recent agreement for the forcible repatriation by the U.S. of future Cuban boat people would seem to be a victory for Castro, in the sense that it amounts to our recruiting him as the most efficient jailor we can find. However, by removing the escape valve of immigration to the United States, the accord may actually increase internal pressures for political change—more rapidly and even more explosively than anyone, least of all the Clinton administration, had in mind.

The United States, then, is supremely relevant to Cuba's future without possessing the powers to determine its ultimate shape. But the dilemma facing the island is far worse: if, as so many of our authors contend, the driving force of Cuban politics remains today—as it was fifty or sixty years ago—a peculiarly perverted version of Ruritanian nationalism, more's the pity, since there is nothing (save plunging the entire North American continent under water) that can relieve the island of "unreasonable comparisons and inordinate expectations."

Nor is there anything that can be done to reassure the Cuban government that in the event of normalization of relations with the United States, its "sovereignty" will be respected. The terms of this argument are remarkably antique, since nowadays it is not treaties but impersonal economic and demographic forces which govern relations between large states and small. What kind of sovereignty is it, anyway, that is only available as a gift from a self-effacing neighbor? The fact is that Cuba's alleged aspiration to survive as an entity wholly independent of the United States can only be met by prolonging its isolation indefinitely. (Critics of U.S. policy like Gunn, so worshipful of Cuban sovereignty, fail to see the contradiction.) Such isolation exacts a horrible price from the population as a whole, which is why one is inclined to wonder whether the island's political culture is really quite as frozen in time as we are so often told.

If there is a correlation between the external and internal dynamics of Cuban politics it is certainly not the one that Gunn has suggested. Rather, the operative relationship is between Cuba's geopolitical weakness and its deliberate political choices. Even if we assume that those choices were made freely by the majority at some point in the past—a debatable proposition, to say the very least—there is such a thing as the right to change one's mind. (Most people on the island today were not even around when the country supposedly opted for its present dispensation.) The Cubans Gunn happens to know tell her that they do not wish to abandon the existing economic model, and would rather starve to death than return to the U.S. sphere of influence. Perhaps. But until all Cubans can be freely consulted at the ballot box, the rest of us have the right to remain skeptical—of the regime, of its claims to legitimacy, and of the peculiar refractions of both in the lens of American social science.

Notes

1. *Cuba and the New Caribbean Economic Order* (with Jonathan D. Levine) (Washington, DC: Center for Strategic and International Studies, 1993).
2. Cuban estimates of tourist revenues need always to be carefully balanced against the high cost of inputs, since the island is so poorly equipped to provide what is readily at hand elsewhere in the Caribbean. For example, one estimate puts gross tourist revenues for 1993 at $530 million, but discounting profits, commissions, transportation expenses, and direct imports to feed and water the visitors, the Cuban state probably netted about $265 million. "Bridging the Gap: Tourism in the 1990s", *La Sociedad Económica*, no. 29, 19 April 1993.
3. New Brunswick, NJ: Transaction Publishers, 1993.
4. Cambridge: Cambridge University Press, 1993.
5. New York: Oxford University Press, 1993.
6. Though she cites the recently published volume on Cuba for 1958–60 in the *Foreign Relations of the United States* series, she does not seem to have

read it very carefully. Among other things, it clearly reveals that the Eisenhower administration's problem with the Cuban Revolution had nothing to do with economics and everything to do with Castro's decision to align his country with the Soviet Union.

7. New York: Twentieth Century Fund, 1993.

15

The Other Cuba

The decision of the Clinton administration to revoke a thirty-year precedent and turn back people on rafts seeking to escape Castro's island has once again put the Cuban-American community in the headlines. It has also revived a long campaign of vilification by the prestige media, centering on the supposition that it is a handful of reactionary émigrés, rather than Castro himself, that constitute the chief obstacle to democracy and freedom on the island.

Indeed, no article on Castro's Cuba these days seems complete without some "balance"—which means a look at the Miami alternative, against which ordinary Cubans are said to recoil. As *U.S. News and World Report* put it not long ago, while the exiles' clout in American politics is obvious, "it is less clear whether their goal is promoting democracy in Cuba or restoring 1950s–style rule by a wealthy elite."

Or here is *The Los Angeles Times Magazine* in May 1992:

> Most of [the] exiles [are] of the white upper class. Today in Cuba, 65 percent of the islanders are black or mulatto. If they have not exactly prospered under Castro, at least they have running water, electricity, and access to education. They owe their loyalty to Castro, no matter what freedoms they lack, and many fear that rich white exiles...will return them to their pre-Castro peasant status.

The most recent major attack on the community came in the form of a sensational piece, in *The New Republic* ("Our Man in Miami," 3 October 1994) by Anne Louise Bardach. The ostensible subject is exile leader Jorge Mas Canosa, founder of the Cuban American National Foundation, whose portrait Miss Bardach paints with a brush as wide as the Mississippi—and just about as muddy. (Among other things, she describes him as a

207

member of the "roughest, toughest crowd this side of the maja-
hedin," and a man "born and bred by the CIA.") Her purpose is
to conflate Mas, the Cuban-American community, Miami vice,
and exile fringe groups into an undifferentiated whole. (Her idea
of a Cuban-American "moderate," appears to be Francisco Aruca,
who runs the Marazul charters to Cuba and is a close personal
and business associate of Castro.) The placement of the article
in *The New Republic* was particularly inspired, since alone of
American liberal journals it boasts an unblemished record of
opposition to Castro and all his works.[1]

When mainstream magazines are repeating these old clichés,
something is in the air. Partly, it is the "Anglo" media's distaste
for the emotionally extravagant tone of Cuban émigré politics,
combined with a lack of sympathy for immigrant communities
that appear to lack adequate commitment to left-liberal political
values. In addition, it is the use by some American journalists of
the Cuban-American story as part of a grand effort to provide a
soft ideological landing for the agonizing Castro revolution, the
final repository of New Left illusions. In this sense the
demonization of the Cuban-American community is an attempt
to influence American policy toward Castro by convincing ordinary Americans that their government has been manipulated into
pursuing policies contrary to their interest by a tiny but powerful
minority supposedly armed with limitless financial resources and
ruthless political cunning. The time has come to reexamine the
assumptions on which this myth is based.

E Pluribus Unum

Although most Cuban-Americans live in Dade County, Florida,
there are communities in almost all of the major metropolitan
areas, including New York City, Boston, Los Angeles, Chicago,
and Houston. They are the product of three consecutive (but
quite different) waves of emigration. The first, from January 1959
to October 1962, comprised about 250,000 men and women (and
their children) drawn from the business and professional classes.
Most were "white"—that is, of Spanish origin—but few were associated with the Batista government. Between December 1965 and
April 1973 another 400,000 people emigrated, this time from
virtually all socioeconomic classes. Finally, in 1980 the Mariel

boatlift produced a third wave—nearly 120,000 people—including many unskilled workers and (for the first time) numerous blacks. A handful of common criminals and mental patients also arrived, but these were deliberately introduced by Castro to bedevil U.S. authorities and discredit the exile community as a whole.

In spite of the differences in their origins (and the falling social level of immigrants gives the lie to the notion that Castro's policies have benefited the poorer segments of Cuban society), the three communities have gradually melded into one. To be sure, the diaspora continues to display the tendency toward factionalism, schism, and infighting which so bedeviled the political life of the island in its pre-Communist days. On the other hand, there is little in its background to suggest a historical penchant for exotic right-wing ideologies.

In fact, between the end of the Cuban war of independence in 1898 and Castro's seizure of power in 1959 there was no Right at all in Cuban politics. Those forces which might have supported the such tendencies—the Spanish merchant community, the upper hierarchy of the Roman Catholic Church, and the military and naval establishment—had been on the "wrong" side of the struggle for nationhood and, once defeated by a combination of U.S. and patriot arms, were compelled to depart for Spain or accept political marginalization.

A new Cuban army, created after the departure of the American occupation forces in 1901, might well have become a vehicle for conservative authoritarianism in Cuba (as it did elsewhere in Latin America) were it not for an extraordinary "sergeants' rebellion" in 1933. This movement effectively ousted the officer corps of the Cuban army, and then linked up with a cohort of radical students and middle-class revolutionaries. The principal figure in that enlisted man's coup was Fulgencio Batista, a sergeant-stenographer who (raised to general officer rank by his own recognizance) became, first, the power behind a succession of weak civilian presidents, and then, in 1940, the elected chief of state with the support of the Communist party.

Since he has become such a bogeyman for those determined to tar the Cuban-American community with his brush, it is interesting that by the standards of the day Batista's first presidency was remarkably progressive. Its major landmarks were a land-tenancy law that effectively enfranchised more than a hundred thousand peasant families, educational reform that brought schools to remote country villages, and an urban labor law that made it almost impossible to fire any employee. (In the 1940s, American businessmen spoke of Cuba in the same tone of voice as Mexico—as a lovely country which, alas! had been "ruined" by an unpleasant social revolution.)

When Batista completed his first term in 1944, he was succeeded by his quondam ally in the 1933 revolution, Dr. Ramón Grau San Martin, and then, in 1948, by Grau's protégé (and former student revolutionary), Carlos Prío. Both men were members of the Cuban Revolutionary Party, known more commonly by its sobriquet Auténtico. The Auténticos professed social democratic and Christian-social ideologies, but the administrations of both Grau and Prío were extraordinarily corrupt. Indeed, in the early 1950s, Auténticos offended by the cynicism of their leaders hived off a new party known as the Ortodóxos. One of its promising figures was Fidel Castro, who would have been elected to Congress in 1952 but for General Batista's military coup.

Although most Cubans either welcomed Batista's return to power or remained indifferent to it, by the mid-1950s an economic slump combined with increasing repression had turned the entire Cuban political establishment against the dictator. At the same time, in an attempt to reactivate the Cuban economy, Batista began to lift some of the restrictions on labor mobility and foreign investment dating to the 1930s—a wise move from an economic point of view, but fatal in the absence of basic political legitimacy. The Communist party, which had originally regarded the young Fidel Castro as a "putschist" and "adventurer" when he took up arms against Batista, severed its ties with the dictator and found its way to Castro's headquarters.

Left-Skewed Spectrum

To the day of Castro's accession to power, then, the ideological geography of Cuban politics extended from the center to the left—with competing versions of populism crowding out all other dispensations. The failure of Cuban politics was an inability to move from personalities to institutions. Unlike in other Latin American countries, social and economic issues were not particularly divisive. Cubans were accustomed to a large government role in economic and social matters, and they continue to feel comfortable with it in their American exile.

A recent survey by Rodolfo de la Garza and his associates records that over 95 percent of Cuban-Americans believe that the national government has a primary responsibility for solving problems, as opposed to 85.6 percent of "Anglos." A significant minority—as much as 45 percent—believe strongly that the government should guarantee jobs or housing to those in need. On issues ranging from crime and drugs to education, health, child services, and the environment, Cuban-Americans believe that spending should increase even if it means an increase in taxes. They strongly favor bilingual education and, until the measure was turned back by an "Anglo"-dominated referendum in 1980, the diaspora had actually managed to have Miami declared officially a bilingual city. Nevertheless, 48.5 percent describe themselves as "conservative" or "slightly conservative," though only 6 percent as "very conservative."

The de la Garza study also revealed a startling degree of similarity between Cuban-Americans and two other Hispanic immigrant groups generally regarded as more politically correct—Mexican-Americans and Puerto Ricans. Nearly as many Mexican-Americans describe themselves as "very conservative" as Cubans, and the Puerto Ricans actually outdo the Cubans (7.8 percent) in this category. Moreover, in the "slightly conservative" category the Mexican-Americans edge out the Cubans by a fraction of a percentage point.

To be sure, both Mexican-Americans and Puerto Ricans tend to cluster slightly further to the left on the ideological spectrum. A larger percentage describe themselves as moderate (35.4 and 24.7 percent, respectively, compared to 22.5 percent for Cuban-Americans). On the other hand, Cuban-Americans are slightly more tolerant than the other two groups of the rights of groups they particularly dislike (in this case, communists and homosexuals). The one area of difference appears to be voting patterns; at the national level at least, most Cuban-Americans vote Republican, most Mexican-Americans and Puerto Ricans vote Democratic. Even so, Democrats who are liberal on domestic issues but notably tough on foreign policy can win Cuban-American support in local races, as illustrated by former Senator Dick Stone

(D-FL), former Representative Dante Fascell (D-FL), Florida Governor Lawton Chiles, and Representative (now Senator) Robert Torricelli (D-NJ).

The importance of foreign policy in defining political identity is not, of course, unusual in ethnic minorities in America. The American Jewish community, which has successfully organized itself on behalf of the survival of the state of Israel, is the most obvious example, and one that has deeply influenced the Cuban-Americans. But in their basic approach to education, lobbying, and dispensing political contributions, the Cuban-Americans proceed no differently from other groups such as Irish and Greek-Americans, and latterly (on South Africa and Haiti) African Americans. While it is true that the State Department and those with other fish to fry periodically express frustration or resentment over this form of lobbying, it is well within the tradition of American interest-group politics. Furthermore, most Americans have no great enthusiasm for opening diplomatic relations with Castro's Cuba. Cuban-Americans owe much of their lobbying success to the simple fact that they are sailing with the political wind at their backs.

So Close to Home

In one way, however, Cuban-Americans are different from other ethnic and minority groups. While all the revolutions of modern history have produced sizable exile communities, in no other case has the diaspora been so proportionately large, so wealthy, so well organized, so geographically concentrated, and so physically proximate to its country of origin. The result is a cultural hybrid—a community that is functionally American, but dwells spiritually in a cloud of imminence.

Miami's climate and vegetation are so similar, and the Cuban-American community so numerous, that it has been possible there to preserve in exile many traditional social practices, institutions, and consumer preferences that other immigrant communities in the United States have been forced to abandon. The result, paradoxically, has not been to put old ghosts to rest but to keep them alive. The periodic arrival of new refugees from the island sharpens the sense of loss, and keeps the wound from healing.

In this environment not everyone responds in a wholesome manner. For years, fringe groups like Alpha 66 and Omega 7, made up of recalcitrant veterans of the Bay of Pigs and their sympathizers, have continued to drill in the Everglades, convinced that the day will soon arrive when they can somehow retake Cuba by force. Their talk (and occasional use) of violence against others make these groups exciting news copy. Yet they are utterly marginal to the life of the community.

Much confusion arises out of the fact that Cuban-Americans are pitched at a rather higher emotional level than "Anglos," and tend to make extravagant use of eschatological language when arguing about politics. However, the distinction between deeply felt emotion and a propensity to violence is huge, and has not always been grasped by news reporters.

A case in point is the press treatment of the Cuban-American National Foundation (CANF), and very particularly its founder, Jorge Mas Canosa. A man of enormous energy and political imagination, Mas emigrated to the United States at the age of seventeen, penniless and speaking no English. Today he is a millionaire many times over, and a major force in politics in Florida and beyond. The foundation that he established in 1981 is principally known for its political-action committee, whose campaign contributions have bought it access to both sides of the congressional aisle and to the White House in both Republican and Democratic administrations. (In 1992 Mas got candidate Clinton to endorse the Cuban Democracy Act—which tightened the U.S. trade embargo on the island—before the Bush White House had gotten around to doing so.) But it is also responsible for the creation of both Radio and TV Martí-U.S. government broadcasting to Cuba—and the EXODUS program, a private immigration agency that has helped to resettle thousands of Cubans in the United States at virtually no cost to the American taxpayer.

Mas is not—as Miss Bardach and others suggest—a mobster or a right-wing terrorist. Indeed, his preference for working within the system has led some extremists to characterize him as a "sellout," and he has shown up on Alpha-66 hit lists more than once. However, like many self-made men, Mas has made a lot of enemies and he has not always chosen his targets well or played according to the genteel rules of Anglo-American politics.

When the *Miami Herald* refused to endorse the Cuban Democracy Act, instead of simply pointing out that this was a curious position for a paper that had supported a trade embargo to bring democracy to racist South Africa, Mas called upon Cuban-

Americans to boycott the paper (and its Spanish edition, *El Nuevo Herald*). According to *Time*, "Mas launched a city-wide billboard campaign to protest. Anonymous callers phoned in bomb threats, and the paper's vending machines were jammed with feces." What Mas called for, however, was a boycott—not bomb threats or night-soil brigades. By eliding the three *Time* puts him in the position of either calling off his boycott altogether or accepting responsibility for actions over which he has no control.

Mas's quarrel with the *Miami Herald* is particularly unfortunate, because no newspaper in the United States has done a better job of covering the Cuban story from both sides of the Florida Keys, or given more Cuban-Americans an opportunity to express their views (many of which are, needless to say, contrary to its own). Nor has the *Herald* followed the general media line of depicting the Miami community as nothing but a bunch of Batistiano thugs and reactionaries. In fact, not long ago it took issue with a report issued by the human-rights organization, Americas Watch, which characterized the environment in Miami as uniformly repressive and intolerant. The report, editorialized the *Herald*, "smears the many for the boorish acts of relatively few," and "unfairly ignores the advances that pluralism has grudgingly made in the Cuban exile community since the 1980s."

Ex Uno, Plures

One manifestation of this pluralism is the increasing multiplicity of Cuban-American political groups. While the CANF remains the largest and best-financed, many Cuban expatriates prefer the Independent and Democratic Cuba (CID), which is run by Huber Matos (a twenty-year veteran of Castro's prisons), or Carlos Alberto Montaner's Cuban Democratic Platform, which unites Social Democratic and Christian Democratic groups. There is even a democratic socialist group, small in number but high in intellectual candle power, led by Enrique Baloyra and Marifeli Pérez-Stable.

These groups are separated by personalist loyalties, but also by differing attitudes toward the "original" (that is, pre-Communist) Cuban revolution in 1959–60. The Cuban-American National Foundation tends to attract people who saw through Castro's democratic mask from the very start. To call such people "Batistianos," however, is not merely libel but a factual error; the

Foundation's leaders are too young to have done anything but attend high school in 1958 and 1959.

Per contra, Independent and Democratic Cuba includes many who supported Castro from his days as a guerrilla leader from 1956 to 1958, and well into his first agrarian reform in 1960. (Huber Matos fought alongside Castro in the Sierra Maestra and was one of the original heroes of the anti-Batista movement.) They broke with him only when he reversed the result of trade-union elections, collapsed his 26th of July Movement with the Cuban Communist Party, and deliberately marched his country into the Soviet camp.

Another fault line is introduced by differences of opinion over the desirability of "dialogue" as a means of resolving Cuba's current political impasse (the Foundation opposes it, the Platform and the democratic socialists favor it). The *dialogista* position is often characterized in the American press as the more "liberal" one, since it seems to suggest somehow coming to terms with the Castro dictatorship. Actually, the *dialogista* position is more complicated than this. Carlos Alberto Montaner has repeatedly stated that he understands "dialogue" as something that must take place first and foremost between the Cuban government and its own people, not as cozy accords reached between Castro and the State Department, or even between Castro and the exile community. Moreover, lost in accounts of the differences between Mas and his rivals is the stubborn fact that the overwhelming majority of Cuban-Americans are firmly anti-Castro, and do not favor U.S. policies likely to rescue him from the consequences of his misrule.

As if to respond to this point, the American press has recently gone digging for exile groups on which to bestow approval. What they have found are Alfredo Durán and his Cuban Committee for Democracy, Lisandro Pérez of the Cuban Research Institute, Eloy Gutíerrez Menoyo, founder of Cambio Cubano, and Ramón Cernuda, who represents the dissident Elizardo Sánchez in the United States. Some of these people are Cuban-American Gorbachevs (we must reform socialism to save the achievements of the revolution); others are sincerely afraid of civil war if the pressure of the U.S. trade embargo is not lifted. Still others are convinced that "dialogue" with Castro is a possibility in spite of all countervailing evidence. No doubt some have been misunderstood by the mainstream community, a few even threatened by fringe groups. In any case, they represent so small a portion of the whole that their only political significance lies in the need of others to find Cuban exiles who will go on record as opposing American policy towards Castro.

Back to the 1950s

Of all the charges leveled against the Cuban-American community, perhaps the most bizarre is the notion that its members plan to return to Cuba, there to impose a lifestyle and political order evocative of the 1950s. Chronology alone rules out such eventualities. Most Cuban-Americans active today in business and politics have roots too deep in the United States to contemplate such a possibility; at most their elderly parents can nourish the hope of moving to retirement condominiums in their homeland.

In fact, a recent poll taken in Dade County reveals that 64 percent of those surveyed have no intention of reestablishing themselves in Cuba (24 percent think they would, 12 percent are undecided). Moreover, 60 percent believe that those who have left should not be allowed to simply reclaim homes and businesses which they abandoned. In addition, fully 73 percent believe that "socialized medicine and free education must continue in democratic Cuba."

On the other hand, we know virtually nothing about the opinion of Cubans on the island, since they have not been allowed to vote or even respond to opinion polls for nearly four decades. While presumably they do not wish to hand over control of their country to exiles in Florida, neither is it certain that their commonly reported views about "Miami" are either sincere or firmly held. In the fullness of time the Cubans may come to appreciate a well-placed ethnic lobby in the United States.

An even more outlandish notion is that the United States is preparing Jorge Mas Canosa to be its puppet president of a post-Castro Cuba. Here, for example, is Wayne Smith, former director of the U.S. Interests Section in Havana, a tireless critic of U.S. policy since his retirement from the foreign service: "The only chance for Mas to come to power in Cuba," he told Anne Louise Bardach, "is a complete collapse of the country, a civil war, leading to a U.S. intervention to install Mas. It's the old 1950s school of CIA thinking about how to get rid of their guy and install our guy."

It *is* 1950s CIA thinking—except that we are not living in the 1950s, and (as both the Bush and Clinton administrations have demonstrated) nowadays the United States intervenes in the Caribbean only to install leaders who have been previously elected. It is, of course, not inconceivable that civil disorder in Cuba could produce pressures for U.S. intervention. But even if such pressures were to bear fruit, the United States would certainly not install someone who has not lived in Cuba for more than thirty-five years. At the most, the United States might sponsor free elections in which Mas would be free to participate.

Moreover, even if the next Cuban election were restricted to Cubans living in Dade County, it is not at all clear that Mas would win in a walk. The poll cited above revealed that in a hypothetical race for the Cuban presidency, Mas would win only 44 percent of the vote (11 percent went to Tony de Varona of the Autentico party, 25 percent "don't know," the remainder expressed preferences for other candidates). Clearly, Cuban-Americans are beginning to disengage emotionally from Cuban politics—to see the island's political destiny as linked to, but yet separate from, their own. This is surely as it should be.

The Cuban-American story is one of the most dramatic sagas in recent American history—partly because it is so deeply enmeshed in conflicts within the United States about America's world role, and also about the particular value we attach to our own culture. Just as Castro's revolution was the first serious challenge to our way of life in this hemisphere, the success of the Cuban diaspora in the United States has forced "Anglos" to revise their notion about what Latin Americans are capable of achieving, given the right economic and legal circumstances. The Cuban-Americans have also demonstrated that it is possible to sink deep roots in a new country without necessarily surrendering one's own identity, and in so doing have formed a remarkable bridge between the United States and Latin America. They deserve a chance to be seen in all of their complexities, rather than refracted largely through the fantasies and resentments of others.

Note

1. Since these lines were written, *The New Republic* has agreed to an out-of-court settlement in response to Mr. Mas's charge of libel—$100,000.00 and a printed apology.

16

Why the Latins Still Love Fidel

The scene was a popular television studio in São Paulo, Brazil, last March, a taping of the popular "Face to Face" interview program. The guest was Cuban president Fidel Castro, on his first visit to Brazil in thirty years: the host, Maria Gabriela, one of her country's leading television personalities. The format was not one that the guest, who exercises total control over his own country's print and electronic media, might have relished: a no-holds-barred discussion, complete with questions from an audience selected at random, not from individuals chosen by Cuban government functionaries.

If Castro entered the studio with apprehensions, however, he must have lost them almost immediately. The questions from the audience were respectful, even obliging; at no point did anyone try to put him on the spot. And Senhora Gabriela. though known to Brazilian politicians as a formidable and relentless interviewer (a local version of Barbara Walters), was strangely passive. Over-awed by her guest, she gushed, giggled, blushed, and at times coyly flirted with him. More to the point, she blunted even her toughest questions with obsequious asides.

On the obligatory subject of free elections in Cuba, for example, she rushed to preface her question with the remark, "You are wonderful. I would also vote for you, by the way." And after Castro had given his stock excuse for three decades of personal dictatorship (he maintains that not all countries need elections)—with no end in sight—she could only enthuse, "You are Cuba's living history, both the free and extraordinary history of Cuba." The audience roared approval.

What was going on here? In an extended season of democratic renewal in Latin America—spreading now even to Paraguay—one might have thought that by now the continent's last surviving dictator would languish beyond the pale of respectability. Yet what occurred on Maria Gabriela's television program is a key cultural indicator of broader political trends in the region. After years of exclusion (and in some cases marked hostility), Fidel Castro has finally succeeded in winning an unusual measure of acceptance, respect, even political support from his colleagues in some of the more important Latin American republics.

Here are some recent examples:

• Since 1988, Castro has been an honored guest at the inaugurations of the democratically elected presidents in Ecuador, Venezuela, Peru, and Brazil. He was also invited to the inauguration of President César Gaviria of Columbia, but for undisclosed reasons chose not to attend. Brazil refused to allow Cuban security agents to bring into the country their massive array of weaponry to protect their chief during the visit, but there was no reason to worry in any case: in Rio, Brasília, and São Paulo (as earlier in Quito and Caracas and later in Lima), the visiting Cuban dictator was showered with attention, sometimes adoration, by politicians, the media, and crowds in the street.

• In 1989, the Group of Eight, a diplomatic coalition of the largest and most important Latin American countries. came out in favor of Cuba's unconditional readmission to the OAS, a body from which it was expelled in 1962 for attempting to subvert its neighbors and for striking a military alliance with an extra-hemispheric power (the Soviet Union). Venezuela's president Carlos Andrés Pérez, leaping over monumental political distinctions at a single bound, justified the decision this way: "Cuba is part of Latin America. Our purpose now should not be to isolate it."

• In Bolivia, where Castro's legendary associate Che Guevara died in 1967 attempting to "turn the Andes into the Sierra Maestra" (that is, to replicate in Bolivia and throughout South America the success of guerrilla warfare that had brought Castro to power in Cuba) Foreign Minister Isidoro Malmierca of Cuba was awarded that nation's highest decoration. Moving on to neighboring Peru. he received a still more effusive welcome from President Alan García, who said, "I believe that every Latin American who values himself, who is proud of being a Latin American, must at this time defend Cuba."

Defending Cuba sometimes means taking otherwise incomprehensible positions in the company of unlikely (and unsavory) partners. This was amply demonstrated in March 1990 when the Latin American members of the United Nations Commission on Human Rights (with the exception of Panama, which had just been liberated from General Noriega) pointedly refused to support a U. S.-sponsored resolution condemning Castro's treatment of dissidents. In the final vote, Argentina, Brazil, Colombia, Peru, and Venezuela abstained, along with Botswana, Madagascar, Pakistan, and Somalia. Mexico went further, voting "no" in the company of some of the world's most egregious human rights offenders: China, Ethiopia, Iraq, the Ukraine, the U.S.S.R., and Yugoslavia. This put the Latins at odds with not just the United States, but also the resolution's co-sponsors (Czechoslovakia and Poland), and with all of the major Western democracies, including Spain and Sweden—both of whom have maintained cordial relations with Castro in years past—and finally with two of Cuba's former allies of the "socialist camp," Bulgaria and Hungary.

All of this would be understandable if the Latins themselves were moving left or if Castro were gradually steering his country toward democracy or at least a less-suffocating brand of authoritarianism. But neither, in fact, is the case: most of the elected governments in the region are pursuing moderate-to-conservative economic and social policies, while Castro, far from developing his own version of *perestroika* and *glasnost*, has deliberately staked out a position as the last defender of Marxism-Leninism in the West and, if need be, the East as well.

Nor is Cuba regarded as much of a model by other Latin American countries. Although Latin politicians who visit the island are quick to praise its allegedly superior health and educational services, none have gone so far as to try to replicate them at home. The combination of macroeconomic failure (Cuba's decline from being the third most developed Latin American country in 1959 to the twentieth or twenty-first today) and the unyieldingly authoritarian texture of the country's public life have led even serious left-wing politicians to question whether the Cuban road is necessarily applicable to their own countries.

To be sure, in private many Latin leaders have expressed some modest disappointment with Castro's rigidity. For example, Premier Felipe Gónzalez of Spain and President Carlos Andrés Pérez of Venezuela took the occasion of their recent visit to Brazil for the inauguration of President Fernando Collor de Mello to meet with Castro and give him a bit of advice. They urged him to initiate at least a few reforms lest he completely lose control of Cuba, suggesting that if he does not he may end up a Latin version of Romanian strongman Nicolae Ceausescu. In some tellings of this story, the two clinched their argument by adding that such a situation "could only benefit the *gringos,*" deliberately using the contemptuous Latin slang to refer to citizens of the United States.

In public however there is a studied reluctance by major Latin American democratic leaders to criticize Castro at all, particularly on any issue where they could be seen as siding, even indirectly, with the United States. The only exception—an important one—is former Costa Rican president Oscar Arias. who has flatly referred to him as "an anachronism...the Kim Il-Sung of the Caribbean." But a high-ranking Venezuelan official who accompanied President Pérez to Washington in April more neatly expresses the conventional Latin wisdom on the subject: Cuba, he told the *Washington Post,* does not have a "traditional dictatorship" like the former strongman regimes in Argentina, Uruguay, and Chile. "Cuba is different from our point of view...Communist is one thing, dictator[ship] is another."

A Diminished Threat?

The most immediate reason for this change in attitude toward Cuba is the fact that most Latin countries—Venezuela included—feel considerably less threatened by Cuba than they did twenty or twenty-five years ago. During the early 1960s, Castro made no secret of his intention to export his system forcibly to the rest of the continent. Havana became a center for training and indoctrinating aspiring guerrilla leaders drawn from more than a dozen republics. This was highly disruptive to the region's larger populist movements like the People's Revolutionary Alliance (APRA) in Peru, Acción Democrática in Venezuela, and the National Revolutionary Movement (MNR) in Bolivia (whose major activities were centered around the electoral process and patronage), and also to its more hidebound, traditionalist communist parties (that evinced no enthusiasm for guerrilla warfare). Both lost some of their more promising younger leaders to schismatic revolutionary movements formed to replicate the Cuban example. During this period, Havana's hand became immediately apparent in new rural insurgencies in Venezuela, Bolivia, Colombia, Peru, and even Che Guevara's own Argentina.

Since Guevara's death in Bolivia in 1967, however, these movements either have been crushed by the military (as in Argentina and Bolivia) or have demobilized voluntarily (as have the National Liberation Armed Forces [FALN] in Venezuela and, more recently, the M-19 in Colombia). In fact, the only serious guerrilla insurgency in South America today, Sendero Luminoso in Peru, has no apparent Cuban connections at all. Central America is the one subregion where Cuba and Castro continue to be active and therefore are still viewed with concern. This is true even in firmly democratic Costa Rica, which presumably has much less to fear from revolutionary challenges than the weak, divided societies of Guatemala or El Salvador.

The sense of diminished threat is not without foundation: over the years, it has been demonstrated that most of the major Latin American armies are fully capable of neutralizing small guerrilla bands, whatever their origins and regardless of their international connections. And outside of El Salvador, Peru, and by some reckonings Brazil and Chile, the left, whether revolutionary or otherwise, is a political cipher.

Meanwhile, Castro himself has somewhat altered his public attitude toward other Latin American governments. During the 1960s, he used to refer to democratically elected regimes in Peru, Venezuela, Colombia, and Chile as—"oligarchical," no more worthy of respect than the harsher military regimes of Guatemala, Honduras, and Nicaragua. He even treated Chile's elected Marxist president Salvador Allende with undisguised condescension, repeatedly warning him—in public—that sooner or later he would have to break with democratic institutionality.

Today, however, Castro no longer insists that his particular brand of revolution is necessary for other countries. On another television program in Brazil last March, he explained:

> We have said many times that the number one problem of Latin America is not the construction of socialism. The number one problem of Latin America is the independence and sovereignty of the Latin American countries. The number one problem is the solution of their great economic and social problems, the solution of the foreign debt problem, the solution of unfair trade relations, the need for the establishment of a new international economic order approved by the United Nations, and the integration of the Latin American countries—without it, we have no future.

In many ways, this is the language of the precommunist Fidel Castro who toured South America just after his victory in 1959, stirring up anti-Yankee passions and declaring the need for greater independence from the United States. yet leaving unclear what he expected to put in place of the traditional hemispheric relationship. More than a generation later, having long since mortgaged his political fortunes to a now-bankrupt Soviet model, Castro seems to be reverting—to be sure, for external consumption only—to an earlier version of his political persona. Whatever else one can say about this latest kind of rhetoric, it is certainly not threatening to the other Latin countries or their leaders. Quite the contrary: it resonates with the deep chords of self-pity resident in Latin America's traditional political discourse. The notion that the problems of those societies have nothing whatever to do with how they are ruled or organized internally but instead are the fault of outsiders is eminently acceptable to the Latin political class—far more so, at any rate, than the earlier, more "sociological" analysis of Castro's long middle period.

Castro also enjoys a huge reservoir of what might be called "racial" sympathy throughout Latin America—after all, blood *is* thicker than water. To the extent that Castro can make his quarrel with the United States seem nothing more than a spat between two ethnic gangs contending for control of a neighborhood, he can automatically count on some support from other Latin countries. This was true for many years in Spain as well: although Generalíssimo Francisco Franco regarded communists *at home* as objects deserving of torture and extermination, he always saw Castro—safely removed in far-off Cuba where his activities could have no impact in Spain itself—as a horse of a different color. For whatever else Castro had done (including the expulsion of a large Spanish clergy and the expropriation of Spanish shops, businesses, and land holdings), the caudillo in Madrid appreciated the fact that his fellow dictator (the son of a Spanish émigré, a former artillery sergeant in the war of Cuban independence) had at least evened the score with the United States. That is, by wresting from the U.S. sphere of influence the country considered to be most firmly in it, Castro had compensated the mother country (at least psychologically) for its humiliations at the hands of the United States: defeat on the field of battle in 1898 and the subsequent loss of her last colonial possessions—Cuba, the Philippines, and Puerto Rico.

Times have changed in Spain, however. Earlier this year, Spanish Minister of Culture Jorge Semprun (himself an ex-communist who had spent many years in France and gained fame as a novelist and screenwriter) unleashed a gratuitous blast against Castro at a ceremony awarding a literary prize to Paraguayan novelist Augusto Roa Bastos. After praising Bastos's work—a fictional depiction of Paraguay's ruthless dictator, Dr. José Gaspar Rodríguez de Francia (1766–1840), Semprun suddenly turned to a metaphorical Latin American novel "unfortunately not yet concluded" that he called *The Autumn of the Caribbean Patriarch.* "Thirty years—and the people [of Cuba] are still forced to incline before rifles, while the Patriarch drones on without end, a monolithic monologue which pretends to speak in the name of the people, but only monopolizes its enforced silence." And even more provocatively, he expressed the hope that "someone, someday, soon" would bring *that* story to an end.

Semprun's remarks, which nearly provoked a major diplomatic incident with Cuba, aroused heated indignation in political and cultural circles in Mexico, Argentina, Brazil, Venezuela, and Chile. (The letters section of the Madrid liberal-left daily *El País* was full of correspondence from these countries for weeks.) Semprun's plain-spoken criticism illustrates the way in which democratic Spain now differs not merely from its fascist predecessor but from most of the Latin American republics. Its political culture has finally emerged from what might be called the slough of cultural despond—where the operative rule was The Enemy of My Enemy Is My Friend. It suggests as well that Spain is now a "European" country in more than just a geographical sense.

The Insider Mentality

Some Latin solidarity with Castro is based on a faulty reading of Cuban history, particularly the assumption that the Cuban dictator was pushed into the arms of the Soviet Union by a harsh and uncomprehending United States (People in Western Europe and a surprising number of otherwise well-informed Americans also believe this.) That the United States supported a succession of Cuban strongmen prior to Castro's seizure of power in 1959 is not in doubt, but it was prepared to support him as well. In fact, the new Cuban leader had to instruct his finance minister *not* to ask for aid on his initial trip to the United States in 1959, leaving the poor man and the Americans with whom he met somewhat at a loss for topics to discuss. Since then, the Cuban dictator has repeatedly insisted that the decision to enter the Soviet Bloc was his own and entered into freely rather than under pressure. This is one of those cases in international politics in which the facts seem to matter not at all: in any confrontation between Cuba and the United States, Castro can count on being regarded by most of the other Latin countries as the innocent victim, and nothing that anyone (even Castro himself) can say seems to have much effect to the contrary.

There is another "racial" aspect to the Cuban question that is often overlooked. Latins are frankly fascinated by Castro, susceptible to his charisma in the same way they have been over the years to other overpowering political personalities—another was the late Argentine leader Juan Perón. (Some diplomats present during Castro's appearance in Ecuador were unsure whether his warm popular reception there was due to political sympathy or simply to his being an instantly recognizable media personality; relatively few world-famous people come to Ecuador.) But even conservative Latins secretly admire the way the Cuban dictator has raised his country—under other circumstances, a rather unimportant Caribbean island—to the status of a quasi-world power. Of course, they know that to accomplish this the Cuban people have had to pay a terrible price, and they wouldn't trade places with them. For these critics, Castro's Cuba is like an pornographic movie: they wouldn't want to do those things themselves, but they enjoy seeing them done by someone else.

Of course, Cuba's artificially inflated international stature is not simply a consequence of politics; it rests upon having the second-largest army in Latin America (after Brazil, a country more than ten times its population and twenty times its size) and a huge diplomatic-cum-intelligence apparatus deployed throughout the world, particularly in what used to be called the Third World. Cuba can maintain both, however, only because it receives a Soviet subsidy estimated at $6 million *a day*, a point other Latins tend to overlook. Nonetheless, the fact of Cuba's apparent importance speaks to one of the particular frustrations of Latin intellectuals and politicians: the sense that neither they nor their countries really matter on the stage of world history. Whatever else one can say about Castro's stewardship of Cuba, he certainly has eliminated this problem, though perhaps not permanently, particularly if—as now seems likely—the Soviets seriously reassess the costs of their sponsorship. The handwriting is on the wall: after 1991, Cuba will have to pay for Soviet oil and other products in hard currency, a radical departure that will alter the quality of the relationship.

Castro also benefits from the historic tendency of Latins to measure U. S.-Latin American relations in rigidly antagonistic terms: that is, if something is bad for the United States, it has to be good for Latin America and vice versa. For example, in a poll taken in July in Colombia on Castro's impending (but subsequently canceled) visit, the 65 percent in favor of the visit said it would be "a great opportunity to learn from Castro how he has resisted U.S. pressures and maintained a regime different from that of the United States over the past thirty years."

Remnants of anti-American feelings are understandable. In countries like Venezuela and Chile, for fifty years or more the principal natural resource (oil and copper, respectively) was owned and exploited by American companies. Not surprisingly, the relationship of these countries (and others like Guatemala and Honduras, where the major foreign employer was the United Fruit Company) with the United States was dominated by what could only be a zero-sum game, namely, the amount of money an American firm could take out by way of compensation for its initial investment. In the 1920s, a specific literature grew up around this antagonism, and while original causes have long since disappeared (copper and oil have been nationalized in Chile and Venezuela, and United Fruit no longer dominates any of the Central American economies), the mind-set that it engendered lives on.

It may also be that Cuban policy is one of the last areas where Latin leaders can still stake out a dramatic policy difference with the United States. The end of the cold war has meant that "nonalignment" has no meaning, radically reducing the Latin margin to maneuver on major geopolitical issues. Certainly on economic issues, the ideological gap has narrowed dramatically; on major choices for trade and growth, virtually all of the continent's leaders (except Castro, of course) are admitting at least implicitly that the United States was right all along. Opening up economies to foreign investment or dismantling huge, inefficient public sectors threatens to exact serious political costs at home; what better way, then to deflect criticism from public-sector unions and the left in general than to draw blood with the Yankees over Cuba?

Perhaps Castro's principal asset today in marshaling support within the region is the Latin American tradition of supporting nonintervention in each other's internal affairs. (This has not always prevented Latin nations from actually mixing in each other's business, starting with Castro's Cuba itself, but as a principle the doctrine is defended with near-religious fervor.) The Latin American position on nonintervention is best expressed by the Estrada Doctrine of 1930, which holds that diplomatic recognition is accorded to countries, not governments; hence, to differentiate between elected and de facto governments is prima facie evidence of unwarranted intervention. In practice, this means that at the level of international policy there is a lack of democratic commitment in Latin America—what goes on in neighboring countries is their business or their good or bad fortune. To Americans, whether liberal or conservative, this seems a strange or even perverse way of approaching foreign policy, but few Latins have raised their voices against it. One who has, poet and philosopher Octavio Paz in Mexico, has been subjected to a sustained campaign of slander and vilification in his country's (largely government-controlled) media. As long as the fate of the Cuban people—as distinct from the Cuban government—arouses no great interest among the leaders of neighboring countries, outsiders will have ample reason to question whether Latin America's democratic political culture in Latin America is matching the apparent progress of its institutions.

It is the issue of nonintervention that explains why, above all, so many Latin leaders oppose any kind of U. S pressure intended to bring about political change in Cuba. The most recent such controversy was Washington's decision to broadcast television to Cuba (TV Martí) to open further the unauthorized window on the world that Radio Martí brought the Cubans in the 1980s. (The Latins opposed Radio Martí, too.) While they clearly prefer democracy in their own countries. they are content to let Cuban affairs settle themselves in whatever way is most convenient and comfortable for Castro himself. Here, for example, is President

Carlos Andrés Pérez this last May, responding to a Honduran television reporter's question about elections in Cuba:

> Well, that is an issue the Cubans must settle in their own way, and I believe that their leader, Fidel Castro, is a man of great talents. He has proven this, even though we may not agree with his ideology. Also, he is a man with a great deal of experience, and he has been in public office for many years, leading his country and keeping in touch with all the complexities of international politics—which I am sure will give us new and fruitful ideas to sponsor a political project according to the world's new reality.

Seen from the south, then, Castro's Cuba is no threat at all. The lack of democracy there is due primarily to U. S. support of all the governments prior to Castro and U.S. refusal to accept social change on the island once the revolution came to power. Cuba is being persecuted, so this line goes, not for its alliance with the Soviet Union, or its attempt to export violence and terrorism to its neighbors or even its announced intention to make hostility to the United States the organizing principle of its national existence, but because of its refusal to knuckle under to U.S. pressures and subordinate its foreign policies to Washington. If the United States wants Cuba to become democratic, it should remove pressures, not apply new ones, and let Castro effect political change when and how he wishes. If no change takes place at all, that is all right, too; anything, including the lack of democracy and human rights, is better than intervention in the internal affairs of a Latin American country, particularly by the United States.

This is a harsh and even slightly distorted caricature of a more complicated set of feelings, but it accurately charts the distance between North and South, between two political universes that, for all that has happened in the last decade and a half, are still much too far apart.

Part IV

Argentine Hours

17

Orange Juice with General Perón: A Memoir

In the fall of 1967 I went to live in Argentina for a year's research on my doctoral dissertation, a study of the ideological origins of Peronism. Even then, the subject was far from purely academic. Though a dozen years had passed since General Perón had departed in disgrace for foreign exile, Peronism—an ill-defined mélange of populism, personalism, and nationalism—remained the defining political faith of at least four out of ten Argentines. Though the Justicialist movement, as it styled itself, was technically proscribed by the military government of the day, there were Peronists all over the place. After less than six months in the country, it became apparent to me that Perón himself (then living in far-off Madrid) was recovering much of the support that he had lost in his final years of power (1954–55), when his quarrel with the Catholic Church and his mismanagement of the economy had turned the Argentine middle class—and even more important, the Argentine armed forces—decisively against him. I became convinced that if an honest election were ever held during his lifetime, he would be returned to power by a decisive majority.

Like most foreigners, I was fascinated by the persistence of Peronism, an ideology that defied conventional classification in social science: whatever it might be, Peronism was clearly something more than just a South American variety of fascism. My working hypothesis (I admit now that it was far from remarkable) was that this phenomenon could only be understood on its own terms—that is, within the very peculiar context of Argentine history. Thus I decided to center my research on the decade-and-a-half immediately before Perón's appearance on the political scene.

233

A Look Backward

The best place to start my quest was the first floor of the old National Library, where the dusty bound volumes of period newspapers were then stored. As any scholar who works with old periodicals soon learns, some of the most useful information is gleaned not from articles dealing with the ostensible subject of the research but from the apparently superfluous addenda—even social notes or advertisements. In the 1930s Argentina possessed three or four daily newspapers of serious quality, and working through them gave me an extremely illuminating look into the country's worldview. In spite of distances, Argentines felt very much involved in the great events of the day—the Soviet Five-Year Plan; the Italian invasion of Ethiopia and Mussolini's decision to flout the League of Nations; the Spanish civil war; the rise of National Socialism in Germany; and finally, the Second World War. These events were heatedly debated, not only in press and parliament, but also on streetcars and in cafes.

There were, I think, two reasons for this. One—the most obvious—is that like the United States but unlike other Latin American nations, Argentina was and is a country of immigrants, the most "European" country of Latin America. In this case, most of the newcomers came from Spain and Italy, countries deeply affected by the ideological convulsions of our century. Moreover, Argentines of Italian or Spanish origin—here an important difference with the United States—managed to maintain a close and continuous relationship with their countries of origin. Until war put an end to easy transatlantic travel, there was much movement back and forth by families or parts of families. Thus events in 1930s Europe were laden with more than just academic interest.

The other reason is that massive European immigration—concentrated in a few short, intense years just before the First World War—tended to postpone the evolution of a genuine sense of Argentine nationality until well into mid-century. True, children of immigrants were dutifully taught Argentine history and patriotic myths in school, and Spanish (spoken with a slight, actually quite lovely Italian lilt) remained the language of politics and public business. But taken as a whole, as late as the 1930s the "melting pot" had not melted all that much. Of course, this did not make Argentina "European" in the fullest sense of the word. Rather, it had become one of those curious principalities living on the periphery of European culture and receiving everything from it a bit distorted and secondhand—somewhat like late 1930s Romania as depicted by Olivia Manning in her magnificent *Balkan Trilogy*.

The resemblances between the two countries for my period were uncanny. Like Romania, Argentina possessed an elite that preferred French to the local language to distinguish itself from the hoi polloi; a capital city consciously modeled on Paris; a particularly reactionary form of Catholic Christianity, which in turn nourished a low grade (but persistent) anti-Semitism; a fragile and uncertain commitment to economic and political liberalism; above all, a pervasive fear of missing the bus of history—or worse still, of accidentally jumping on the wrong line.

But the comparison with pre-war Romania can be carried a bit too far. True, many Argentines of the period imagined that some sort of fascism was the wave of the future, and they were attracted to such colorful epiphenomena as uniformed "nationalist" movements. But by no means everyone in the country was so certain that democracy was finished—and considerable anti-Fascist militance emerged within the ranks of organized labor and the intellectual classes. There was, for example, very strong support for the embattled Spanish Republic; Argentina even sent several hundred volunteers to fight in the International Brigades. Partisans of the democratic cause in Parliament managed to establish a Committee on Un-Argentine Activities (no misprint) to investigate the role of Axis agents or other purveyors of "foreign political ideologies." While the Argentine government remained neutral in the Second World War, people interested in politics divided in half, though the fault line ran, I learned, rather irregularly. This reflected an ambivalence toward bourgeois democracy that pervaded many elements of national life—not just those on either extreme of the political spectrum.

The principal difference with Romania, however, was that, thanks to extreme geographical remoteness, Argentina completely escaped the most important consequence of the Second World War—the radical partition of Europe into communist and non-communist territories, and with it, forcible ascription to one of two opposing ways of life. Evidently, the country avoided Soviet influence altogether, but unlike, say, Italy or Germany, it did not replace the prewar structures with a more modern version of capitalist democracy. Instead, with the coming of Perón and his own "-ism" in 1946, the country lurched into an ideological experiment of its own, in which all of the competing political trends of the prewar period were jumbled together in new and confusing combinations. That is, both Peronists and anti-Peronists were drawn from pro- and anti-Fascist political forces of the prewar period.

Thus whatever its unpleasant features, this new Argentine political phenomenon was not to be confused with classical fascism. Rather, Peronism was a kind of Argentine New Deal, complete with new government agencies that preempted much of the economic space formerly reserved for a handful of private businesses and agricultural enterprises. It created a modern labor movement, the most powerful in Latin America. It gave women the right to vote. And it delivered services like education, housing, medical services, and nutrition to long-neglected regions and social groups. Like the New Deal, too, though it often brandished the language of radical economic redress, in the end it strengthened the power of the middle class even more than the labor movement.

To be sure, these things were not done in a particularly gentle way, and not always efficiently or honestly either. Loyalty to the leader, his wife, and their movement became the overarching criterion of civic virtue—and, often, eligibility for government largess. Up to that point, Perón's quasi-dictatorship simply replicated the experience of neighboring Latin American countries.

What gave Peronism a peculiar sociology of its own, however, was the way it cleaved Argentine society along vertical rather than horizontal planes. The controlling vectors of Peronism and anti-Peronism were, in fact, values and sensibilities rather than just conventional economic interest. Instead of pitting class against class or party against party, Peronism systematically divided each down the middle—conservatives who believed in the rule of law and the sanctity of contract versus those who preferred to sacrifice these to order, hierarchy, and the styles of authoritarian rule; labor leaders who cherished the autonomy of their own institutions versus those who were prepared to support whomever could "deliver the goods"; businessmen who preferred "sweetheart" deals with the government versus those who chafed at bureaucratic restrictions and structured inefficiencies; clerics avid to control the state's educational system versus those churchmen troubled by an emerging idolatry of President Perón and his wife; intellectuals obsessed with anticommunism versus those for whom democracy was a virtue above and apart from specific electoral outcomes.

To make matters more confusing, the fall of Perón in 1955 did not cleanly reverse the pattern and impose virtue and probity in place of personalism and demagoguery, jobbery and corruption. Too much had happened in the meantime to embitter old-fashioned liberals and conservatives, or even socialists. This meant that in practice not all triumphant anti-Peronists turned out to be democrats, and not all democrats were willing to stand by their values if free and fair elections threatened to restore the Unspeakable to power. Thus if Peronism was difficult to define ideologically, so too, was anti-Peronism. It could be of the Left or the Right, either civilian or military, Catholic or anticlerical. The only thing that was certain was that until the two halves of the apple of discord were somehow reunited, the country would remain almost impossible to govern.

The Reperonization of Argentina

After going through the public prints, I decided to seek out old Peronists to cross-examine ideologically. The multiplicity of types, I must allow, was frankly bewildering. As I expected, quite a few had started out in the old Radical party, the country's largest populist force before the advent of Perón, but some had begun their political life in the old Conservative or Socialist parties; there was even an occasional ex-Communist. Each was convinced that his version of Peronism was the genuine article, had the support of the exiled leader, and would be restored to power in the fullness of time. By closing off debate and political competition, the Argentine establishment had thus assured the survival of a coalition of often contradictory interests that would eventually dislodge it from power.

The old Peronists were held together, of course, largely by the conviction that times had been better during the general's period of rule. In this they were not wrong, at least in the narrowest technical sense. Things had been better in the late 1940s. But, as a few upperclass people of my acquaintance were quick to point out, the country's decline actually began during Perón's second term in the early 1950s, the consequence (they insisted) of his ruinous mismanagement of national resources. In many ways they were right. But resurrecting pre-Perón Argentina lay beyond the realm of possibility; the proof, if one required it, was the inability of any government, military or civilian, to rule successfully in its place. On the other hand, as long as Perón remained alive and in apparent readiness to return, it was possible to fantasize an immediate restoration of good times gone by.

This led to a perceptible seepage back toward Peronism on the part of the Argentine middle class. But it was evident as well among the younger generation, though there it assumed a somewhat different guise. I discovered this on my own at the University of Buenos Aires, where I was auditing classes on modern Argentine history. At first glance, the Communists appeared to be the leading political force on campus, which, given their superior discipline and organizational skill, was not really surprising. A closer look, however, revealed Marxism to be in sharp decline as an ideological force, slowly but firmly being supplanted by the argument that, whatever the order of the day might be in other Latin American countries, the way to be revolutionary in Argentina—to be really revolutionary—was to be some sort of Peronist.

This was quite a departure, since during Perón's presidency Argentine universities had been a virtual hotbed of student opposition. And no wonder: during the 1940s Perón had packed the administrations with Catholic Fascist lawyers, who in turn cashiered many distinguished socialist and liberal academics. But Perón had also strengthened and greatly expanded the Argentine labor movement, causing workers to abandon their traditional loyalties to the Socialist and Communist parties. Both these groups had important student branches, and opposition to Peronism put their militants in the 1940s in the rather uncomfortable situation of having to take up positions opposite the very working class on whose behalf they claimed to speak. After Perón's fall, the traditional left-wing parties rushed to recapture the ground they had lost in the labor movement. Although Peronism was officially proscribed, they never succeeded in doing so. Argentine workers remained—in 1955, in 1960, in 1968—unshakably loyal to the exiled leader.

Over time this was bound to have an important influence on academics and intellectuals. For anyone who thought of himself as "of the Left"—and that of course included many students and not a few professors—it was becoming increasingly difficult to maintain a firmly anti-Peronist stance, since as far as the Argentine working class was concerned, Peronism remained the only political show in town. Leftist intellectuals, most of them from middle- or even upper-middle class homes, were also very sensitive to the charge that their anti-Peronism constituted an indirect endorsement of the military government of the day, and with it the hateful status quo. (The fact that the argument was specious and self-serving did nothing to temper its ideological sting.)

Meanwhile, a group of prominent ex-leftists had begun to rewrite the history of the Peronist period from a decidedly "revisionist" point of view. Their gravamen was that the Socialists and Communists had made a serious historic error during the 1940s; instead of surveying the Argentine situation and accurately assessing the real situation of workers, they argued, their comrades had gotten bogged down in European ideologies irrelevant to the local situation, or they had allowed foreign powers (in this case, Britain, the United States, or the Soviet Union) to dictate what should have been a purely Argentine agenda. One of these dissident Marxists, an ex-Trotskyite by the name of Juan José Hernández Arregui, electrified a student audience in my hearing by declaring that "the choice is to be with Perón and the working class, or to be against the working class. I, for my part, am with the working class."

Somewhat after my time in Argentina, an entire theory was hatched to explain how, objectively, Perón, once returned to power, *would have no choice* (the emphasis was always added) but to implement the Marxist revolutionary agenda. I found these theories frankly bizarre, though they played no small role in the events surrounding Perón's reelection in 1973 and the sanguinary events that followed his death in 1974. But Perón himself did little to discourage them, even to the point of receiving in Madrid Argentine student leaders of a type that would have ended up in his jails or in exile a generation before.

At a certain point in a research project, the material often raises more questions than answers. This was certainly the case with me. Was Peronism, I wondered, becoming something different from what it had originally been? But then, what had it been originally? Why was it possible to find so many different kinds of people responding to the same political label? What would happen if the founder and leader of the movement were to return to Argentina and, therefore, be forced to choose among them? In effect, what would happen if past and present were suddenly compressed into one?

A Successful Long Shot

The one person with whom it would be most useful to discuss these matters was living on another continent and presumably no more accessible to an American graduate student than His Holiness in the Vatican. There is such a thing as a successful long shot, however, and I decided to take it. One evening I was having dinner with one of my professors at the university, a quiet, modest man who had come over to Peronism from Christian Democracy. I knew him to be one of the country's rising Peronist intellectuals, and therefore presumably in contact with the exiled leader in Madrid. At one point in our discussion I asked, as casually as I could manage, whether he thought it would be both useful and possible for me to discuss my thesis topic with General Perón himself. Much to my surprise, he looked up from his plate and said, "Absolutely. I think it would be an excellent idea." "Do you really think you can arrange it?" I asked. Without hesitating, he said, "Yes."

I wrote Perón a letter outlining my work and asking for an interview sometime during the next two months. I enclosed a letter of introduction from my professor. Both of these went into an envelope addressed, not to Perón, but to a young functionary of the Spanish Falange who had apparently been delegated to receive correspondence from Argentina on his behalf, thus circumventing local postal censorship. A couple of weeks later, returning from a brief visit to neighboring Uruguay, I found an unfamiliar envelope in my accumulated mail bearing a Madrid postmark and no return address.

It was a fairly lengthy letter from Perón, full of references to the topic and offering to see me within the time frame I had suggested. He even included his private phone number so that I could arrange my appointment with his secretary, José López

Rega (the name meant absolutely nothing to me.) There was nothing left to do but buy an airline ticket, shut down my Buenos Aires operation, and fly off to Spain, a country I had never before visited. I went about my business in a state of barely contained euphoria until the time came to leave.

The trip from Buenos Aires to Madrid took about seventeen hours, flying at night with stops in São Paolo and Rio de Janeiro in Brazil, thence across the Atlantic to the Canary Islands, touching Spanish soil shortly after noon the following day. Accustomed to the somewhat down-at-the-heels appearance of Buenos Aires, I was stunned by the order and cleanliness of Madrid. While the Franco dictatorship was reputed to be far more repressive than the one I had just left behind in Argentina (and for all I know, was), the general air was more cheerful and optimistic, and people seemed more prosperous and better dressed.

As far as I could gather, the relationship between Franco and Perón was curious and delicate; officially the two men had never met (a story that almost nobody believed). Perón was personally very popular among working-class Spaniards; one of the principal avenues of the capital was even named after him in gratitude for the shipments of wheat he had sent to the peninsula in 1946 and 1947, when the United States, Great Britain, and the Soviet Union were jointly trying to oust Franco from power by means of an economic embargo (or as the Spaniards put it, "when you were trying to starve us to death").

After allowing myself two days to get used to the change in time, I drew out Perón's letter and phoned his villa. López Rega was not there when I phoned, but when he returned my call we agreed to a date at ten in the morning two days hence. Perón's secretary urged me to take careful notes on how to get to the house; this proved to be sound counsel, since no taxi driver was familiar with the area, and without the instructions I doubt we would ever have found it. The villa was, in fact, situated at the end of a maze of heavily wooded streets in Puerta de Hierro, a luxurious if then somewhat distant suburb of Madrid much preferred by foreign embassies for their residences.

The house itself was not visible from the road. Instead, there was a high wall and a huge sheet of metal painted black that masked the driveway. Into this a small access door had been cut. Standing in front of it was a conservatively dressed Spaniard in shirtsleeves whom—for reasons to be explained later—I have since concluded was an officer of the Spanish Civil Guard. I paid the driver and approached the sentinel, whose only remark to me was, "Your last name, please?" When I gave it, he pointed to the access door and bid me enter.

The driveway, it turned out, descended some feet to a large stone house sitting in the center of a European-style park. Before I had a chance to take all this in, I noted a familiar figure on the veranda. Even in a crowded room I would have had little difficulty picking him out. With his dark glasses and commanding stature (well over six feet), Perón looked like nothing so much as an exiled South American dictator at leisure. As I descended the driveway, I debated briefly how to greet him. Finally I decided it was best to fall back on Argentine military protocol; I saluted him and said, "*Buenos días, mi general.*"

That seemed to touch the right button. He shook my hand, asked what brought me to Spain, expressed feigned disbelief that I had come only to see him, and bid me inside. We passed through a long hall and turned left into a study that ran half at least the depth of the house. The room was sparsely furnished, with a globe and two Louis XIV throne chairs at one end and a large desk at the other. Perhaps to impress me with his strength and vigor, he picked up one of the throne chairs and carried it all the way to the front of the room, where he deposited it for my use in front of his desk. He signaled that I should sit down, clapped his hands, Spanish-style, and ordered a servant to bring us some orange juice.

According to his official biography, Perón was then seventy-three years old. He did not seem it until one looked closely at the details of his face. The broad features were familiar but had lapsed into a coarse replica of the mask that adorned so many posters on walls or small banners in buses or taxis. In particular I noticed a red splotch (I could not determine whether it was a birthmark or some degenerative condition) just below his eye on the right-hand side. It was too large to overlook, yet it never showed up in any photograph, which leads me to believe that he never went anywhere without covering it with some cosmetic application.

Perón had a very distinctive style of speaking, employing his hands frequently for emphasis. I would say of him what Clarence Darrow says of William Jennings Bryan in the stage version of

Inherit the Wind: he was capable of strutting even while sitting down. Perón did not, in fact, converse in the ordinary sense, at least not with strangers like me. He did not even discourse in the way of many chiefs of state I have since met. Instead, he gave a speech, in which there was very little opportunity to interrupt, pose a question, or follow it up. The only thing missing was the balcony and the adoring masses below it. I had been warned that if he was bored he wouldn't smoke, but in fact he lit up almost immediately, and during the more than two hours we were together he consumed two full packs. ("I don't believe cigarettes cause cancer," he said. "You've proved it," I replied.) His smoking not only reassured me but also marginally improved the prospects of dialogue, since almost the only time I was able to get a word in edgewise was when he was spitting into the wastebasket.

I sat down and looked around. The house was, I confess, greatly different from my expectations. Perhaps too much under the influence of Hollywood films, I imagined that it would be somewhat baroque in style, with heavy red drapes and dark furniture, and a sinister aide lurking behind every arras. I expected, too, a rather elaborate secretariat, with maps of Argentina and the latest in communications equipment. None of this turned out to be the case. The house was large and comfortable, but it was modern, unpretentious—tastefully austere. And, as far as I could gather, political business was conducted from Perón's hip pocket. Late in the interview, for example, López Rega arrived with the day's mail, and they sorted it out together.

A Curious Lecture

As soon as I activated the small cassette tape recorder I had brought with me, Perón launched into a lengthy lecture on world history since 1917—seen, of course, from his very idiosyncratic perspective. The leitmotif was the struggle for the world between the United States and Great Britain, with the latter finally conceding the Western hemisphere to the United States in—of all things—the Atlantic Charter. Then, suddenly, he shifted to the autobiographical, recounting his experiences as Argentine military attaché in Europe in 1939 and 1940. He chose to settle in Italy because "a very interesting experiment was under way there."

"An interesting experiment, you mean fascism?" I asked.

"From 1917 on, the world was divided into huge, let us say imperialistic poles," he lectured me. "In the face of these two colossi of domination, one communist, one capitalist, there emerged a third position within the sphere of ideologies." That position, he emphasized, could best be characterized by the term "national socialism." This was not to be confused with fascism alone, he added, since national socialism is, after all, "the ideology of two-thirds of the countries in the world today."

I must have expressed some surprise, because he then went on to say—and now I am quoting verbatim:

> Look at the Nordic countries—the most civilized in the world; they are socialist monarchies. The Low Countries, too, are socialist monarchies. The British Empire [sic] is a socialist monarchy.... Germany—one sector is Social Democratic, that is to say, Marxist, and one, Christian Democrat, that is to say, neocapitalist. They have joined forces and are governing together, with a neosocialist system.
>
> Italy is the same way. The Middle East, all socialist republics. In Africa, the thirty black nations, all with socialist systems. This country [Spain] they call a state, a kingdom, which is national syndicalist because [and here a pause for effect] they are afraid of the word "socialist." [laughter] But what they say—I'm not sure it's what they really do—but what they say has the genuine flavor [of fascism]. Naturally, because these people were Fascists during the civil war. The side that was victorious, without doubt it was Fascist.

Returning to the subject of Mussolini's Italy, Perón expressed serious reservations about the way it had put "national socialism" into practice.

> I didn't like it—I didn't like it in the *form* it assumed. I spoke an hour with Mussolini. I told him. The form of execution was bad. But Italy was Mussolini at that time. In contrast to Germany: Hitler might have been Germany, but if he hadn't existed his place would have been taken by someone else.

"What do you mean about the form?" I pressed. "Could you go into that in greater detail?"

"In the ideology they did not err; the proof is that today, forty years later, two-thirds of the world is in the position they advocated.... But the methods they used to achieve this—there is where they went wrong."

"How did Mussolini fail in his realization? I mean, not so much in international policy but in the internal politics of Italy?"

"I'll tell you how he failed," Perón replied.

> I told *him*. In 1939 Mussolini received me in Rome.... The entire realization of their ideological conception [was based] on three grand promises...(1)

"Fascism or death," fascism or nothing, civil death; (2) the monarchy should be replaced by a republic; and (3) a popular militia should replace the standing army. If they had done all of this, well, fascism would have consolidated itself in Italy, would have moved forward, in spite of everything.

But what happened? All the while that Mussolini was in government...there persisted a living socialist party, international, dogmatic, Marxist—which was in open warfare against him.... Mussolini didn't create the republic he promised. He created a popular militia, but he failed to supplant the army. The two forces subsisted side by side.

These three, labor, monarchy, army, were potential enemies (*enemigos en potencia*).... The moment Mussolini weakened...the three threw out their restraints and took power under Bagdolio, the Army, by order...of the King. And who supported it? A popular sector, which is socialism....

Mussolini was a great man, no denying that. A great man. But Italy was a very difficult country in which to carry out a project like that.

These were, I knew, the views of many Italian Fascists who played a role in the Salò republic after 1943 and whose apologias sold very well in Buenos Aires bookshops. But at the same time, what Perón had to say about Italy could be said *pari passu* about his own regime in Argentina. Despite its claims to being "revolutionary," it left most of the structures of economic and social power intact—particularly the great landowners, the church, and the armed forces. Was this Perón's form of indirect self-criticism? Or was this his way of seeming more left-wing than he really was? Or did he really regard the Italian experiment as something upon which he had improved?

Before I could press this line of questioning, Perón had moved on to talk about his travels in Western Europe. Besides Italy, he said, he went to Germany, then to Spain (where the civil war had ended a mere six months before). Here I saw another ideologically pregnant topic and pressed for his views on the Spanish conflict. All he would offer is that he went around talking to "both the Republicans and the Nationals...so that I could impartially form an idea of what this was all about." He studiously avoided drawing any lessons from the Spanish tragedy, even though his biographers in Argentina habitually emphasized that his firsthand view of the consequences of civil war had influenced not only his policies of economic redistribution, but also his decision to quit the country in 1955 rather than call upon his followers to rise up in his defense.

Perón continued his travelogue—to Russia, along the eastern Prussian frontier, Portugal, the Low Countries, Scandanavia. "I formed a concept," he concluded. "Intuitively, I sensed the direction of the future." The coming war was an attempt to stop "a nascent evolution." "Neither National Socialist nor Fascist, but an evolution which cannot be stopped by cannons. On the contrary, war tends to accelerate these evolutions."

Perón returned to Argentina in 1940 and began to speak to his fellow officers about these things. ("Military men said I was a Communist. Me! Naturally, I had to speak about the phenomenon of socialism—I myself have no problem with the word 'socialism' [ha ha ha], but when they hear the word they see you coming with a bomb in your hand!") Then, he claimed, a group of young officers, mostly his former students at the National War College, came to him in late 1941 or early 1942 and urged him to stage a coup to put these (murky) concepts into practice. This I knew to be, at best, about 20 percent of the truth; the coup out of which he emerged as the most important single figure (but over a period of nearly two years) was made by others, with very different initial objectives.

Perón was right, though, to characterize the country to which he had returned as awash in conspiracies. These had largely to do with the efforts of President Roberto M. Ortiz to end a system of electoral fraud that had been in place since 1932, to which he owed his own accession, and which virtually assured the rule of a coalition of conservative parties in perpetuity. In 1940, however, President Ortiz was forced to take an indefinite medical leave because of severe diabetes that affected his vision. His vice president, Ramón S. Castillo, a hardliner who had a more astringent view of universal suffrage, immediately reversed his predecessor's policies. Argentines were scheduled to select a new administration altogether in late 1943, and Castillo had already decided that his successor should be Conservative Senator Robustiano Patrón Costas, whose huge personal fortune included sugar refineries, oil, and railroads in Argentina's arid north.

At the same time, the Second World War was reaching a decisive phase. Most Argentines still anticipated an Axis victory, a prospect that was viewed with mixed emotions by the Argentine establishment and Conservative party. Though Castillo himself was a firm partisan of neutrality, his designated successor—like many Conservatives—had strong business, personal, and cultural links with Great Britain and was therefore reputed to be pro-Allied. On the other hand, the apparent invincibility of Axis forces seemed to suggest a new "wave of the future" on which side it would do well for Argentina to range itself. This was particularly the view of the sons of the elite, many of whom joined quasi-fascist "nationalist" groups.

Neither Conservative fathers nor nationalist sons saw anything wrong with electoral fraud, but the latter saw no reason to go to the polls at all if the prearranged result was someone like Patrón Costas. The latter's allegedly pro-British attitudes also deeply troubled junior and middle-level officers in the Argentine army. Whether these fears were really justified is beside the point; it was to prevent an apparently pro-British Conservative from taking power (and conceivably, compromising the country's neutrality) that the military had overthrown Castillo on 4 June 1943.

I found it interesting that Perón expressed no interest whatsoever in the "nationalist" groups, even though they constituted an important part of his early civilian constituency. ("It was a nationalism of lyrical expression," he told me. "It was always that in our country. It still is.... Afterwards, nationalism was taken over by gangsters and fell into the hands of whoever gave its leaders money.")

The truth is that Perón knew how to use Argentine nationalism when he needed it and discard it when he did not. (The reverse was also the case.) Between 1943 and 1944, first as war minister and then as vice president, he posed as the firmest advocate of neutrality; when the tide turned and it was obvious the Axis was going to lose the war, and Argentina was in danger of being excluded from the emerging United Nations Organization, he had no difficulty switching sides, even to the point of approving a very tardy declaration of war against Germany and Japan. Moreover, during the early years of his presidency, people recruited from nationalist groups fleshed out most of the government offices having to do with education, culture, and religious affairs; once he began to quarrel with the Roman Catholic Church, they were relieved of their posts or resigned. (Many found their way into the conspiracy that eventually deposed him.)

Now Perón launched into a wildly favorable account of his two presidential terms, the second of which was, of course, truncated by a coup. It was embarrassing to listen straight-facedly to things I knew to be contrary to the truth, but I saw no point in interrupting him. Apparently not a single mistake was ever made, even by one of his aides. He did not even attempt to explain why it was that after nine years of uninterrupted economic growth and social betterment he was overthrown to wide (if temporary) popular acclaim.

Now Perón was really warming to his subject, which was current affairs. Pounding the table, he assured me that "if national socialism does not triumph in the world, then international socialism will." The United States, he insisted, was pursuing policies contrary to its own national interests. ("The U.S. is playing the game of Moscow without meaning to.") He particularly objected to countries such as Argentina having to pay royalties on foreign patents, or being obliged to repatriate capital earned on foreign investment. "Bad as is your economic policy," he continued, "your political methods are worse, your political methods are worse.... If you don't like the policies of any Latin American government, you start a revolution against it." He even claimed that the United States and Britain had played a vital role in his overthrow; when I started in amazement—it was the first time I had ever heard this—he said, "Yes, by provisioning the rebels with ammunition from the Malvinas (Falkland) Islands."

I sighed, "I can't imagine why."

He replied, "You're right: I don't know why either—we weren't enemies of the United States."

Unexpected Observations

I could see Perón was getting tired and perhaps a bit bored, since he now jumped from topic to topic in no particular order. Try as I might, it proved impossible to get him back on the track of Argentine events, particularly those relating to the period of my dissertation. But it may be of some interest to record a few of his remarks nonetheless. On the Alliance for Progress: "At the time of the meeting at Punta del Este, I wrote a letter to President John Kennedy. He sent an aide out to speak to me for three days...what was his name? Some Irishman. Kennedy agreed completely with the concepts in my letter." He spoke approvingly of Vice President Hubert Humphrey, who was then fighting to succeed Lyndon Johnson (like most Latin Americans, Perón disliked and distrusted Richard Nixon). On Czechoslovakia, then under the reform government of Dubček: "We want the socialism of fatherlands, not the reverse.... Look how much better the Soviets handle the national aspirations of countries in their sphere of influence." On Israel: "I don't see anything wrong with it; why shouldn't the Jews have a state of their own? The Spaniards refuse to recognize it because they are, you know, *pro-Arab*." ("Arab" pronounced like a horrible disease.) On Vietnam: "Here you have a case where spiritual forces can compensate entirely for the lack of material resources." (But then, "What the Vietnamese want is food. Why not give them that, and that will stop them.") On Che Guevara, killed less than two years before in Bolivia: "I am anti-communist—I always have been. He was a communist, but a great man...killed by your American Green Berets. It was a Bolivian matter. Why was the United States involved?" On the U.S. presidential campaign, then underway: "I wouldn't want to be President of the United States. Too many problems."

Toward the end of the meeting a visitor was announced, brought in by López Rega, whom I now met for the first time. It was Juan Atilio Bramuglia, whose deceased father, a former labor leader, had been Perón's most respected foreign minister. Indeed, the elder Bramuglia had done such a good job in the late 1940s burnishing the prestige of the Argentine government at the United Nations (then not a particularly friendly forum) as to arouse the jealous ire of Eva Perón, who contrived to get rid of him. The younger Bramuglia must have been a teenager when Perón was overthrown; whatever grudges the family might have harbored against Evita in the meantime had obviously not been transferred to her husband.

Bramuglia had just returned from a business trip to the Middle East, and he wished to have a few moments alone with Perón. López Rega gently guided me out of the room and out of the house. We took a slow promenade around the grounds, during which Perón's secretary regaled me with the story of his life. He had originally started out to be a poet, he said, but "they" (the Argentine literary establishment?) purposely ignored his work because of his political views. He had been with Perón twenty-five years, he said; it was amazing to watch the way old opponents were coming around to supporting him. ("I've seen some Argentine politicians come to this house, people who've been against him their entire lives, and leave with tears in their eyes.") Mentally I calculated that López Rega must have been in the

Argentine military, perhaps an NCO? How else could he have been with Perón since 1943?

By this time we were rounding the bend and coming back to the house, and Perón and Bramuglia were standing on the veranda, with a woman I immediately recognized as the general's third wife, María Estela Martínez de Perón (or Isabelita, as she was later known). She was far less attractive than her photographs in the study, but it was a hot summer day and she had not bothered with makeup. I do not think we were even introduced. Since I knew her to be a former cabaret dancer who was barely literate, I harbored no great desire to meet her. Too bad for me: within six years she was to become Latin America's first woman chief of state.

Bramuglia offered to give me a ride back to downtown in a chauffeur-driven car that was waiting for him outside the gate. Perón accompanied us through the small access door, and as we waited for the car to pull into place I saw something that had entirely escaped my notice when I arrived. On a hillock looking down on the house, and controlling all the access routes, was a uniformed squad from the Civil Guard crouched around a machine gun mounted on a tripod. These precautions were probably gratuitous (during Perón's long stay in Spain there were never any security problems), but they had the desired dramatic effect, at least on me. The chauffeur rapidly dismounted to take the opportunity to shake the great man's hand.

Riding back to the center of Madrid, I reflected on the fact that Perón's ideological views remained firmly fixed in the interwar period. Nothing that had happened since, including the political collapse of fascism in Italy or its military defeat in alliance with Nazi Germany had made much of an impression on him. Nor did he seem to see the relationship between fascism and the outbreak of the Second World War, which had left Soviet Communism—not "national socialism"—in control of much of the European continent. His confusion of Scandinavian social democracy and the populist-authoritarian regimes in Egypt and Syria made no sense to me, but it obviously served to appeal to the most diverse range of supporters in Argentina. After all, his country was something of a maverick among nations, half-European, half-Third World. But what would happen if he had to put these theories into practice?

Fast Forward to 1973

The next time I saw Perón was on American television, re-turning to his country in 1972 at the invitation of a military re-gime that—having exhausted all other alternatives—finally chose national reconciliation through a political opening. The gener-als thought they could have it all ways, however: they rigged the rules so that Perón himself could not be a candidate in new elec-tions. Perón remained unruffled. After a three-week stay he re-turned to Spain, from whence he designated that Héctor Cámpora, a dentist who had served briefly as president of the Chamber of Deputies during his first presidency, should stand in for him. In May 1973, Cámpora—a charming mediocrity—won 49 percent of the vote and was inaugurated for a six-year term.

In the event, Cámpora served less than six weeks. By mid-June, under orders from Perón, he and his vice president resigned to clear the way for new elections. This time there would be no proscriptions, and Perón could run on his own. This of course was an eventuality that surprised nobody. What was rather unex-pected was the peculiarly "leftist" texture of Cámpora's brief presidency, since there was nothing about the man's political background to prepare one for it. All of a sudden the Interior Ministry—that is, the agency in charge of the judicial system and the police—as well as the state-controlled television network, were taken over by "revolutionary Peronists." One of Cámpora's first measures was to offer a blanket pardon to "political prisoners"—that is to say, to urban terrorists who over the past three or four years had been convicted for bank robberies, kidnapping of wealthy Argentines for ransom, and occasionally assassination of military men and conservative politicians. Perón himself was widely reported to be shocked by the disorder that overtook his country, although in fact he himself had done nothing whatever to restrain these youthful terrorists, since their activities did much to convince the generals that the price of remaining in power was becoming prohibitive.

Who were these people? Many of them were the Marxist-influ-enced students I had known in a more hesitant ideological guise during my stay in Argentina. After 1968 they moved more or less en masse into the Peronist youth movement ("to infiltrate Peronism from within") or into two different urban guerrilla movements, one of which was more or less loosely allied to it. For a few short weeks the gamble paid off. But then, all of a sudden, in Madrid Perón had shaken his finger and the whole structure collapsed. A provisional government was named to prepare the way for new elections in September. Perón himself returned for good in late June. The spectacle was too good to miss; I bought a round-trip ticket and prepared to spend six weeks in Argentina.

A Return to Argentina

"You will find things greatly changed here," a friend had written me before my arrival. That was quite literally the understatement of the decade. Peronism was not merely no longer proscribed; it was, in fact, the declared political preference of almost anyone who heeded the counsels of fashion—or prudence. The principal issue of the day was not whether Perón would be reelected—all surveys showed him winning hands-down—but who his running mate would be. He was, after all, by then nearly eighty years old and probably would not survive the six-year term. What Peronism now was, and where it could be expected to go over the longer term, would therefore be defined largely by whom Perón selected to be his vice president. This question, I found, dominated all others in Argentine politics.

In my effort to elucidate matters, I started looking up old friends and acquaintances. Some decided not to return my calls, presumably because I was an American—a condition that, in the ideological delirium of the moment, apparently established that I was working for the CIA. (I was not.) But others simply expressed their regrets; they did not have the time, since they were spending their days and nights at meetings. The purpose of these, it appeared, was to force upon Perón one or another vice presidential candidate. This was particularly true of the Left, members of which, having done much to make Perón's return possible, believed that he owed it a massive political debt.

There was certainly no shortage of people willing to be Perón's running mate. They included a labor leader from the province of Córdoba, who brandished Marxist clichés like a lethal weapon, as well as an active-duty general who, until recently, figured among the most repressive of military authorities. It was obvious to me—

though not always to my friends—that the second most important figure in the country was now Perón's former secretary, José
López Rega, who now presided over the ministry of social welfare. As the agency in charge of handing out pensions to the
elderly, this was a political powerhouse in its own right. But López
Rega's reach extended somewhat further afield. He was rumored
to have strong connections in the Argentine political underworld,
which included groups that were later identified in the world
press as right-wing "death squads." His son-in-law was serving as
provisional president, pending Perón's reelection several weeks
hence. And he was so closely tied to Perón's wife politically that
the gossips had it that the two were lovers.

From extensive journalistic coverage, I now learned more about
the man with whom I had taken a brief morning stroll around
Perón's villa some five years before. López Rega was a former
policeman who had served on Perón's security detail during his
presidency; he had returned to the general's immediate circle in
the mid-sixties after having proved his usefulness to Madame
Perón during an important visit she paid to Argentina as her
husband's representative in 1964. There was nothing in the papers about his supposed early vocation as a poet, but much about
his intense interest in astrology, and about how both the Peróns,
but particularly Isabelita, were reputed to set great store in his
"readings." When—to the surprise of many—Perón passed over
more logical running mates to name his wife, there were many
ways to interpret the decision, but none of them suggested that
López Rega would play a minor role in the next administration,
less so that it would be tilted toward the Left.

I would have liked to have discussed all of this with my old professor, the one who had made possible my meeting with Perón,
but this proved very difficult. In the intervening years the poor
man, and his wife, too, had succumbed to a form of schizophrenia
that manifested itself in flights of irrationality and extreme delu-
sions of grandeur. The walls of their apartment were covered by
homemade "diplomas" naming him to such high posts as—I am
not exaggerating—field marshal of the Chinese armies. During
dinner the only topic of discussion was what Western European
embassy Perón should give him after his imminent return to power.
(Humoring them along—what else could I do?—I helped them finally decide upon Brussels.) Subsequently, both were committed

to institutions, where each was to spend many long years. Their two children were turned over to her sister to be raised.

As for Perón, he confined his campaign appearances to television, where he was interviewed by panels of friendly journalists. He had aged considerably since I had met him, and his pronouncements were banal in the extreme; they lacked even the idiosyncratic cutting edge that had so surprised me during our morning together in Madrid. The principal burden of his message was that the world was a hungry place and that countries like Argentina, which were in a position to supply it with foodstuffs, would have a disproportionate amount to say about things. Only the first half was true. Ahead lay two oil shocks that would greatly undermine the purchasing power of countries most in need of foodstuffs, and in other ways the Argentine economy was in less than optimal condition; those who could were already sending their liquid wealth out of the country.

A few days before I left to go back to the United States, one of the two urban guerrilla movements attacked an army post just outside of Buenos Aires, killing an officer and a conscript. The nation was profoundly shocked, but particularly so were those people who expected that with Perón's return to power now imminent, the country could at least put such episodes behind it. ("This is what these people wanted," a friend's mother, a lifelong anti-Peronist, bitterly remarked. "Why are they rebelling against it?") The answer, of course, was that as the moment of his return approached, Perón suddenly revealed his true colors which were the very same shown to me in Madrid six years before. "Socialism," yes, but "national socialism"—which is to say, not socialism as understood by Marxists of any stripe. Perón had already begun to confront his own Left, which was now beginning to strike back.

I was luckier than most of my Argentine friends: I could watch the unfolding drama from a safe distance. It included Perón's reelection, his futile attempt to harness the forces he had unleashed to return to power; his sudden death a year later; his replacement by his widow; the growth of political violence on the Left and Right—and finally, in 1976, a coup that caused at least nine thousand people to be "disappeared." My old professor—immured in his schizophrenia and in a foreign embassy of his imaginings might have been able to make sense of these events, but for the rest of us, fate seemed to make of Argentina nothing less than a great sad madhouse itself.

18

Between Two Fires:
Terrorism and Counterterrorism
in Argentina, 1970–1983

Between 1970 and 1983, Argentina—one of the most refined and civilized countries in the world—experienced a sharp regression towards barbarism, the likes of which had not been seen since the Second World War. During those years uncounted thousands of persons were abducted, tortured and killed by revolutionary and counterrevolutionary forces, both regular and paramilitary, in conjunction with or with the approval of members of the clergy, judiciary, press, business, and intellectual and labor communities.

In broadest outlines the events were these: between 1970 and 1973, armed formations loyal to former President Juan Perón engaged in an urban guerrilla war against a de facto military government. The characteristic methods were kidnapping and outright assassination; the ultimate purpose was to undermine the morale of the armed forces and compel it to call elections so that Perón, the leader of the largest political party in Argentina who had been expelled in 1955, could return to power.

The strategy eventually bore fruit. In 1973, the generals decided that discretion was the better part of valor; elections were held; and the Peronist party in fact returned to government. However, acts of terrorist violence—this time against a government that terrorists had once sought to establish—continued until 1976, when the armed forces once again seized power and initiated blanket repression. In 1983, having been defeated in a humiliating war with Great Britain over the Malvinas (Falkland) Islands in the South Atlantic, the armed forces were compelled to step down; elections were again held; and Argentina passed into a period of democratic rule.

To say anything more than this is to enter immediately into a polemical minefield. To put matters simply, virtually every aspect of the problem is fraught with ideological implications; both sides of the civil war continue to struggle over the writing of recent history. There is, in the first place, absolutely no agreement on the number of victims of either terrorism or counterterrorism. The U.S. government, reporting to Congress in early 1977 on the state of human rights in Argentina, found that some 2,000 Argentines died between 1973 and 1976.[1] In contrast, the National Commission of Disappeared Persons (CONADEP), appointed by President Alfonsín in 1983, found only 600 such instances prior to the March 1976 coup.[2]

Nor is there any consensus on the number of victims of counterterrorism, or state repression. Prior to the collapse of the military government in 1983, estimates ranged widely; the Argentine Permanent Assembly on Human Rights (APDH), an organization known to be close to the Communist party, claimed 6,500 such cases (1976–1979). A special commission of the New York City Bar Association that visited Argentina in 1979 put the number at 10,000. Amnesty International preferred an estimate running between 15,000 and 20,000.[3] After Argentina's return to civilian government, CONADEP was given extensive facilities to pursue its investigation; as its report explains, it sent representatives to interview victims, relatives, or witnesses not only throughout Argentina, but in Mexico, Western Europe, and the United States. In the end it documented just slightly less than 9,000 individual cases. It was not, however, satisfied to leave matters there. As its report explains, "We have reason to believe that the true figure is much higher. Many families were reluctant to report a disappearance for fear of reprisals." CONADEP's final report speaks somewhat cavalierly of "tens of thousands" of victims.[4]

The matter is further complicated by the fact that both terrorism and counterterrorism overlap administrations. Between 1970 and 1973, the principal perpetrators were armed formations of the Peronist Left attacking a de facto military dictatorship. But between 1973 and 1976 there were three kinds of violence—between the terrorists and an elected government they had helped to install but found they could not control; between the terrorists and the armed forces and police; and between paramilitary

formations and parallel organizations of the police loyal to the
Peróns' Social Welfare Minister, José López Rega. After the 1976
coup, some Peronists fell victim to outright military repression
and suddenly discovered the virtues of human rights. Others,
however, did not; instead, they took advantage of the military
sweep to collaborate in the dispatching of their rivals. Thus, while
individual Peronists may clamor for justice, the party as a whole
has no particular reason to look too closely into the events which
occurred in the two years prior to the military coup.

Finally, there is no agreement on the sources of strategy and
political doctrine which inspired so much political violence. The
terrorists of the early 1970s had evidently drunk deeply at the
wells of Marxist ideology. Yet the report of CONADEP has nothing whatever to say about this; in fact, it denied that its job was to
"look into the crimes committed by those terrorists," which in
any event, it argued, were adequately documented by the military government and by the press of the period.[5]

It was less reticent about the doctrinal sources of counterterror,
which it placed at the hands of the United States and France, particularly the former. In an appendix to its report, by cleverly stitch-
ing together various quotations from U.S. and Argentine officials,
it blurs crucial differences between the counterinsurgency doctrine of the Kennedy and Johnson administrations and the actual
conduct of the Argentine armed forces a decade later. The report
thus serves two needs at once: to transfer all responsibility to the
United States and to discount completely any linkage between
Marxism and the conduct of terrorists who undermined civilian
political institutions in Argentina in 1973–76.

The result is that any evaluation of the Argentine experience
must be provisional and tentative. In this chapter we propose to
examine the setting and context; the personalities and doctrines;
and the implications for the future course of Argentine society.
But we make no pretense to offering more than a cursory explo-
ration into a very complex and difficult subject which by its very
nature eludes rigorous analysis.

The Setting and Context: Why Argentina?

All societies display certain political pathologies; not all of
them, however, experience terrorism. The United States, for example, is thought to be a violent country, and in fact is so, if we

base our judgment wholly on the number of violent crimes committed annually, adjusted proportionally to population. Yet the United States has suffered relatively little from political terrorism, in spite of the presence of diverse national, cultural, and religious groups within its boundaries, some of which harbor serious grievances against authority, or at any rate, against the resident representatives of foreign powers (the Soviet Union, Turkey, Great Britain, and so forth).

Conversely, countries with a more "peaceful" social environment (the United Kingdom, France, Italy) have been primary victims of terrorism in recent years. This paradox should warn those searching for simple explanations of complex problems. It is possible to find within any society reasons why terrorism occurs, without the presence of those factors effectively explaining anything. This much said, there are certain features of Argentine life which cannot be ignored in any discussion of the subject; in considering them, however, we leave open the question of how important (or unimportant) each might have been.

Lack of Legitimacy in the Political System

Argentina led South America in political development before the First World War, electing its first truly representative chief executive in 1916. Since 1930, however, at least a significant minority of citizens have felt disenfranchised most of the time. In 1930 the military seized power and deposed President Hipólito Yrigoyen. Though new elections were held in 1932, fraud and exclusion prevented the majoritarian Radical party from registering its true strength. The same was true in 1938; the 1944 elections were never held.

A military coup in 1943 radically shifted the direction of Argentine politics by introducing a new alliance between the armed forces and the labor movement. Its leader was Colonel Juan Perón, who combined nationalism, populism, and personalism to capture a solid majority of voters in new elections convoked in 1946. While some fraud and intimidation seems to have occurred, Perón's real problem was his governing style, which confused loyalty to the leader and his movement with loyalty to the Argentine nation. Exploiting class and regional resentments, Perón purposely polarized Argentina into Peronist and anti-Peronist camps; it became impossible for anyone to remain neutral on the subject of his person or policies. The anti-Peronist front was extremely broad—stretching from the Communists on the Left to the Conservatives on the Right; in its totality it supported the coup which brought the president down in September 1955.

Perón's flight into exile did not bring Argentines closer together, nor impart greater legitimacy to the political system. The victors and the vanquished merely changed places, with the important difference that the former fell to quarreling among themselves over the way to deal with Perón's followers. One group, led by the armed forces (particularly the navy) and seconded by the conservative political and business community, favored a thorough purge of Argentine society, hoping to extinguish Peronism as a political force. The other, made up of sections of the Radical party and the Left, sought to co-opt Perón's followers and harness them to a new majority. Thus the leading Radical politician of the 1950s, Arturo Frondizi, struck a deal with the exiled Perón to re-legalize his party if the latter supported his presidential bid in 1958. For keeping his promise in 1962, however, Frondizi was deposed by the armed forces.

The following year new elections were held in which political exclusions were so complete that Dr. Arturo Illia, a Radical from a more rigidly anti-Peronist branch of the party, limped into office with a mere 23 percent of the vote. When he was deposed in 1966 by a military coup, many Peronists and anti-Peronists joined hands to applaud. On the other hand, the new military regime, the so-called Argentine Revolution, quickly divided between "liberals" (that is, conservatives) and "nationalists" (that is, fascistoid Catholics and their military allies). Meanwhile, the vast majority of Argentines—Peronist, Radical, and independent—went unrepresented.

Between 1966 and 1973 Argentine society underwent what can only be called "re-Peronization." The causes were several. Economic deterioration, which actually began in the late Perón period, but accelerated sharply in the 1960s, led many Argentines to confuse the earlier Peronist era with better days, which in fact they were, since they coincided with high agricultural prices following the Second World War. A new student generation emerged which had no memory of the Peronist period and which, not unnaturally, linked the lack of popular representation with the poor performance of the economy. And the exiled leader—

now in Madrid—demonstrated a remarkable capacity to be all things to all people. In general, by the early 1970s Perón subsumed all of the anti-status quo elements in the country: to Catholics he represented opposition to the increasing secularization of society; to conservatives, the last, best hope to restore order and greatness to Argentina; to the young, particularly the youthful left, the Argentine version of a socialist revolution.

Quite obviously, Perón could not possibly be all of these things simultaneously—except in exile. By 1972-73 the military recognized that sooner rather than later elections would have to be held, and though they designed the rules to prevent Perón from presenting a candidacy of his own, he outmaneuvered them by naming a loyal subordinate, Héctor Cámpora, to stand in for him. Shortly after his victory, Cámpora resigned; new elections were held; and Perón was elected president of Argentina for the third time with 60 percent of the vote.

Perón's final period of power (1973-74) was brief and turbulent, characterized by growing difficulties between the aging chief executive and the left wing of his own party, which had already begun to mesh with the guerrilla movement. After his death, his spouse María Estela ("Isabel"), who had been elected with him as his vice president, assumed the presidential office, but was increasingly dependent upon sinister advisers. Moreover, she lacked Perón's magic, so that as both internal security and the economy deteriorated rapidly she became the object of considerable popular discontent. Her overthrow by the armed forces two years later was widely supported.

The "process of national reorganization," as the military government of 1976-83 was known, immediately turned its attentions to a full scale counterguerrilla war, which enjoyed considerable popular support. This, combined with an economic policy which vastly overvalued the peso, led to a period of free spending on imported goods and foreign travel which neutralized much potential opposition to the regime. By 1982, however, the economy began to show signs of serious deterioration, leading President General Leopoldo Galtieri to embark upon a military adventure in the South Atlantic—the recuperation of the Malvinas, an archipelago of islands seized from Argentina by the British in the early nineteenth century and thereafter more widely known as the Falklands.

The reconquest of the Malvinas temporarily rescued the government's popularity; Galtieri overnight became the idol of the Argentines, and his regime suddenly reacquired all of the quasi-legitimacy it had enjoyed in its first days. But the defeat of the Argentine armed forces by a hastily assembled British expeditionary force suddenly turned the political tables, and the same crowds which had been wildly cheering the dictator now demanded his resignation. The defeat in the Malvinas war without doubt deprived the military of its will to continue in power, and, in new elections convoked in November 1983, Dr. Raul Alfonsín, a Radical sternly critical of the military, was elected by a strong popular majority.

From this cursory recital of names, dates, and events, two somber facts stand out. First, all military governments in Argentina have enjoyed a kind of quasi-legitimacy in their first days of power, but all have rapidly lost them. Second, no Argentine government was legitimate in the conventional, democratic sense of the term between 1928 and 1946; none were accepted as fully legitimate by most Argentines between 1928 and 1973; and Alfonsín is the first civilian since Hipólito Yrigoyen to come to power by elections in which there were no exclusions.

The prolonged crisis of legitimacy not merely encouraged some to resort to terrorism; it deprived others of the moral resources to extinguish it once it had appeared. Thus, during the government of President Gen. Alejandro Lanusse, an entire legal apparatus was put into place to deal with the terrorist problem; had the administration been democratically elected, such mechanisms could have been employed with minimal damage to civil liberties, as in the case of Italy. As it was, however, the new Peronist government, which came into power in May 1973 through the first free elections in a decade, felt obligated to reverse all acts of its predecessor. Not only was the counterterrorist machinery dismantled, but a blanket amnesty released from Argentine jails many perpetrators of terrorism who resumed their activities almost immediately.

Cosmopolitanism and Provincialism

Argentina is a "European" country in social customs, structure, and aspirations. It is also a melting pot of nationalities—particularly Italian and Spanish, but also French, British, Irish, and Russian Jewish. Unlike the United States, however, these groups do not fully identify with their country of birth and residence, but hold on to what links, however tenuous, they can claim with their ultimate country of origin.[6] An extraordinary number of Argentines continue to maintain family and other ties with the old country, and many young people have studied and traveled there—particularly since the advent of jet travel in the 1960s. There are, of course, many Europes. Like all colonial or quasi-colonial peoples, Argentines have been selective in their adaptation. In general the more positive Western European trends since 1945—political liberalism, market economics, educational reform—have appealed far less than the surviving remnants of prewar culture (Franco's Spain or Gaullist France for the Right), or the revolutionary effervescence associated with the 1968 movement in France, Italy and West Germany (for the Left). In particular, young Argentines studying in Western Europe during the 1960s tended to come under the influence of Marxism, and those who spent time in Italy were exposed to one of the most creative and energetic terrorist movements of modern times.[7]

The relationship between Argentine and European terrorism is something more than literary and platonic; as Claire Sterling has pointed out, both the Montoneros and the People's Revolutionary Army (ERP) had extensive overseas connections. As early as 1971 the ERP was represented at a terrorist conference held in a Jesuit college in Florence, which included representatives of sixteen movements including the Irish Republican Army, the Basque ETA, and the Palestinians.[8] Five years later police in Argentina raided one of the ERP's safehouses and discovered a document revealing a plan to launch a "Europe Brigade" in order to recycle Argentine terrorism at one of the points of origin. For their part, the Montoneros were trained by the Basque ETA, who landed in Cuba in the early 1970s and later fanned out to South America.[9] At times the Montonero leadership operated from abroad, shifting headquarters from Rome, to Madrid, Mexico City, and Havana, and then back.[10]

It is entirely possible that even without these linkages Argentine terrorism would have assumed much the same configuration as it did. Certainly the Montoneros and the ERP were *sui generis* in inspiration and ideology, perhaps taking from foreigners certain techniques, but not answering in any way to foreign control. Yet the more pathological features of European society fit neatly into Argentina precisely because the country experienced little institutional development after the 1930s. Indeed, many visitors to the country in the 1960s and 1970s noted that obsolete issues that once agitated prewar Europe (political pluralism, the rights of religious and racial minorities, secularization of education, and women's rights) had miraculously survived in Argentina. Similarly, it was the Italy of the 1930s, not the 1960s, which the Argentine authorities ultimately copied to suppress terrorism, sacrificing in the process representative political institutions and an independent judiciary. At the same time, the terrorist Left operated on assumptions about the accessibility of state power that would have been more appropriate to anarchists and anarcho-syndicalists in Barcelona or Madrid during the mid-1930s, and eschewed the gradualism that characterized the Spanish transition in the 1970s. Thus it is at least possible that, had Argentine political development not been frozen in 1939-40, the society would have been open to cosmopolitan influences of a more wholesome sort.

Confusion between Left and Right

The lack of democratic continuity in Argentine political development and the evident illegitimacy of most governments since 1930 bred a culture of resentful populism, whose principal themes were xenophobia, anti-intellectualism, and the conviction that constitutions, courts, and the republican system were a conspiracy to prevent the "real" will of the people from being represented. Of course, this was technically true for much of the time.

Exclusion and alienation were the twin points at which all kinds of political ideologies crossed and met. Right-wing Catholics at times shared with left-wing revolutionaries the notion that all foreign influences in Argentine culture and education (most of them from democratic countries) were corrupting. The same, of course, could be said for foreign investment, so that left- and right-wing "anti-imperialism" overlapped. The centrality of the Peronist movement—which in a certain way was a populism, if not a fascism, of left, right, and center all at the same time—meant that antidemocratic currents could meet within the same broad church.[11] Finally, the culture of violence itself tended to blur ideological distinctions in the maelstrom of praxis.

There seems also to have been a process whereby many young men and women trained at Catholic private schools—presumably in the doctrines of sword and cross, if not throne and altar—made the passage from right to left with no perceptible difficulty. Juan José Sebreli, a remarkable Argentine sociologist, points out that the lines between Catholic left and Catholic right became blurred during the 1960s; one characteristic personality, Father Carlos Mujica, "divided his time more or less equally between slum towns where he preached the social Christian revolution and the most elegant circles of the oligarchy, to which he belonged by birth, parentage, and association." Above all, Sebreli notes, Catholicism left indelible marks on the Montoneros, "which endured well into their Marxist phase: irrationality, sectarianism, asceticism, the cult of individual sacrifice for the greater good, a preference for absolutes, a near-longing for death and martyrdom."[12]

The Peculiarly Urban Nature of Argentine Society

During the early 1960s, the Cuban revolution was the dominant model for revolutionary forces in Argentina as it was elsewhere in Latin America. However, unlike Cuba (or Bolivia, Peru, or Guatemala), Argentina possessed no peasant class, which, according to the theories of Che Guevara, was the "motor" of a social revolution in Latin America.[13] The earliest attempts by the guerrilla leader Ricardo Masetti to replicate the Cuban revolution in the province of Salta, near the Bolivian border, ended in disaster. By 1970, however, the revolutionary Left was looking elsewhere for theoretical sustenance: to the writings of Abraham Guillén, a veteran of the Spanish civil war who had settled in Argentina, and to the writings of Alberto Methol Ferré, the "theoretician" of the Tupamaros in neighboring Uruguay.

Argentina is not merely an urban society, but a metropolitan one as well—approximately a third of the country resides in and around Buenos Aires. This made the capital a perfect setting for urban terrorism, in which the guerrillas were indistinguishable from the population as a whole,[14] and could take advantage of the anonymity provided by population density. However, the urban setting also made counterterrorism a matter of systematic police dragnets, rather than endless days slogging in an inhospitable countryside, and deprived the guerrillas of one of their traditional advantages.

The Overproduction of Intellectuals

Higher education in Argentina is provided free of charge by the state, and in an immigrant or immigrant–descended society many families look to the university degree as the logical avenue of social mobility. The result has been huge enrollments at public institutions; during the 1960s, for example, the University of Buenos Aires carried more than 80,000 students on its rolls.

A heavy emphasis on liberal arts and the social sciences (introduced during the Frondizi presidency) resulted in bumper crops of sociologists, social psychologists, and psychoanalysts—most with no conceivable outlet for their talents. The combination of a highly theoretical education, with a heavy Marxist bias, and lack of employment opportunities generated immense frustration. Over time, increasing numbers of university graduates sought an outlet in either individual or collective liberation. Many young professionals underwent psychoanalysis, and in fact Argentina in the 1970s had the largest per capita number of practitioners of any country in the world. Others went on, with or without analysis, to terrorism and direct action.

A Strong Bias against Intellectual Independence

Historically pluralism has ranked low in the hierarchy of Argentine virtues. Power is respected above all things. All governments enjoy a supportive *oficialista* press. Political movements aspire to complete hegemony, including democratic parties like the Radical Civic Union. The lonely dissenter enjoys little respect in a society in which the practical outcome between success and failure is so enormous.

Among other things, this means that Argentines display a "herd instinct" that pushes them from one position to the other almost overnight, with no apparent contradiction. It explains how so many of the same people could favor the government of the Peróns, its overthrow by the military three years later, the counterterrorist campaign, the war in the South Atlantic, and the return to democracy in 1983. It also accounts for the fact that so much of the human rights movement in that country comes from political forces which historically have been somewhat outside the mainstream.

Who Were the Terrorists?

Origins

There were five large terrorist groupings active in Argentina from 1970. They included the People's Revolutionary Army (ERP); the Armed Forces of Liberation (FAL); the Peronist Armed Forces (FAP); the Revolutionary Armed Forces (FAR); and the Montoneros. The ERP was vaguely related to the Fourth (Trotskyist) International; the FAL was Marxist-Leninist and not (initially) Peronist, a schismatic offshoot of the Revolutionary Communist party, one of the many factions into which the Argentine party had divided in the 1960s. Some members of these organizations were trained in Cuba; others were trained by those who had taken courses there. The Montoneros were actually an outgrowth of militant Catholic youth groups, particularly Tacuara, a fascistoid organization active in the early 1960s that later merged imperceptibly with a "revolutionary" Catholic left. By 1973, all of these groups except the ERP had merged with the Montoneros, subsuming their individual doctrinal identities in a praxis of violence which took on a logic of its own.

Whatever their initial ideological orientation, most of the leaders of Argentine terrorism came from mainstream political backgrounds. Fernando Vaca Narvaja's father was deputy governor of Córdoba province in the 1950s; Juan and Julio Storni were related to one of the principal figures of the "Liberating Revolution" of 1955–the Catholic nationalist movement which overthrew Perón. Raúl Mende was the son of a Peronist minister, while Domingo Sosa Barber's father was a provincial minister during the Radical administration of Arturo Illia. Pablo María and Sebastian Llorens came from a similar background, while Sergio Paz Berlin was the son of a wealthy industrialist. Diego Muñiz Barreto, a landowner and Peronist deputy (1973–76) friendly to the Montoneros, had been a technical adviser to the military dictatorship of Juan Carlos Onganía. In effect, then, all of the pathologies of Argentine politics–left, right and center, traditional and avant-garde–met and coexisted in this movement.

Methods

The earliest urban terrorist organizations in Argentina probably received some resources from abroad, but by the early 1970s they were entirely self-sufficient, usually financed by bank robberies or kidnappings of Argentine or foreign businessmen who were ransomed for huge sums. For example, the Born brothers, heirs to the vast Bunge y Born cereal fortune, yielded their abductors $60 million, the largest single ransom ever paid anywhere in the world. In short order the Montoneros were generating so much income that they had their own brokers investing on Wall Street, with interest payments from their accounts averaging as much as $130,000 a month.[15] It has been rumored as well that David Graiver, an Argentine financier who disappeared in a mysterious plane crash in Mexico in 1980, was the "banker" for the Montoneros in New York and Brussels.

While some of the resources generated by ransom were used periodically to distribute (with great flourish) food, clothing, and medicine in the slums of Buenos Aires and other Argentine cities, most of the money raised by ransom was invested in overtly political activities. For example, in 1973 the long-defunct Argentine daily *El Mundo* was revived by ERP financiers. The Montoneros owned *Noticias,* and it is even possible that they held a major interest in the most serious Argentine newspaper of them all, *La Opinión,* unbeknownst to its publisher, Jacobo Timerman, whose business partner was David Graiver.

Between 1970 and 1973 the Montoneros and the ERP were known largely for what Timerman has rightly called "the eroticism of violence."[16] First, there was the murder of individuals thought to be standing in the way of a truly "revolutionary" trend within the Peronist movement, such as union leaders Augusto Vandor (1969), José Alonso (1970), and José Rucci (1973) Second, there were "executions" of individuals for shock or symbolic value, most notably former President Pedro Eugenio Aramburu (1970). Third, there were attacks on members of the military establishment or their families, intended to undermine their morale and willingness to bear the costs of remaining in power. For example, the wife of the paraplegic son of President General Alejandro Lanusse (1970–73) perished through a letter bomb. Fourth, foreign diplomats were abducted and military establishments or prisons temporarily seized in order to obtain the release of incarcerated comrades. Fifth, bombs were planted in public places where the well-to-do tended to gather, an updated version of the earlier Russian anarchist doctrine of "the propaganda of the deed." Finally, the guerrillas sought direct confrontation with the armed forces, convinced that by selective encounters and assassinations they could destroy the latter's capacity to sustain the political structure.

In retrospect it seems remarkable that a movement which probably never amounted to more than four to six thousand persons (even this number is controversial) could seriously entertain thoughts of seizing political power in its own right. Nonetheless, in 1972 and 1973 it acted as if this was only a matter of willpower, directly assaulting army and navy installations, killing officers and enlisted men in the process. The Montoneros were particularly active in the northern province of Tucumán, a part of which it succeeded in actively controlling for more than a year.[17]

Moreover, for a few weeks in mid-1973, when Dr. Héctor Cámpora was serving as a presidential stand-in for Juan Perón, it was possible to contemplate taking over the government by infiltrating existing institutions. Cámpora's interior minister Estéban Righli was widely rumored to have close ties to the Montoneros; one of his first acts was to declare a blanket amnesty for convicted terrorists then serving sentences in Argentine prisons. At the same time, the state-controlled national television network evidently came under the control of the revolutionary Left, and it appeared that the national school system might do so as well. Once Perón himself returned to Argentina and to power, this trend was immediately reversed, leading to an open break between Perón and the Montonero leadership in 1974; a new round of terrorist violence followed in the weeks and months after the president's death and the shaky succession of his widow.

One final point: by mid-1975 many people had become afraid to go out at night in Buenos Aires and other major Argentine cities. The sense of insecurity was overwhelming, trust in major government institutions and particularly in the security forces was at an all-time low, since many perceived (not inaccurately) that the military was deliberately allowing things to get out of hand so that when it returned to power it would be with broad popular support. In this sense, the terrorists succeeded in half of their agenda—undermining an elected, civilian government, however incompetent and corrupt. But their assumption that the military's reluctance to move against them with full force was due to fear or even supposed ideological affinities proved to be a grave error. Once Isabel Perón was placed under house arrest, they felt the full blast of forces the army had kept in reserve.

Who Were the Counterterrorists?

Origins

The counterterrorist offensive was, as one might expect, initially the responsibility of the armed forces and federal police. What made the Argentine case unusual was the fact that there was no apparent centralization of effort; instead, the country was divided into geographical and functional "security zones," each under the command of a different branch of the service. Among other things, this meant that different policies prevailed in different zones; there was considerable interservice rivalry; some victims were spared because they (or their family) had contacts within the particular branch which conducted sweeps in their zone, while others perished for the lack of them.

In addition, during the presidency of Juan and Isabel Perón, the Ministry of the Interior, the labor unions, and the Ministry of Social Welfare were involved in antiterrorist activity, which necessarily overlapped with other agendas favored by the "traditionalist" leadership of the Peronist party. These included elimination of left-wing and dissident Peronists within the movement, particularly within the Peronist Youth. Since some of these were, in fact, actively involved with urban guerrilla activities, two tasks were accomplished at once.

To add to the confusion, over the years the Ministry of the Interior and police periodically recurred to "parallel" (that is, extraofficial) formations of the police. Some of these overlapped imperceptibly with Argentina's criminal underworld; others with labor unions or shady business operations; others with extreme right-wing political groups. Since not much is known about these except for the fact of their existence, it is difficult to say how important a role they played during either the Perón government (1973–76) or the "process" (1976–83). The important point is that it was never possible to demarcate clearly areas of responsibility, even when the counterterrorist offensive was in full tilt.

Methods

Perhaps the most important feature of the antiterrorist sweep, or "dirty war" (1974–1979), was its covert nature. The Argentine military were much impressed with the international ostracism to which their Chilean counterparts had been subjected after the coup in that country in 1973 and sought to avoid the same fate by proceeding in secret. As the report of the National Commission notes, "no kidnapping was ever stopped, not a single detention center was ever located, there was never news of those responsible being punished for any of the crimes." Argentina was "engulfed by an ominous silence."[18]

This was made possible in large part by the conduct of the Argentine press, which, with the exception of the English-language Buenos Aires *Herald*, exercised rigorous self-censorship, and by widespread public complacency. Many Argentines—not wholly without reason—regarded the repression as distasteful but inevitable and necessary.[19] Though thousands of families were affected by "disappearances," the matter never became a burning public issue until after the military had been humiliated on the field of battle. In fact, public opinion surveys throughout the period showed that only a small minority of Argentines regarded human rights as an important issue, even within those sectors of the population disproportionately affected by "disappearances"—students and labor.

In an environment in which there were no restraints—either on the part of the judiciary or public opinion—what started out as a counterterrorist drive inevitably acquired wider dimensions. Some military and police officials took advantage of the situation to enrich themselves with the property of their victims. Others saw the campaign as an opportunity to eliminate not merely terrorists but people who happened to figure in their address books. The line disappeared not merely between suspicion and guilt, but between presumed guilt and presumed guilt by association.

In addition, the counterguerrilla offensive made it possible to settle outstanding political and cultural scores. As James Neilson, editor of the Buenos Aires *Herald* has written, "Many [victims], it is clear, were merely people in such suspect professions as journalism, psychology, or university education—people whom the men in charge of the government's antiterrorist squads believed, at a time of high hysteria, were the "intellectual authors of terrorism."[20] These suffered far out of proportion to the actual number of their colleagues who actually participated, in various action groups, impoverishing still further the country whose intellectual capital had been depleted by decades of military rule, Peronist anti-intellectualism, and budgetary neglect.

In a certain sense, the "dirty war" was the final installment of a long campaign the Argentine conservative community and military have waged against their adversaries since at least 1930. But whereas earlier military coups were concerned with overthrowing specific civilian governments (Yrigoyen, Frondizi, Illia), the "process" was intended to alter permanently Argentina's political and cultural landscape. In spite of the allegations of the National Commission on Disappeared Persons, and even of some of the army officers cited in its report, it is clear that no counter-revolutionary doctrine needed to be imported. What is more, had the armed forces met with greater success either in the management of the Argentine economy or the recuperation of the Malvinas Islands, it is likely that they would have succeeded in transforming the nation's political foundations.

Just what Argentina might have looked like under those circumstances is as difficult to say as what it might have resembled had the Montoneros or the ERP seized power. Even within the armed forces and their civilian allies there was (and is) no agreement on the kind of country Argentina should be—whether "liberal," that is, open to the world as a partner in the Western community, or "nationalist," that is, withdrawn behind a spiteful curtain of self-absorption[21]. As it was, the country had to pass through a crucible of both terrorism and counterterrorism before any democratic synthesis was possible. In any event, it is difficult to see how it might have otherwise occurred.

Long-term Implications for Argentine Politics

From the very beginning, Argentina's military government (1976–83) was faced with a dilemma entirely of its own making. Because it proceeded against terrorism without the slightest reference to the rule of law, a graceful exit from power at some future date was utterly impossible.[22] This explains why, at a moment when the economy was rapidly deteriorating and serious discussions with the opposition should have been the order of the day, President General Leopoldo Galtieri chose instead to embark on a military expedition in the South Atlantic. Had Great Britain possessed a different prime minister, the gamble might have worked. As it was, what appeared to be one of the strongest military governments in Latin America collapsed within a matter of days. Nonetheless, some of the problems created by Argentina's bloody decade have survived into the current period of democratic government.

In the first place, it has not been possible to fix full moral and personal responsibility for the events. Though the present government is Radical, the Peronist party remains the largest single political force in the country, and its cooperation is essential if democratic institutions are to survive. For their part, the Peronists obviously have no great interest in looking too closely into events which occurred on their watch (1973-76), nor in exploring the relationship between the armed forces, the trade unions, and other agencies who worked together in the past.

Nor is the matter much simpler with regard to the armed forces themselves. Though the Alfonsín government has brought the commanders-in-chief of the armed forces to justice, it cannot go much further short of disbanding the military establishment itself. This explains why it proposed "full-stop" legislation to the Congress, setting an early terminal date for victims and relatives of victims to file charges in the federal courts. As it is, there have been several minor military uprisings, including some promoted by younger officers—many of them combat veterans of the Malvinas war—who oppose the allegedly supine attitude of their superiors toward the government.

For its part, the Argentine human rights community and its allies abroad have no particular interest in closing out investigations and further judicial action on past abuses. Quite apart from the fact that so far only a tiny fraction of the guilty have even been brought to trial, this is the only conceivable issue which the Argentine left can hope to use to advance its other agendas. Given the constraints of the political system and of military-civilian relations, it is likely that the issue of "disappearances" will continue to bedevil Argentine politics and whichever party wins the 1989 elections.

Finally, an important minority of Argentines—perhaps 20 percent—view with a certain cynicism the human rights policies of the present Argentine government, since it has brought to trial only one terrorist, Montonero leader Mario Firmenich, extradited from Brazil in 1984.[23] A new organization, Families and Friends of the Victims of Terrorism, has placed frequent advertisements in the press to protest what it regards as a one-sided approach by the government and, particularly, by the National Commission on Disappeared Persons. The latter attempted to finesse this charge in its report by asserting that "it was not our task to look into the crimes committed by those terrorists," and that, in any event, "none of the relatives of the victims of that earlier terror approached us, because those people were killed rather than "disappeared."[24]

On balance, then, the Argentine experience with terror and counterterror has inflicted wounds upon that society which will take many years to heal. Nonetheless, something positive must be said about the capacity of the political system to face up to this legacy, in however limited a fashion.[25] Without doubt it has reversed a long-standing tendency for political forces in Argentina to seek an understanding with the military rather than bargain frankly with their rivals and counterparts. It has convinced a younger generation of Argentines that anything is better than military dictatorship. It has strengthened the country's prestige and credibility internationally. And it has set the stage for a serious revival of the republican tradition, one which once distinguished Argentina among Latin American nations, and may yet do so again.

Notes

1. Human *Rights Practices in Countries Receiving U. S. Security Assistance*, 95th Congress, First Session (Washington, DC, 1977), 101.
2. *Nunca Más* (London, 1986), 10. It should be noted that this report has inspired a response, entitled *Definitivamente–Nunca Más: La otra cara del informe de la* CONADEP (Buenos Aires, 1985).
3. *Country Reports on Human Rights Practices for 1979*, 96th Congress, Second Session, joint Committee Print (Washington, DC, 1980), 239.
4. *Nunca Más*, 5, 10.
5. Ibid., 6.
6. This includes the Argentine Jewish community, which is more actively Zionist than its American counterpart. This was obviously not the case

with those Jews who—somewhat out of proportion to their actual numbers—participated in the terrorist movement; like their predecessors in czarist Russia, they saw revolutionary Marxism as a larger identity within which they could finally belong to the Argentine national community.

7. It is perhaps worth noting here that a small number of students from right-wing and Catholic homes went to Spain on scholarships from Franco's *Instituto de Cultura Hispánica*. According to one informant, they came back "vomiting stupidities about the church, the army, and tradition." Some of course eventually ended up working as civilians in the military government of 1976–83, providing a gloss of ideology to the entire repressive sweep.

8. *The Terror Network* (New York, 1981), 44.

9. Ibid., 98.

10. Pablo Guissiani, *Montoneros: La soberbia armada* (Buenos Aires, 1984), 67.

11. One Montonero intellectual once told Pablo Guissiani that "the Germans, after all, were not far wrong in voting for Hitler, since Hitler, after all, raised genuinely popular banners." Ibid., 151.

12. *Los deseos imaginarios del Peronismo* (Buenos Aires, 1983), 170.

13. In *Guerrilla Warfare*, Brian Loveman and Thomas M. Davies, Jr., eds. (Lincoln, NE, 1985).

14. Costa-Gavras's motion picture *State of Siege* (1970), based on the Uruguayan experience but obviously similar in many ways to Argentina, emphasizes the "ordinariness" of the Tupamaros. In one unforgettable scene we are shown block wardens of the movement, who include not only students and intellectuals but also housewives and even an Army officer.

15. Richard Gillespie, *Soldiers of Perón: Argentina's Montoneros* (Oxford, 1982), 180–83, 252.

16. *Prisoner without a Name, Cell without a Number*, Toby Talbot, tr. (New York, 1981), 14. "We had to do it," a guerrilla leader confessed to a friend after the assassination of labor leader José Rucci. "Our people were going soft in their office jobs. From time to time they have to be rescued by putting them back into military action." Guissiani, *Montoneros: La soberbia armada*, 49.

17. Tucumán was subsequently the scene of "Operation Independence," the bloodiest example of repression anywhere in Argentina after 1976.

18. *Nunca Más*, p. 3.

19. M. E. Aftilión et al., *Qué nos pasa a los argentinos?* (Buenos Aires, 1985), pp. 83–84.

20. "Argentina: The Process and the Puzzle," *Encounter*, January 1981.

21. See James Neilson's reflections on this point, loc. cit.

22. Dr. Angel Robledo, defense minister in the last cabinet of President Juan Perón, remarked to me in 1983 that in 1978 he told some of his high-ranking contacts in the military that the moment was opportune to promulgate a blanket amnesty for both sides—terrorist and counterterrorist. "Instead," he remarked, "intoxicated with the arrogance of power, they chose to put the matter off. And now you see where they are."

23. At this writing (fall 1988) Fernando Vaca Narvaja is awaiting sentencing.

24. *Nunca Más*, p. 6.

25. We can never be reminded too often that the Nuremburg precedent is not wholly applicable here, since the Argentine authorities were not liberated from their responsibilites by invading armies, but were forced to confront the issue *motu propio*.

19

The Falklands Conflict Revisited

In the dawn hours of 2 April 1982, a task force of Argentine soldiers and marines landed on the Falkland Islands—an archipelago some three hundred miles off the coast of southern South America. The islands, referred to on Argentine maps as the Islas Malvinas, had been continuously occupied by British authorities and settled by British nationals for nearly two hundred years but claimed by Argentina for at least as long. Logically, their status occupied a prominent place on the agenda of Anglo-Argentine relations, and litigation over their ultimate disposition had been under way in one form or another since the late 1960s. Nonetheless, the event itself—the seizure or "recuperation" of the islands by force—was totally unexpected.

It is not difficult to see why. Argentina had not fought a war in more than a hundred years, and Britain had been steadily divesting itself of its fleet and its overseas responsibilities for nearly two generations. The Falklands were—in the words of one British official—"the bin ends of empire." How could possessions so small, so remote, so inhospitable, even be worth fighting about? It reminded more than one political cartoonist of Gilbert and Sullivan's *HMS Pinafore*. Nonetheless, there was nothing comic-opera about the war or its outcome. The British mustered an expeditionary force of soldiers, sailors, airmen, and Royal Marines in record time, dispatched it halfway around the world, then met and defeated the occupying force—all things widely believed to be beyond their capability. Both sides lost ships and men—the Argentines, the cruiser *Belgrano*; the British, the battleship HMS *Sheffield*.

The political costs were no less dramatic, though different in quality and kind. The Thatcher government, considered in deep political trouble, was reelected shortly thereafter in a burst of

British patriotic fervor, consolidating what has subsequently become an extraordinary hold on power. The ruling junta in Argentina collapsed, and its leader, General Leopoldo Galtieri, was brought up on criminal charges by a democratic government elected the following year. General Alexander Haig, Jr., the U.S. secretary of state who attempted to mediate between the British government and the Argentina junta, lost his job. With him went the policy of "quiet diplomacy," or as some would have it, collusion with South American dictators to meet the threat to U.S. security in Central America.

These are fairly significant outcomes for a small war in an out-of-the-way place; yet, until recently, the conflict itself has been treated largely as a historical curiosity, rather than a crisis that illuminates some of the important strategic and political issues of our time. This deficiency has now been remedied in large part by the publication in Great Britain of *The Little Platoon: Diplomacy and the Falklands Dispute*,[1] by prize-winning BBC journalist Michael Charlton, best known to American readers for his earlier books, *The Eagle and the Small Birds* (1987) and (with Anthony Moncrieff) *Many Reasons Why: The American Involvement in Vietnam* (1978).

Like *Many Reasons Why*, *The Little Platoon* draws upon radio interviews done for a series of eight programs for BBC's Radio Three, reincorporating much material that had to be excised to meet time constraints. Charlton spoke not only with a vast range of British personalities and policymakers, but interrogated key American and Argentine authorities in Washington and Buenos Aires. The result is a remarkably multifaceted study, a book that rises considerably above parochial or monographic interest, casting much new light on British defense policy, British domestic politics, and Anglo-American relations. It also gives us a much clearer notion of Argentine motivations and puts to rest several myths about the war.

The Roots of Conflict

Charlton characterizes the Falklands War as the logical outcome of a situation in which Britain could not make up its mind—with regard both to its world role and between the continental and maritime schools of strategy. It is the story, too, of a nation whose goals were at cross-purposes with its resources, or rather, its willingness to expend resources. It illustrates, more than anything else, what modern democracies are capable of in wartime when they possess the requisite national will. In that regard at least, Britain's experience has considerable relevance for the United States—in Central America, the Persian Gulf, and elsewhere.

In effect 2 April 1982, constitutes the point of convergence of two intersecting lines. One of these was British retrenchment overseas, a process that began in the 1950s and accelerated in the following decade. In 1966 the Labor government of Harold Wilson decided that there would be no more strike carriers, and—in the words of Admiral Lord Lewin[2]—"successive governments had told us that 'never again' would we be called upon to fight a limited war, without allies, outside the NATO area, or to fight a war outside the range of shore-based air support." Within this context, Britain's abandonment of its naval base at Simonstown, South Africa, and the retirement of its South Atlantic squadrons removed the principal deterrent to an Argentine invasion. As Admiral Sir Henry Leach[3] told Charlton, "Thereafter...Britain had been relying increasingly on bluff in the South Atlantic. Nothing remained to forestall Argentina from taking the islands if her ambition was not satisfied by negotiation."

Ironically—in light of subsequent events—the Thatcher government carried this policy even further, driven by a determination to reduce budget deficits. The 1981 defense review cut so deeply into Britain's naval strength that "if the Falklands crisis had occurred let us say two years later," Sir Henry Leach recalls, "*Invincible* would have gone, *Hermes* would have been scrapped.... I doubt we could have expedited the in-service state of *Ark Royal* sufficiently." In such circumstances, he told Charlton, "I would not have advised the operation.... It would not have been a practical proposition. It would have been suicidal."

It is not surprising, then, that since the late 1960s the British had been conducting talks with successive Argentine governments with a view to altering the status of the islands. All of this took place in an atmosphere of cordiality and goodwill hard to imagine today. Diplomat Robin Edmonds[4] reminded Charlton, however, that "the Argentines, figuratively if not literally, are our oldest friends in the subcontinent. They were in many ways our best friends."

General Juan Perón, living in exile in Madrid (but still the most important figure in Argentine politics), privately assured the British ambassador there that, while recuperation of the islands was important, he was in no particular hurry. Nicanor Costa Méndez, Argentine foreign minister (1966-69),[5] left the Foreign Office people who met with him in the summer and autumn of 1968 with the impression that "we were all looking ahead to decades, not years. It was all very relaxed; a normal, civilized, and long-term diplomatic negotiation."[6] What was contemplated, nonetheless was—again, in the words of Lord Chalfont—that there would, one day, be a "final settlement which would recognize Argentina's sovereignty over the islands from a date to be agreed." This concession to principle had already been made in the Memorandum of Understanding that guided the talks—though the British public did not learn of it until later.

The other line was the resistance of the 2,000-odd islanders to any change in their status, a resistance that found remarkable resonance within Britain itself. For the Argentines, the issue pure and simple was decolonization—expressed, however, in purely geographic terms. For the British political public, however, it was self-determination, no more no less. The idea of turning British nationals over to a foreign power expressly against their wishes—a power, moreover, as unappealing to local tastes as the Argentine—aroused the widest range of opposition. This was what the Foreign Office people discovered when the subject eventually reached the floor of Parliament.

Argentine accounts of the dispute make much of the "Falkland Islands lobby" in Britain—that is, representatives of the Falkland Islands Company, chief employer and sole concessionaire of the archipelago. Such a lobby did, in fact, exist, and it cast a remarkably long shadow over British policy. But, as Charlton's book shows, its influence rested upon an extraordinarily wide base of political support. While the lobby's foot soldiers in Parliament tended, predictably, to come from the right wing of the Conservative Party, it could enlist some support from Fabian socialists, "who saw in the evolving Commonwealth a secular agency for good," and from environmentalists who had little confidence in the stewardship of Latin American governments over natural resources. Charlton reminds us, too, that the lobby was also linked to "great names that stirred the memory, like the last of the great imperial adventurers, Scott of the Antarctic, an Agamemnon dead on the ice and a reminder of the moral quality in the British contribution to the Antarctic—unprofitable, but magnificent.

Its constituency included advocates of British economic expansion into the Antarctic, including some who convinced themselves that the South Atlantic continental shelf might be "the largest remaining unexploited oilfield in the world"[7]an argument (whatever its merits) bound to compel attention after OPEC declared a fourfold increase in energy prices in 1973. It also mobilized the maritime strategists, whose argument was summarized by Sir John Biggs-Davison, MP:[8] "There were two decisive naval actions, in two world wars, fought in those waters." Should Panama be put out of commission in another world war, "it was...vital that the Falkland Islands should be in reliable hands."

Moreover, the Falklands issue touched a particularly sensitive nerve in British domestic politics—the Irish question, or rather, what remained of it in Ulster. As Biggs-Davison explained, if the "Kelpers" (that is, the Falkland Islanders) could be off-loaded onto the Argentines, it was only a matter of time before Protestants in Northern Ireland found themselves in the same boat. His concerns were shared in a slightly different way by Peter Shore, then Labor's shadow foreign secretary, who believed that in both Ulster and the Falklands Britain had the obligation "not [to] abandon its own people, even if its power has been greatly reduced."

But, of course, the most compelling argument against a change in the status of the islands—the one to which the islanders and their supporters could always return—was the simple fact that those most nearly concerned did not want it and could not be persuaded to endorse anything that seemed to lead to it. Nor did this seem unreasonable to British politicians or to the British public generally, once they became aware of the issue. "This is British sovereign territory," Biggs-Davison told Charlton. "It is inhabited by a population that is certainly more British than the population of London. There is no reason therefore why those people should not be allowed to live their lives in peace, and it was the duty of any British government to defend that right." The fact that Argentina was under military dictatorship during much of the 1960s and 1970s—and in the late 1970s, under a particularly hideous form of dictatorship—was an argument the Tories could deploy with telling effect in the Labor and Liberal benches. "By what right," asked Sir Bernard Braine,[9] "did a fascist dictatorship next door demand that sovereignty over [the islanders] should be transferred?"

The Diplomatic Labyrinth

Actually, the Foreign Office had considered this problem rather thoroughly prior to launching discussions with the Argentines in 1966 and 1967. "The simple fact of the matter is," Chalfont explained, "that you really cannot, in the long run, conduct the foreign policy of an important international power according entirely to the interests, and certainly not to the wishes, of a couple of thousand inhabitants of some islands in the South Atlantic." Unless sovereignty was seriously negotiated, and ceded in the long term, "we [were] likely to end up in a state of armed conflict with Argentina." Perhaps so, but this was not the way the world looked to people outside the Foreign Office.

The islanders themselves, alerted that a change was about to take place, appealed to Parliament. A full-scale debate in December 1968 sent the government and the Foreign Office into full retreat. When he tried to defend the negotiations, Foreign Secretary Michael Stewart was howled down in the House of Commons—an experience neither he nor his party ever forgot. In the process Stewart was forced to promise that in all future consideration of the islands, the wishes of the inhabitants would remain paramount. "After a bit it became almost impossible to say anything to the islanders," British diplomat Henry Hankey[10] complained, "because you risked being accused of trying to throw the game away"—a charge that could have immediate political consequences at the constituency level. That is the way matters remained up to the day war broke out.

Between December 1968 and April 1982 the Foreign Office attempted to split the difference between domestic politics and the interests (as they saw it) of British foreign policy. Basically this called for side-stepping the sovereignty issue, or approaching it by radical indirection. The Foreign Office encouraged the Argentines to approach the islanders and invite them to the mainland, where they could meet others of their origin and culture who had lived uninterruptedly (and for the most part, happily) under Argentine rule for decades. A communications agreement established regular air service between Port Stanley, capital of the archipelago, and Buenos Aires, made available to the islanders for the first time sophisticated medical treatment, education for their children in British schools, or merely fresh fruits and vegetables. The plan to link the islands to ease the islanders into a relationship with the Argentines proceeded apace. But the political ends sought—to make them want to be Argentines—stayed securely out of reach.

This was followed by a British proposal in 1974 for a condominium—that is, joint sovereignty, an arrangement presumably similar to the one Britain and Egypt had once shared (on very unequal terms) in the Sudan. When this failed to elicit Argentine interest, a commission under Lord Shackleton proposed instead joint economic development of the islands and the southwestern Atlantic. In other words, as Ted Rowlands[11] put it, to *divide* sovereignty "and split it up as between resources and people." The Argentines were unenthusiastic about this idea; moreover, the Shackleton report qualified the recommendation by requiring the assent of the islanders, which all but buried it. The British government was temporarily rescued from having its bluff called on this particular by the collapse of the government of President Isabel Perón in March 1976.

The following year the Foreign Office came up with what Charlton calls "the most elegant solution of all"—a leaseback arrangement. This combined the idea of British administration (what the islanders wanted) under the fiction of residual Argentine sovereignty (what the Argentines claimed). When this proposal was finally presented to Parliament in 1981, the reaction was predictably violent; as Richard Luce[12] later put it, "the Foreign Office could negotiate, it seemed, with almost everyone except the vigilant body of opinion in its own Parliament."

Sovereignty proved indivisible because, strange as it might seem to diplomats and international civil servants, people in the Falklands cared deeply about symbols and about their own identity—far more, in fact, than they did for any conceivable economic incentive. As Rowlands discovered on a visit to the islands in 1977, the inhabitants "just wanted to be left alone...we were fighting for their right to decline, not for the right [to] develop.... It was their right and desire to be themselves." He went on to tell Charlton that they would not have minded, I think, Argentina developing resources, but they did not want them [the Argentines] strutting around the island[s]. That was a major interference in their style of life. It had a profound effect on my views about leaseback; it gives you the right to strut about and put up flags.

The View from Buenos Aires

The Argentines, of course, cared no less about symbols; indeed, in many ways it was all they cared about. In the words of Oscar Camilion, who served the junta briefly as foreign minister in 1981, the issue was not merely one of sovereignty, but "in some ways also of...dignity....It is maybe, metaphysics. From the point of view of the British it was just a far-away territory. It was not a problem of the essence, of the being, of the state, as it was for Argentina."

This radically different view of the problem tended to greatly distort perceptions; as Charlton's interviews reveal, more than once the Argentines misread British intentions (or capabilities).They were intimately familiar with the Foreign Office viewpoint, and they presumed it to represent the British government in every meaningful way. This notion was underscored by the trend lines in British defense budgets, particularly the 1981 estimate. As Camilion's successor Nicanor Costa Méndez put it, "My first conclusion [upon reading the latter] was that either Britain was losing interest in the zone, or because of the defence budget, Britain was compelled to leave the zone and pay less attention to the area. We thought that these economic reasons would at least offset the power of the Falkland Islands lobby."

Other signs seemed to corroborate this view—the withdrawal from the area of the ice patrol vessel HMS *Endurance*, a bill working its way through Parliament in 1981 that would deny the islanders certain rights of British citizenship, and the intended closing of the British Antarctic survey, the only British presence in South Georgia, one of the islands in the Falklands chain. The Argentines were also strongly impressed by the Thatcher government's decision in the same year to cut its losses in Rhodesia. They failed to grasp, perhaps understandably, that in terms of Conservative Party politics, *that* particular sacrifice was simply too expensive to be repeated too often.

In a broader sense the Argentine military, particularly the Argentine army, suffered from a kind of folkloric misunderstanding of the British national character—the product, figuratively if not literally speaking, of Bertie Wooster novels and Ealing studio comedies. Possibly they extrapolated too generously from the precipitous economic and social decline of their own British expatriate community, which before the Second World War had been the proudest and most affluent of any outside of India. Certainly in the purely military sphere they appear to have taken no cognizance whatever of the activities of the British army in Northern Ireland, duties that had raised its skill in small-scale infantry operations to superlative levels. Above all, they tended to confuse the relative deterioration of others with an automatic increase in their own capabilities. "They had this view of Britain as a sort of fallen major power," recalled General Vernon Walters, who accompanied Haig to Argentina at the height of the crisis. "At one point one of [the junta members] said to me, 'It is a world in which there are two major powers, and everyone else is equal.'"

Perhaps the biggest error of all was to reach simplistic conclusions from Britain's humiliation at Suez. The Argentines failed, for example, to read the various ways in which that event was playing itself out a quarter century later—in British domestic politics, in American strategic thinking, and in Anglo-American relations. No doubt Suez had inflicted what Julian Arnery[13]calls "a great streak of defeatism" upon the British civil service and establishment. But, he added, the same spirit "did not enter into the gut feeling of the representatives of the British people in the House of Commons."

There is some reason to believe, in fact, that the Suez precedent strengthened rather than weakened the British penchant for unilateralism, at least under certain given circumstances. As Charlton's interviews show, once the Falklands operation began, the British government and naval authorities were determined to carry it to its conclusion regardless of the position of the United States.

Such precautions turned out to be entirely gratuitous. Much soul-searching had taken place on the other side of the Atlantic since 1956, and a strongly "revisionist" attitude toward Suez had gained considerable ground at the level of senior American policymakers. Amery told Charlton that

> I had a very interesting letter from ex-President Nixon...in which he said
> that, looking back, he thought that the American action at Suez had been
> disastrous. It had led not just to the boost it gave to Colonel Nasser, but to

the withdrawal of France and Britain from accepting responsibilities in the rest of the world. He added that he had talked to President Eisenhower, by then ex-President Eisenhower, who had agreed with him.

The Americans, once so anxious to dismantle other people's empires, now "realized...how alone they were in the world after Vietnam, and that without European support it was going to be a very difficult ride. Maybe they have understood this now and the Falklands was the first evidence of it." The Reagan administration seems to have absorbed this lesson very fully: Once the war began, Haig explicitly informed British Ambassador Sir Nicholas Henderson that both he and President Reagan were determined that "whatever attitude they adopted about our resistance, they would not, what they called, 'repeat Suez.'"[14]

The matter was not merely one of American attitudes reshaped by subsequent experience, however, but of new defense arrangements that qualitatively altered the Anglo-American relationship. Since the late 1960s, Britain's adoption of the Polaris submarine led to a unique intimacy in the strategic and intelligence fields, particularly between the two navies. Whereas in 1956 the United States, Britain, and France were seen (and to some extent, saw themselves) as more or less coequal maritime powers, in 1982 the United States had no choice but to go along with the British if it did not want to be "alone...in the world after Vietnam."

Run-up to War

After the leaseback proposal was howled down in Parliament, Sir Anthony Williams, British ambassador in Buenos Aires, urged his government to tell the Argentines that frankly it could not "deliver" the islanders, and therefore could not continue in good faith to negotiate the question of sovereignty. This would have implied heavily fortifying the area against a possible Argentine invasion ("Fortress Falklands"), an expensive proposition that was vetoed, predictably, by the Treasury. Instead, throughout 1981, British diplomats were forced to tread water in their discussions with the Argentines until something turned up. What turned up, Charlton remarks dryly, was the invasion.

The original Argentine plan—as revealed to Charlton by Rear Admiral Carlos Busser—was "to recover the islands with a small force, and leave a small force there." This, according to Costa

Méndez, would have the virtue of breaking diplomatic deadlock; even if it did not lead to an immediate agreement, it would at least activate the talks. The operative assumption was that the British would recognize Argentine restraint for what it was and respond in kind. Or even if it did not, it would be compelled to resume negotiations under pressure from others—the UN Security Council or the United States.

Instead, by invading, the Argentines transformed what in Britain had been a vexing technical question (how to divide sovereignty) into a deeply compelling national cause. To aggravate matters, the same event unleashed a wave of nationalist hysteria of unanticipated dimensions within Argentina itself. The mission of Argentine troops on the islands, originally conceived as an elaborate diplomatic ploy ("'giving a nudge to diplomacy' by landing five hundred troops"[15]), could now be none other than an exercise in outright recuperation of *terra irredenta*. This in turn escalated the potential political costs of failure, whether on the battlefield or at the conference table.

Having miscalculated on the initial British response, Argentine authorities plunged still deeper into a sea of illusions. These, according to the Americans who accompanied Haig to Buenos Aires were, first, the notion ("the absolute conviction," Walters calls it) that in the end the British would not actually fight; or that if they did, that the United States would remain neutral; or, at worst, that it would intervene diplomatically to separate the warring armies and thus protect its new ally from outright defeat on the battlefield.

These assumptions, which sound wildly eccentric today, were slightly less improbable at the time. U.S. relations with Argentina had dramatically improved since Reagan took office in January 1981—part of a new policy toward anti-Communist dictatorships in the Third World subsumed under the title "quiet diplomacy."[16]

There had been much coming and going between Washington and Buenos Aires in the previous months, though virtually all of it was in connection with Central America, where the Argentines were quietly assisting the United States in Nicaragua, Honduras, and El Salvador. If, however, the Falklands were supposed to be some sort of quid pro quo, the Americans remained blissfully unaware of the fact.[17]

The Argentines could perhaps be excused for misjudging their country's value to the United States by Haig's decision shortly after April 2 to mediate between them and the British. Certainly the unusual spectacle of the secretary and his staff—leaving all other pressing matters to subordinates in Washington, triangulating back and forth across the Atlantic in April and May—did nothing to dissuade the Argentine generals from their belief that "there are two major powers, and everyone else is equal." Nonetheless, once the crisis actually began, the Argentines could persist in their comforting notions only by purposely ignoring actual events (the immediate response of the British government, Parliament, and public opinion), as well as repeated disclaimers from Haig himself to the effect that the British would fight, and that if it came to that, the United States would be compelled to support its traditional friend and ally.

Actually, the Argentines were right to perceive a deep ambivalence in both British and American policy. What they failed to see was that *if choices were posed sharply enough*, the dominoes might stack totally against them. That is, by invading the islands in the first place, the junta forced the British to make up their minds how much their honor was worth to them, and the Americans, in turn, to decide how much their alliance with the British was worth to them. These two eventualities were the very ones the Argentines were wholly unprepared, psychologically and materially, to meet.

Was Conflict Avoidable?

Almost to the last days of the crisis, rumors persisted that some sort of diplomatic solution would nonetheless be found. Certainly Haig's team cannot be faulted for lack of trying. The American secretary's problem was, quite simply, that nothing he could come up was acceptable to the Argentines if it did not award them at the conference table what they sought on the battlefield. As Thomas Enders[18] put it, "the Argentine leaders had put themselves in a position from which they believed, and quite possibly they were right, there was no retreat, without the destruction of their regime." Unable to retreat, they were then beaten.

Camilion stated the matter somewhat differently. "The real, critical problem for Argentina," he told Charlton, "was that its minimum goals were never well determined in Buenos Aires. For that reason the negotiations failed." He might just as easily have said that the invasion itself collapsed the difference between minimum and maximum goals, and that therefore—once the battle was joined—there was nothing to negotiate but the surrender of one army to another.

Even today, in Argentina and in liberal-left Britain, many nonetheless cherish the belief that a diplomatic solution ostensibly crafted by President Fernando Belaúnde Terry of Peru failed only because of Prime Minister Margaret Thatcher's decision to sink the Argentine battleship *Belgrano*. Or worse still, that Thatcher ordered *Belgrano* sunk precisely to avoid imminent Argentine acceptance of the Peruvian proposal. Charlton shows that both versions are wholly fictitious.

Actually, the "Peruvian" plan was not really Peruvian at all; it was devised by Haig's team and brokered by Belaúnde at Washington's request. Nor was the British Admiralty apparently aware of it until after the naval engagement in which the *Belgrano* was sunk. Most important of all, Admiralty never requested specific permission from the prime minister to sink the ship. Rather, it asked for a change in the *rules of engagement*, so that the HMS *Conqueror* could off-load British troops, which it could not do, as Lord Lewin puts it, "with a couple of Argie destroyers about, armed with Exocet missiles." No doubt, he admits, this had the effect of sinking the *Belgrano*; "We *hoped* it would be the effect." Anything else would have been a dereliction of duty to his own troops.

These crucial distinctions were later lost in the tangle of partisan politics in Britain, as well as the understandable revulsion in world opinion provoked by the high casualties suffered in that action by the Argentine navy. Lord Lewin himself was appalled; it showed "a remarkable lack of professionalism or preparedness."

> My understanding of the *Belgrano* [he added] is that a large number of the watertight doors were open. They were not at any level of "damage control"; some of the men were in their bunks in underpants and nothing else. I believe that their casualties would have been much less if they had exhibited a higher standard of professionalism. I am sorry to say it, but I think that is so.

Though he himself seems to subscribe to the view that the sinking also torpedoed a promising diplomatic negotiation, Argentine Admiral Gualter Allara, commander of Task Force 79 aboard the aircraft carrier *Veinticinco de Mayo,* nonetheless supports his British colleague. "As far as I'm concerned, from a strictly professional point of view," he told Charlton, "I cannot criticize that action. She [the *Belgrano*] was a ship carrying out a war mission, and this military mission was connected with the conflict."

The Lessons of War

The Falklands conflict was a very old-fashioned war, pitting a European power against a Third World state—precisely the kind of conflict that conventional wisdom since at least Suez had taught us could no longer happen. The fact that it did suggests that a number of apparently outdated notions of international politics continue to be relevant. First, wars can happen for the very same reasons they did a century ago—because of conflicting national aspirations to the same piece of territory. It was frustration with interminable, inconclusive negotiations (helped along by a dose of political opportunism and the illusion that Britain would not fight anyway) that led the Argentines to invade in the first place; and honor and a felt obligation to "kith and kin," not rational cost-benefit analysis, that led the British to respond.

Second, not all issues are subject to diplomatic negotiation; some goods are indivisible, including sovereignty, honor, and credibility, not to mention self-determination. The Foreign Office had no business negotiating what repeated experience had shown it could not reasonably deliver, and the Argentines were naive to think that it could. On the other hand, having realized that it could not surrender sovereignty over the islands, the British government should have been prepared to pursue "Fortress Falklands" and pay for it, as they ended up doing anyway, although only after much blood and cannon had been expended. This demonstrates the third point, which is that costly choices put off now often prove more costly still later on.

Fourth, the unwillingness of a major power to make strategic choices in and of itself is inherently destabilizing. The British determination to have it both ways—to demand the benefits of a maritime strategy while being willing to pay only for a continental strategy—naturally encouraged the Argentines to assume that a military solution to the Falklands problem was feasible. From this perspective, the United States was equally guilty of allowing others to doubt its own priorities, since until forced to do so it tried to artificially balance its obligations toward Western Europe with its aspirations in the Western Hemisphere. The British officials with whom Charlton talked are convinced, at any rate, that "*only* a declaration of support for Britain at the outset might have given Buenos Aires pause."[19]

Fifth, the Falklands War demonstrates that national power remains preeminently a matter of' national will. The fact that the British won a resounding victory should not lure us into thinking that the outcome was inevitable; as a matter of fact, they were forced to surmount enormous odds just to reach the islands, let alone doing battle there. This point about national will cannot be repeated too often these days, when we are being told that "history" (whatever that is) is on the side of Third World dictatorships and that we have no choice but to bend to their will. Actually, once they make up their minds, Western democracies call still be remarkably efficient.

Finally, victory in war often provides its own justification. Without Argentina's defeat on the field of battle, the country might never have returned to electoral democracy. Nor was the political price in Latin America anywhere near as high for the British and the Americans as was predicted at the time. Indeed, the same crowds in Buenos Aires that cheered Galtieri when he seized the islands were baying for his head the day he announced the Argentine defeat, and a month later it was difficult to find anyone in that country who would admit to having favored the military adventure in the first place. The rest of the continent followed suit.

"It was a very bold, firm and decisive action," former Defense Secretary Caspar Weinberger told Charlton, "and it contrasted very much with the many long years in which a great deal of the West, the United States included, had always allowed contemplation of all the things which could go *wrong* to block the course of action." It remains to be seen whether the West—"the United States included"—will absorb the lessons which a small war in a faraway place has the capacity to teach.

Notes

1. Oxford: Basil Blackwell, 1989.
2. Chief of Defense Staff, 1979–1982.

3. Chief of the Naval Staff and First Sea Lord.
4. Head of the Latin American Department, foreign officer, 1966–68; undersecretary, Foreign Office, 1969–1973.
5. And again in 1981–82.
6. Lord Chalfont, minister of state, Foreign Office, 1964–1970.
7. William Hunter Christie, former British diplomat in Argentina; a founder of the Falkland Islands lobby.
8. Vice chairman of the Conservative parliamentary Foreign and Commonwealth Affairs Committee.
9. Parliamentary undersecretary of state for commonwealth affairs, 1962–64. Conservative front-bench spokesman on commonwealth affairs, 1967–1970.
10. Head of American Department, Foreign Office, 1956; assistant undersecretary of state, Foreign Office, 1969–1974.
11. Parliamentary undersecretary of state, Foreign Office, 1975–1976; minister of state, Foreign Office, 1969–1974.
12. Parliamentary undersecretary of state, 1979–1981; minister of state, Foreign Office, 1981–1982.
13. Minister of state, Foreign Office, 1972–74.
14. Charlton, pp. 194–95. Haig confirmed this point to Charlton specifically, p. 167. In predicting U.S. behavior, Costa Mendez took into account not merely Suez, but Washington's response to the Yom Kippur War between Egypt and Israel in 1973—perhaps an even more unfortunate metaphor. Charlton, p. 120.
15. The view of Argentine Navy Commander Admiral Jorge Anaya, as related to Charlton by Admiral Harry Train, U.S. Navy, supreme allied commander, Atlantic, who personally debriefed his colleague for a classified American study of the war. Charlton, p. 119.
16. For a further discussion of this phenomenon as it pertained to Argentina, see Mark Falcoff, *A Tale of Two Policies : U.S. Relations with the Argentine Junta, 1976–83* (Philadelphia, PA: Foreign Policy Research Institute, 1989), especially pp. 37–48.
17. *Caveat: Reagan, Realism, and Foreign Policy* (New York: Macmillan, 1984). p. 262
18. Assistant secretary of state for inter-American affairs, 1981–1983.
19. Charlton, p. 164

Part V

Latins and Europeans

20

The Strange Case of Erich Honecker

Former East German President Erich Honecker set up house-keeping in the Chilean Embassy in Moscow on 11 December 1991–literally hours before the Soviet Union ceased to exist. In so doing, he narrowly avoided immediate extradition to the German Federal Republic. For months, the German government had been clamoring for his return to face charges of political repression and massive abuse of human rights, a prospect which now suddenly seemed possible with the emergence of a new Russian government under Boris Yeltsin.

Indeed, the morning after the Soviet collapse it appeared that the only thing that stood between Germany and Russia was the sturdy defense of the right of diplomatic asylum by a distant South American country. As long as Chile refused to hand Honecker over to the Russian authorities, there was little that could be done. Worse still, the Germans were confronted by the possibility that Honecker might depart Russia under diplomatic protection for Chile, a country where his daughter (married to a Chilean national) was already a resident. (To complicate matters still further, Honecker had originally requested shelter at the Chilean embassy on humanitarian grounds—namely, that he was terminally ill with cancer. To the consternation of his hosts, a subsequent medical examination revealed this claim to be without foundation.)

Thus began one of the most bizarre episodes in recent diplomatic history: the flight of a dictator of a state which no longer existed to another state only to be faced by *its* sudden disappearance. As if that were not enough, the country under whose escutcheon he took shelter—and in which he now proposed to settle—was itself only emerging from the trauma of sixteen years of dictatorship, and was conscientiously attempting to reestab-

lish its own liberal traditions. By the end of May, Honecker remained inside Chile's embassy compound in Moscow, at the center of a major diplomatic crisis between Chile and Germany,
complete with haggling, high-level negotiations, and not-so-veiled
threats to his hosts.

Why Chile?

But why Chile? Why, above all, *this* Chile, ruled by a coalition
of parties deeply committed to respecting human rights at home
and abroad? The answer to that question sheds some fascinating
light on the way the lines of domestic and foreign policy have
become hopelessly confused as the relations between small countries and large ones have become internationalized over the past
generation or so. It also shows how certain cold war themes continue to resonate and disrupt the lines of communication between democracies.

The story begins with the long and complex relationship between Chile and Germany. During the nineteenth century, thousands of Germans emigrated to Chile, often as farmers,
mechanics, or merchants. Their children and grandchildren became engineers, doctors, lawyers, politicians and soldiers, providing much of the backbone of the country's small but vital
middle class. By 1914, Germany was one of the two "model"
countries for Chile (the other being Great Britain). The German
language was taught in schools; some districts of Santiago came
to resemble the Expressionist quarter of old Berlin; the Chilean
army, trained by German officers for several generations, learned
to march with the goosestep, and its officers acquired a version
of the pre-war German uniform, complete with mandarin collar,
which they wear to this date.

Although the primacy of German culture in Chile was steadily
undermined by the growing economic presence of the United
States after 1920, it never entirely disappeared. Not only did it
survive the Nazi period and the postwar collapse, it also flour-
ished anew in the 1950s and 1960s. Of course, to some degree
this was a natural result of the emergence of a stable, prosperous
democratic state in the West after 1949; the German Federal
Republic reopened diplomatic and economic relations with Chile
in the early 1950s. Within a decade West Germany had become

one of the country's more important trading partners, as well as the source of much new investment and technology. More important still, Chile's small but growing Christian Democratic party established crucial links with its West German counterpart. The election of a Christian Democratic government in Chile in 1964 under Eduardo Frei was due in no small part to the training and financial assistance of the West German Christian Democratic Union (CDU).

The postwar division of Germany into two states, one democratic and Western-oriented, the other socialist and Eastern-oriented, produced a bifurcation in the German image in Chile generally, one sharply reflected within the political community. While Bonn became a crucial point on the map for the Christian Democrats, East Berlin became the mecca for the country's large and well-organized Socialist and Communist parties. Indeed, for the Communist party's stylishly edited daily newspaper *El Siglo*, the country of choice during the 1960s and 1970s was not (as one might ordinarily expect) the Soviet Union—or for that matter even Cuba—but *Alemania Democrática* ("where the only privileged people are the children"). No issue of this paper was complete without a photograph of lederhosen-clad "youth leaders" marching happy-faced children through forests of flowers and balloons. There was even a "Chile-Democratic Germany Cultural Institute" in Santiago, complete with concerts, photographic exhibits, and lectures, to compete with the Federal Republic's larger and more fulsomely funded Goethe Institute.

The relationship between the Chilean left and East Germany only intensified in the 1970s and 1980s. During the brief rule of Marxist Salvador Allende (1970–73), East Germany was one of Chile's principal sources of financial and political support. When Allende was overthrown by the armed forces, many leaders of his government and his Socialist party took refuge in East Berlin. (Communists tended to go to Moscow or Prague.) Some of Allende's people, politically inexperienced and little traveled outside of Chile prior to the coup, were appalled by what they found in East Germany, and moved Westward—to Paris or Madrid. For many it was a pilgrimage as much ideological as geographical, producing an important division in Chilean socialism. Others, however, felt completely at home in East Germany, where they were the object of fulsome hospitality. One was Allende's former foreign minister, Clodomiro Almeyda.

Almeyda's Honor

This same Almeyda was the Chilean ambassador who offered Honecker his hospitality when the latter's world was (quite literally) collapsing around him last December. For the ambassador, it was a matter of personal honor—returning the favor to the man who (in his eyes) had saved him from Pinochet's police. Though Almeyda acted out of impulse and entirely on his own, President Patricio Aylwin, a Christian Democrat and an old adversary of communism in any form, nonetheless backed him up to the hilt. At a press conference on the second anniversary of his government (11 March), the president assumed "full responsibility for the decision" to accept Honecker. While the ambassador had acted precipitously, Aylwin admitted, "if I would have been at the embassy at that time, I would have done the same thing."

When a German reporter asked Aylwin why a Chile "which still suffers from the consequences of a dictatorship, does not allow another dictator, who also violated human rights, to be sent to trial," the president responded that "Chile is not defending Mr. Honecker, nor does it intend to save him from anything. We have made this decision based on humanitarian considerations, bearing in mind this person's old age and delicate condition." And he added, "Because we respect even the human rights of those who may have violated human rights, we act according to law. We are seeking a solution in accordance with the laws and our concept of fairness."

The president's remarks not only angered the German government, which presented a heated note of diplomatic protest, but provoked and acrimonious debate at home. Senate President Gabriel Valdés, historically on the left of the Christian Democratic party, told the press that he was frankly unsure "if Honecker is a guest of the government or a guest of Ambassador Almeyda...I would not like to see relations [between] Chile and Germany tarnished by a situation caused by a person who has no links to Chile and whose past is, at the least, politically doubtful." The Party for Democracy, whose leaders are former Allende Socialists, expressed themselves even more directly. Senator Erich

Schnake said that "we believe Honecker must end his prolonged visit to our embassy in Moscow on his own volition and answer the charges his own nation is leveling against him."

Predictably, Almeyda's own Socialist party called for granting Honecker immediate asylum, with the proviso that the German government could then formally request his extradition. Far less predictably however, Chile's two right-wing parties, led largely by former ministers and technocrats of the Pinochet regime, hedged their bets; the Independent Democrat Union (UDI) confined itself to calling for the resignation of Foreign Minister Enrique Silva Cimma, while National Renewal, through Senator Sergio Romero, asserted that Chile "must not accept pressures from either Germany or Russia," and agreed with Almeyda's people that "Honecker must be taken to Chile for our country's courts to rule on a possible extradition request."

Thus the Honecker case split the Chilean political spectrum at oblique angles, dividing the government and also its opposition. Looked at from a German point of view, this was simply inexplicable, and the confusion of the German reporter at President Aylwin's press conference was fully understandable. In fact however, looked at strictly in terms of recent Chilean history, there is a bizarre logic to the entire affair.

"Political Recess"

At the time of his overthrow in September 1973, President Salvador Allende had so polarized Chilean politics that the coup itself was welcomed by a clear majority of the population, including the Christian Democrats and other parties of the center. It quickly became apparent, however, that the armed forces, and particularly the new junta chief General Augusto Pinochet, regarded all politicians as an unmitigated evil. The country therefore entered into nearly a generation of "political recess," which gave Christian Democrats and leaders of the deposed coalition of left-wing parties plenty of time to renew bonds of friendship and solidarity shattered by the traumatic Allende period. Dialogue was promoted partly by Pinochet's rather indiscriminate rough-handling of opponents, but also by the fact that many Allende Socialists went into exile in Western European countries, particularly Spain, Italy, and France, where Socialist governments came to power in the

1980s. The experience had a profound effect on many; for example, Senator Erich Schnake, a former firebreather of the far left, became a protégé of Prime Minister Felipe González of Spain and a model of moderation and good sense. In the mid-1980s many of these "renovated" Socialists founded the Party for Democracy, now one of the key partners in the coalition.

Meanwhile, the Communists moved in a rather different direction: before and during the Allende government they were actually a restraining influence in the Chilean left. But the experience of blanket repression after the coup, years of clandestinity, and the example of successful guerrilla movements in Central America eventually pushed them in an entirely different direction. In 1981, they formally embraced the "violent road" to power, and their armed formations began to rob banks, assassinate government leaders, and blow up electrical pylons. This shift in tactics by the Communists did the moderate opposition a favor; it made it easy for it to reject any form of alliance with the CP, which in turn had the effect of assuaging the concerns of more conservative Chileans, gaining support abroad (particularly in the United States), and even to some extent disarming the Pinochet government. Those Socialists who went instead to East Germany or other bloc nations, including Clodomiro Almeyda himself, took a middle position: while opposing violence, they argued for unconditional inclusion of the Communists in any future government coalition. This allowed them to keep faith with their friends on the farthest left, while at the same time maintaining their place in the democratic opposition.

The Aylwin government, elected in 1989, is thus a coalition of both former pro- and anti-Allende forces, but both committed to moderate, peaceful change and national reconciliation. The old Socialist party is a rather minor partner these days, with a handful of seats in Congress and a few bureaucratic preferments and foreign embassies. The appointment of Clodomiro Almeyda to the embassy in Moscow was seen by many as a form of gilded exile for an old Socialist warhorse: out of sight, out of mind. Or so it seemed...

Splitting the Coalition

The Honecker affair has split the coalition apart: most Christian Democrats are horrified by the government's refusal to dis-

avow Almeyda, but to do so would force it to break with one of
its most disciplined (and reliable) partners. The PPD (Party for
Democracy) feels differently, partly because its leaders have decisively turned their back on Marxism, but also because the case
serves a useful political purpose at home—namely, to prove to
centrist voters who normally vote for the Christian Democrats
that a "renovated" socialism is a trustworthy alternative. The Socialists, for their part, imagine that by proposing asylum (with
the possibility of later extradition proceedings) they can have it
all ways: get the government off the hook (at least temporarily)
with the Germans, prove that the whole business has a simple
"technical" solution, and (counting on the apparently inexhaustible supply of delaying tactics and legalistic recourses normally
available to Chilean justice) assure Honecker that he will never
have to face the courts at home.

This last is the link that binds Almeyda's people with the Chilean right. Nothing comes more naturally to UDI and National
Renewal than to wrap themselves in the national flag: this is
what they did best and most often during the late Pinochet years,
when the military government—*their* military government—was
under continuous attack from abroad. The case has the additional appeal of serving two other, quite important, domestic
agendas. One is to depict the Aylwin government as ineffective
in defending national interests: at the very same time, by goading it into standing up to the Germans, the Chilean right threatens to divide the president and the Christian Democratic party
from many of their own ministers, members of Congress and
voters. More cynically still, by advocating asylum-plus-extradition
hearings (the identical formula of Almeyda and his Socialist colleagues) UDI and National Renewal deal by indirection with
another case which means far more to them—that of General
Manuel Contreras, retired head of Pinochet's old secret police.

Contreras stands accused by the U.S. Department of Justice
and the U.S. courts of having planned the car-bomb attack which
killed Orlando Letelier, Allende's former ambassador in Washington, a few blocks from the White House in 1976. In spite of
abundant evidence (including the testimony of a former secret
police agent who has fingered Pinochet himself as the ultimate
author of the murder) as well as a new and more sympathetic
regime in Santiago, the United States has still been unable to
obtain Contreras' extradition. For the Chilean right, Contreras,

of course, is a far bigger fish than Honecker; if he were extradited to the United States and told all he knew, it might well implicate an entire network of retired and active-duty officers of the armed forces, a constituency which UDI and National Renewal have assiduously cultivated since the return to democracy two years ago.

Although at his 11 March press conference President Aylwin did his best to minimize the political dimensions of the affair, it is obvious that if anyone other than Clodomiro Almeyda had been ambassador in Moscow, Honecker would not have sought refuge in the Chilean embassy. By an apparently harmless concession to an old adversary, President Aylwin—a man of almost limitless decency—found himself dragged into the maelstrom of post-cold war politics. The crisis ultimately may have to be resolved by Russian and German courts, but it already has left its mark on German-Chilean relations, on Chile's credibility as an emerging (or rather reemerging) South American democracy, and on Chilean domestic politics. One can only wish its diplomacy better luck in the future.

21

Franco, Trujillo, and the CIA

At 10:00 in the evening on 12 March 1956, Jesús de Galíndez, a Spanish Basque refugee living in New York City, entered the subway station at Fifty-seventh Street and Park Avenue. He was never seen again. His disappearance, which subsequently became a cause célèbre in the United States, Spain and the Dominican Republic, is now the subject of a best-selling novel in Spain by Manuel Vásquez Montálban, arguably the finest writer currently at work in the peninsula. Not surprisingly, Vásquez Montálban's book, *Galíndez* (Barcelona: Seix Barral), was awarded the national literary prize in 1991, has gone through ten printings in its original edition and has already appeared in a French translation. It is only a matter of time before it appears in the United States; when it does, it is bound to reopen old controversies.

This is so because Vásquez Montálban is no ordinary writer—he is a committed Marxist novelist armed with a formidable literary talent to recreate atmospheres and textures. The novel moves freely between Spain, the United States and the Dominican Republic; mixing fact with fiction, and shifting events from "past" (1956) and "present" (circa 1985). Vásquez Montálban is, predictably, at his best in dealing with the Spanish background, but he has evidently spent considerable time in the Dominican Republic, and also in the United States, a country which he clearly despises, but which he takes seriously enough to investigate in some detail. Indeed, in spite of some egregious errors, certain details about American life are offered with a telling piquancy. Rarely has a book with a deeply partisan political viewpoint succeeded so fully as art; whether it will have quite the same effect in the area of policy debate remains to be seen.

From Franco to Trujillo

Jesus de Galíndez was a young Basque lawyer and politician whose career was artificially truncated by the collapse of the Spanish Republic in 1939. Like many on the losing side in the civil war, he was hard-pressed to find a country in which to settle; after some difficulties in France he was able to obtain an immigrant visa for the Dominican Republic, where he arrived in early 1940. The choice of countries was dictated by utter necessity, but is nonetheless ironic. Here was a Basque democrat fleeing Franco's rule in Spain only to take refuge under the colors of one of the fiercest dictators in the Caribbean, Generalíssimo Rafael Leonidas Trujillo, who had ruled that tiny country like a personal fiefdom since the late 1920s (and was to rule it for twenty years more). Galíndez spent six years in the Dominican Republic, teaching at the Diplomatic Academy of the Foreign Ministry, and also serving as an advisor to the Labor Department. After the Second World War he was able to get a visa for the United States and he settled in New York, where he found work as a graduate teaching fellow at Columbia University. He also became the representative of the Basque government-in-exile for the United States and Latin America, and plunged in to the netherworld of exile politics in New York City. He may also have maintained some contact with the United States government, which at the time of his arrival was contemplating (jointly with Great Britain) some form of retaliation against the Franco government for Spain's flirtation with the Axis during the Second World War.

Sometime in the mid-1950s the Dominican government became aware through its agents in New York that Galíndez was at work on his doctoral thesis—the subject of which was to be the theory and practice of dictatorship in the Dominican Republic.[1] Generalíssimo Trujillo, who entertained a suspicious regard for U.S. public opinion, was alarmed at the prospect and ordered his people to attempt to persuade Galíndez to desist from the project, even to the extent of offering him $25,000 as an incentive to lay down his pen. When these offers were turned aside, Trujillo ordered Galíndez's liquidation.

In fact, Galíndez was not the first dissident from the Dominican Republic to die or disappear under mysterious conditions in the United States, but he was the first to provoke widespread public comment and a thoroughgoing investigation. There were two reasons for this. Galíndez was not a Dominican but a Spaniard, and as such had a larger and more influential network of friends and supporters. At the same time, shortly after his disappearance, the relatives of Gerald Murphy, an American pilot for the Dominican national airline, reported a similar incident. In effect, Murphy's abandoned Ford was discovered in the slaughterhouse district of Ciudad Trujillo (as the Dominican capital was then called)—with no trace of the owner. Murphy's relatives in Oregon were able to interest both Senator Wayne Morse and Representative Charles Porter in his fate; they in turn goaded the U.S. Department of State and Justice into action.

In due course, the U.S. government learned that a small private plane piloted by Murphy had landed illegally at a small airport near Amityville, Long Island on the night of Galíndez's disappearance. The Basque, either already dead or drugged, was loaded onto the craft, which took off for Monte Cristi on the north shore of the Dominican Republic. Beyond that, neither the fate of Galíndez or Murphy could be traced. Even the mechanic who serviced the plane at Amityville and the night watchman who witnessed the events both subsequently died under mysterious circumstances. This information was sufficient to provoke a serious crisis in U.S.–Dominican relations, but nothing more than this has since been learned; even Trujillo's assassination in 1961 did not uncover any additional information about the case.

These events form the skeleton of the novel. Onto it Vásquez Montálban has mounted a fictitious tale of a young female graduate student from Yale by the name of Muriel Colbert who has decided to write a thesis on Galíndez. Colbert is a young woman from Utah who has broken with her conservative Mormon family to become involved in left-wing political causes. Vásquez Montálban might have gone over the top with this character, but he draws her with skill and some sophistication; although in most ways "politically correct," she possesses a healthy sense of irony and self-doubt, perhaps because she has already been around, and in more ways than one. When we first meet her she has already begun and ended affairs with a Chilean refugee and her thesis adviser at Yale, and is sharing an apartment with

Ricardo, an official of the Ministry of Culture in Madrid several years her junior.

The opening chapters permit Vásquez Montálban to express the full range of his distaste for contemporary Spain, and particularly for Socialist politicians and bureaucrats who have (in his view) betrayed dreams of a more just social order. Ricardo is, in fact, the archetype—an opportunist who takes Muriel to task for her relentless high-mindedness. ("You 'progressive' Yankees have a guilt complex and run around the world saying yes to everybody and everything.") To his Basque uncle, a former Communist militant, he explains that the Spanish socialists believe "things change slowly, very slowly, and the most you can do is to give them a little push forward, so they eventually fall into the proper hole, like a game of golf." He accuses the Communists of the Franco era of having an unhealthy predilection for martyrdom ("they loved being thrown into jail"). When Muriel asks, "What would you have done in their place?" he cynically answers, "I don't like martyrs or heroes either—I only like rock idols or heroines of the bedroom."

In conversation with Ricardo and his friends one evening, Muriel expresses her own , (and presumably the author's) disillusionment with the country. When she first visited Spain as an adolescent, she relates, it reminded her of the works of Hemingway; now it rather recalled the novels of F. Scott Fitzgerald. When pressed as to why, she says, "it is full of the same sensation of defeat, where the world divides once and for all into rich and poor, winners and losers." "You have become a normal country," she adds, "You can calculate your hopes and reject your useless dreams. You have divided into pragmatists who've made it and pragmatists who remain nostalgic for the revolution." Not surprisingly, when Muriel quits Spain for the Dominican Republic she also terminates her relationship with her Spanish lover.

Meanwhile in the United States, the Central Intelligence Agency has gotten wind of what Muriel is doing, and one of its agents calls upon her thesis adviser Professor Norman Radcliffe. The purpose of the visit is to pressure Radcliffe into persuading Muriel to drop or change the topic of her thesis. When Radcliffe tries to find out why the subject is so objectionable to the U.S. government, the agent answers delphically, "he was a piece on the strategic chessboard, independent of his own worth or without knowing it... We are not prepared to let a few melancholy reds resurrect useless corpses." The agent offers to assure foundation support for a new topic—anything Muriel wants, at three or four times her current fellowship. When Radcliffe resists, he threatens various forms of blackmail—from assuring withdrawal of financial support for the professor's own pet project, to making public his (Radcliffe's) predilection for sexually exploiting his female students. Properly intimidated, the professor writes Muriel urging her to shift topics, but without success. The CIA's efforts have been trumped—for the moment.

At this point the novel shifts back to 1956, and allows the reader to witness the interrogation of Galíndez, who wakes up form a drug-induced stupor to find himself in the hands of Trujillo's interrogators somewhere in the Dominican Republic. As best he can, Galíndez tries to persuade his captors that he is an agent and collaborator with the American government and that Washington will be very angry with Trujillo when they learn of his disappearance. These scenes are done with great deftness and care. Even the cameo appearance of the dictator himself is rendered credible.

Galíndez an American agent? Possibly so, Muriel learns (now again in 1985) from a variety of people who remember him in the Dominican Republic or New York. In discursive, gossipy prose Vásquez Montálban reproduces exactly how such people talk—and leaves the reader unsure whether we are supposed to believe them or not. It is repeatedly suggested that Galíndez made a kind of bargain with the devil—in this case, the U.S. government. In exchange for providing information on the Communists in the exile movement, the Basque professor was provided with a visa to study in the United States, possible even money form the FBI. What Galíndez failed to realize, however, was that another American agency, the CIA, had a somewhat higher priority than vetting the Spanish exile movement; it was desperate to keep Trujillo in power in the Dominican Republic. The dictator, confident of CIA support, was thus emboldened to embark upon the kidnapping and the murder. Later, there was hell to pay in the U.S. government, as well as in Washington's relationship with Trujillo, but those points are pushed somewhat vaguely off the screen.

The final chapters deal with Muriel's visit to the Dominican Republic, where when is assembling the final pieces of the monstrous puzzle. Lured to an interview with someone purportedly present at the interrogation of Galíndez by Trujillo's henchmen, she instead falls into the hands of some sinister individuals of indeterminate nationality (Cuban-Americans?) and eventually disappears altogether. Thus Muriel Colbert's career trajectory almost perfectly replicates that of her thesis topic: refusing to accept money (fellowships) to abandon her project, she ends up paying the supreme price, just as Galíndez was "disappeared" for refusing to cease work on his book on Trujillo in exchange for $25,000. As the back cover of the Spanish edition summarizes the point somewhat grandiloquently, "she labors under the common banner of vulnerable idealism in a world in which depredation, barbarism, and venality only permit those who do not partake of them to opt for self-elimination."

In its broadest outlines, the thesis of Vásquez Montálban is at least conceivable—that is, that Galíndez was in fact in the confidence, (if not the pay) of the FBI; that the CIA was unaware of the fact; that Trujillo had reason to assume he was "protected" by the United States government, and (ignorant of the Galíndez-FBI link) was thus encouraged to overstep the permissible bounds of state-to-state relations, leave aside the laws of both countries against kidnapping and homicide. What is irritating about the book is the author's unwillingness to accept our continuing ignorance over the details of the crime as anything but a purposeful cover-up, one that extends a full thirty years after the event.

Indeed, it is precisely Vásquez Montálban's device of putting the main body of the narrative in the near-present-day that saps its credibility. That some operatives in the CIA in 1956 might wish to have protected Trujillo from embarrassment seems logical in the context of the era; but why in 1985 would anyone—in the CIA or elsewhere in the U.S. government—care about Muriel's dissertation, destined in all likelihood to gather dust in the bowels of the Yale University library? The closest answer to the question is offered by one CIA spokesman in the novel, who claims that the Dominican Republic is tottering on the brink of instability because its chief executive, Joaquin Balaguer (an old Trujillo protégé, by the way) "is blind and old, ready at any point to pass into the next world." "If the girl doesn't back off," one CIA agent murmurs in sinister tones, "we have to mobilize the whole process and move immediately to the next phase." Really?

Here we see Vásquez Montálban's real problem with the United States. For him nothing has changed since he 1950s—the country is awash in hysterical anticommunism, and rued by a cabal of right-wing operatives who will stop at nothing to crush the slightest sign of independent thought. All the more so when there exists the possibility that if the truth were known about the disappearance of Galíndez it might imperil the government of the Dominican Republic, presumably the epicenter of U.S. strategic concerns. One might argue that even the 1950s were not like this—indeed, I would so argue—but even if they were, they bear no resemblance whatsoever to the 1980s.

Vásquez Montálban seems not to have noticed that while Ronald Reagan was in the White House during the period described, the U.S. Congress was largely in the hands of a Democratic party considerably to the left of its predecessor thirty years before, and the American press engaged in a daily campaign to discredit the administration's policies both domestic and foreign. To an American reader if not to a Spanish writer it is simply inconceivable that in the mid-1980s any functionary of the U.S. government could dictate grant-giving by any of the major foundations, most of whom are (as any reader of the learned journals can attest) in the business of subsidizing research which sharply questions the economic, social, and sexual status quo. The stability of the Dominican Republic has not been a serious issue in U.S. foreign policy for more than a generation and—unless Dominicans begin emigrating illegally to the United States in the kind of numbers that Haitians have lately begun to do—is not likely to become so again. There is some superficial plausibility to one of his plot devices: the CIA threat to expose Radcliffe's sexual exploitation of female students might well produce a bit of moral leverage. But Vásquez Montálban gets a crucial detail wrong here, too: the professor's problem today would have been with feminists, the Yale administration or the New Haven Human Rights Commission, not the "puritanical Yankee foundations."

Vásquez Montálban seems also not to be very well informed about the American left. He is strongest in dealing with academic liberals, whose folkloric aspects he describes with vicious accuracy. ("The Volkswagen... the external sign of rebellion against the American Way of Life. It is the car of choice of the American progressives....but now [they] have discovered other European

brands, and even switched to bicycles.") But he tends to lump together causes which have little or nothing to do with each other.
Above all, he seem wholly unaware of the sharp divide between
the old (communist-influenced) left of the 1930s and the (non-
communist-influenced) New Left of the 1960s. In this area, (as in
many others) Spanish readers of his novel are bound to have many
ill-founded prejudices reinforced, all the more so since the facts,
or rather the factoids, are rendered in such bold, clear colors.

   Let us concede that the world of Caribbean politics was and is
one of conspiracy—as is the world of exile politics in New York
and Miami. In such a world anything is possible. By resurrecting
the Galíndez case, Vaquez Montálban has managed to serve both
his literary and political agendas. For who can say with absolute
assurance that his theories about the disappearance of Galíndez
are false? Will the appearance of this book in English spur new
efforts to declassify documents under the Freedom of Information Act? Will the American press accept as true the working
hypothesis of the novel? Will it even be possible to disprove it?
As the recent Oliver Stone film *JFK* has shown, in the United
States today fiction has the capability of driving fact. It remains
to be seen whether Vásquez Montálban will match his artistic
triumph with a political coup as well.

Note

1. The book was in fact published posthumously as *La era de Trujillo* to universal success in the Spanish-speaking world, and an English-language
   edition was subsequently printed by the University of Arizona Press.

22

Why the Europeans Support
the Sandinistas

In the preface to *When the Going Was Good* (1946), a selection from his travel books written in the 1920s and 1930s, Evelyn Waugh wrote, without much regret, that his own traveling days were over:

> Never again, I suppose, shall we land on foreign soil with a letter of credit and passport...and feel the world wide open before us.... Others, not I, gifted with the art of pleasing public authorities may get themselves despatched abroad to promote "Cultural Relations."...I shall not, by my own wish, be among them.

I suddenly recalled this passage when I was invited by the United States Information Agency (USIA) to visit six Western European countries this past May to explain our Central American policy. Apparently I had been gifted "with the art of pleasing public authorities," and had to bear the consequences. I knew, of course, that Central America was a subject Europeans did not wish to dwell upon at any length; I knew, also, that most countries were critical of our policies, and some downright sympathetic to our enemies. I had heard of the vast "solidarity" movements which, particularly in West Germany, Holland, and the Scandinavian countries, had sprung up to assist the Sandinistas in their task of Stalinizing Nicaraguan society; but I had heard, too, that the tide was beginning to turn, as the Ortega brothers and Tomás Borge revealed their true colors. Perhaps this was opportune moment to restate our case?

The following reflections are taken from a journal of the trip.

Helsinki, April 27–30

This is the city often used to represent Leningrad in Western spy films—and no wonder: it is full of architecture evocative of the late Russian empire, and seems cold, bleak, and properly Baltic. (I realize for the first time that Tallinn—formerly Revel—Estonia is just forty miles across the water, Leningrad a mere train ride away).

Finns are known to be a reserved, introspective people, but the ones I meet—the very few who are interested in Central America—are voluble enough. Here the issue of Nicaragua is played in two different ways. Either the Sandinistas are confused with Nicaragua ("big country versus small country"), in which case Finland must side with any other small country threatened by a large imperialistic neighbor (in this case, the United States); or the Sandinistas represent one area where Finnish "neutrality" can show its tilt toward the Soviets at low cost and risk.

In any event, there is abundant activity here on behalf of the Sandinistas. As the Press and Public Affairs Counselor at the U.S. embassy explained to me in a letter before my arrival, "Recently, there has been pressure on the Finnish Ministry for Foreign Affairs' Department of Development Cooperation to increase development assistance to Nicaragua. A group of twenty-eight Finnish organizations, including student, union, and church groups, also requested that a group of Finnish peace-corps types be sent to help out." Surprisingly, he added, "*La Prensa* has been represented in the journalists' union house organ (controlled by leftists) as a U.S.-financed paper which stands for reaction, opposes the revolution, and, therefore, does not represent freedom of information but rather an obstacle in the way of progress in Nicaragua. No media voices were raised here against its closing."

During my four days here I have ample opportunity to learn that these observations are not exaggerated. The Finns are basically where the American liberals were about 1982, still hopeful that the Nicaraguan revolution could somehow justify their support, but with the anti-American cutting edge a bit sharper (or possibly merely more explicit). Perhaps the most appalling moment of the visit comes when a young labor leader looks me straight in the eye and says, "The Nicaraguan elections were quite convincing, don't you think?" I manage to respond, "Well, what do your friends in the Nicaraguan labor movement think of them?" "Well," he says a bit uncomfortably, "it is a rather confused situation." When I suggest that the AFL-CIO thought otherwise, he just smirks.

Why a country which has lost so much territory to the Soviet Union should view Nicaraguan affairs in this light is rather difficult to say. Actually, Finland is not "Finlandized" at all; that is, though formally neutral, in most ways it is unambiguously pro-Western—which is not to be confused, however, with being pro-American. The Finns are also deeply anti-Soviet. (A member of parliament says to me, when I remark on the proximity of Leningrad, "Well, yes, that's so. I've never been there, of course." The "of course" is the operative part of the sentence). What makes Nicaragua a cause worthy of Finnish support, then, is not its desire to be part of the Soviet bloc, or even the Sandinistas' supposedly revolutionary achievements at home, but the regime's opposition to the United States. This does not offer us much in the way of constructive suggestions for future policy, except perhaps that we should reduce our national territory by 90 percent and declare ourselves nonaligned vis-à-vis, say, Canada.

Rome-Vatican City-Trieste-Naples, May 1–9

The nice thing about Italy—apart from the food, the wine, the weather, the scenery, and the people—is the political diversity and forthrightness of all parties. This is one of the few countries where you can see wall slogans like SOVIETS OUT OF AFGHANISTAN. Also, when someone applies the slogan VIVA NICARAGUA SANDINISTA he thoughtfully adds a hammer and sickle. Such candor is refreshing; at least we all know what we're talking about.

Latin realism has its charms. The Italians are a cynical people—they have a right to be, given their history—and I find few ardent Sandinista sympathizers. Even the Socialists, who have their own problems with Communists, are beginning to ask hard questions about Nicaragua. At the Foreign Ministry the senior official in charge of political relations with Latin America is mainly interested in learning more about the mess in Washington; clearly, the baroque convolutions of congress and the administration (the Iran-*contra* affair) make our country seem more exotic (and more difficult to understand) than any banana republic. (A mostly undressed Donna Rice is currently adorning the front pages of all the Italian papers; one has as its headline SIGNORINA RICE SAYS GARY HART IS "TOO OLD.")

At the Vatican I meet with two groups—a class at the Pontifical Lateran University and a group of Jesuits at the Gregorian University across town. The former are a polyglot group from the four corners of the globe, including a disenchanted Salvadoran and two Africans, one of whom wants only to discuss South Africa, while the other is mainly interested in practicing, for what I imagine is at least the seventy-ninth time, his maiden speech (in French) for some future UN General Assembly.

The Jesuits are a mixed bag, representing all political points of view. The most leftward by far is an American who has just returned from twenty years' service in the Phillippines. He doesn't know much about Nicaragua, but he has little admiration for our foreign policy generally, extrapolating from what he believes to be our record Phillippines. "There the last thing in the world we had in mind was the welfare of the Filipino people," he repeatedly insists. "This is why we supported Marcos to the end."

Now, I too have read the newspapers, and I think this version somewhat at variance with the facts. Was Ambassador Stephen Bosworth's evident preference for Mrs. Aquino not matter of public knowledge? Who was it that finally got Marcos out, anyway, if not Senator Paul Laxalt? And so forth. Pressing the matter further, I force him into an undignified retreat. But the feelings are still there—my country, wrong or wrong—and nothing will ever make him part with them. He will not lack kindred spirits when he eventually returns home.

Trieste is a city which knows something of communism; it is literally in sight of Yugoslavia, whose soldiers occupied the city in 1945 and killed some 40,000 people. Yugoslavs still come to Trieste nowadays to buy little necessities like soap, toothpaste, toilet paper, hangers and so forth. I remark to the local USIA representative, a passionate Triestino intellectual, that for many people I know—leftist "community organizers" in the United States, Socialists in Spain, Christian Democrats in Chile—Yugoslavia is the *ideal* communist country, a social experiment worthy of emulation everywhere. He is astounded. "That is no communist country!" he insists. I say, "Really, then what would you call it?" "It is a country of corruption, nepotism, where everyone hates everyone..." In other words, the Yugoslavs are a form of animal life too low to aspire to coherent political institutions. I permit myself to doubt this.

Trieste is also a city which reminds one, eloquently, of Europe's troubled history, and the price which is still being paid for the folly of the First World War. It mutely attests, as well, to the permanent damage done to Western civilization by the pernicious ideas of Woodrow Wilson. Once the port of the Austro-Hungarian empire and the home of its fleet, Trieste was ceded to Italy in 1919. In many ways it is closer to Vienna than to Rome, and not just geographically, though the language is Italian. It seems a bit of *alt-Mitteleuropa* pinned in a remote corner of the Adriatic, separated by distance and culture from its nominal parent state, and by accidents of diplomacy and war from the country to which it has greatest affinity. Having seized Trieste from Austria-Hungary in the post-Versailles division of Europe, Italy in turn lost much of the city's hinterland to the hated Yugoslavs after the Second World War. It is full of fascinating literary and cultural associations: James Joyce lived here during and after the First World War, and the cafe on the quay where he used to hold forth looks as if he might walk in at any moment.

Naples reminds me of Lisbon—a fortified port city, shabby, picturesque, and full of life. Here our Central American problems—as indeed our views on SALT, nuclear testing, South Africa, and so forth—lie with the local press, which is intermittently under the control of militants of the Italian Communist Party. However, according to what one of our few friends in the media here tells me, the real damage is done by the *Washington Post*, whose articles are reprinted verbatim by the Neapolitan papers. When I suggest perhaps a bit too facetiously that no one in Washington takes the *Post* seriously as a *newspaper* (we all turn first to the "Style" section to read the gossip, and after that, to the ads, comics, and sports, relying for real news on the *New York Times*) he remarks, "That's all very well in Washington; you have a context in which to place things, and an alternative source of information. Here things are different."

Paris-Grenoble-Lyon-Lille, May 11–17

France is the only really serious country in Europe, if by serious one means having the capacity to address major political questions head-on; unlike the Germanic and Nordic countries, French political culture is concerned with outcomes, not just intentions.

Further, it is the only country in Europe with what might be called a "libertarian Left"—a serious, anticommunist socialism, which for a visitor from the intellectual provinces of the United States takes some getting used to. Finally, because of their own colonial past, the French have far fewer illusions about the Third World; also, of late they have become very unsentimental about terrorism.

My hotel in Paris is around the corner from and eighteenth-century building which houses both the Navy and Finance Ministries: the block is acrawl with policemen in flak jackets leading sniffing German shepherds around. When the French Interior Ministry decides to you are a suspicious foreigner, out you go—no civil-liberties union, no bleeding hearts, no sanctuary movement, no nothing. Whether we would wish to copy such practices is beside the point. Taken together, they bespeak a state of mind which makes France a much less propitious breeding ground for Sandinista sympathizers than other European countries.

This is not to say that there is any active *support* for our policies toward Nicaragua, merely that they are accepted by large sectors of the French political community as an inevitable consequence of certain geopolitical realities. When I explain to some people at the French Socialist party that the real issue in the United States is not what kind of a role we should play in Central America, but whether we have a role to play there at all, the response is frank disbelief. "What nonsense!" one of my hosts bursts out. "You *can't* withdraw from there; it's your sphere of influence. You have vital security interests there!" After I catch my breath I say, "Well, you have to come to Paris to hear that kind of talk nowadays, and then to make sure you hear it, you'd best head straight to the French Socialist party headquarters!"

I was last in France in 1968. It is a different country today: more stable, more prosperous, more self-confident, and therefore more tolerant of foreigners. The real key to the country's current state of mind seems to me to be its emancipation from the bugaboo of Western culture—self-hatred. My description of the political-intellectual situation in the United States to a French friend who's never been there draws the remarkable response, "My God, it sounds just like West Germany." Have I overstated my case? I can only hope so.

Of course, the hard Left still exists here, albeit in diminished numbers and intellectual force. You can still see it in places like the *Maison de l'Amérique Latine,* where I have the dubious plea-sure of participating in a two-day conference on Nicaragua (*"une solution démocratique et pacifique"*). Though the conference orga-nizer, Jean Elleinstien, is supposed to be a repentant ex-Com-munist, no one else seems to be an ex-anything. The audience is the usual mixture of professional Latin American expatriates (some of whose countries have, unfortunately, recently reverted to democracy, in the act heartlessly depriving them of the con-secrated statues of "refugee"), UN bureaucrats, renegade Catho-lic priests in turtleneck sweaters, and intellectualoids of various sizes and shapes.

A panel on "Human Rights in Nicaragua" is allowed to run more than an hour overtime; thus my own contribution, which follows at the end of the day, is delivered to a largely empty hall. (Elleinstein has quit the place, and left one of his assistants to chair this final part of the meeting). The previous panel has es-tablished that there no human-rights problem in Nicaragua, though José Estéban González, the founder of the Nicaraguan Human Rights commission, now living European exile, rises to question the finding with a wealth of facts and figures. Both panel and audience are wholly unmoved; he might as well have been speaking in Bulgarian.

My most vociferous questioners are American expatriates, prob-ing to their French and Latin American friends that in spite of their shameful place of birth, they have somehow managed to rise above it all. This is an invitation to return the compliment with no holds barred, and by the end of the session I am actually enjoying myself. But then, as I have been learning on this trip, compared with the loony grandmothers in the United States who have discovered Central America "down at our church," the Sandinista supporters in Europe are a piece of cake.

Vienna, May 17–19

There is only one topic dominating U.S.–Austrian relations these days, and it isn't Central America. The decision of the Jus-tice Department to refuse entry to President Kurt Waldheim has infuriated everybody, and plunged our embassy people in to a deep, dark funk. Of course, the irony of it all is that if the Austri-ans themselves hadn't insisted on our giving Waldheim a clean bill of health, we could have slipped the whole matter under the rug and pretended the Holtzman amendment didn't exist. As it is, by forcing us to confrontation, they got the worst of both worlds—and so have we.

Waldheim is, of course, a most unappetizing character and by lying about his wartime record, he laid himself open to an exquisite revenge by his enemies. However, one can take little comfort from his comeuppance, since his People's Party is much friendlier to the United States than the Socialists, or rather *was*, as one of its members of parliament emphasizes to me. So, we've punished our traditional allies and, in effect if not intent, rushed to embrace their opponents, whose notion of neutralism is more or less proximate to that of the Swedes. The People's Party only recently forced the Socialists to split their aid to Nicaragua into five pieces, apportioning it equally among the Central American countries. Now it's unclear what will happen.

Zurich-Bern-Geneva, May 20–24

Until recently, Switzerland was known as a neutral country, in the value-free sense of that term. Now some Swiss have discovered the pleasures of having an enemy in the United States (which never hits back) rather than, say, in Germany or the Soviet Union (which just might). This makes it possible to luxuriate in new forms of political expression, such as solidarity with Nicaragua (whose dictatorial aspects can be described as a mere reaction to U.S. aggression) and indignation at El Salvador (whose human-rights violations are said to be glossed over, or even supported, by the Reagan administration). Such posturings have their uses, particularly to distract attention from new and embarrassing revelations of Swiss involvement in other parts of the world. (It was not, after all, *Belgian* banks which acted as intermediaries for the alleged activities of Colonel North in the Iran-contra affair.)

At the same time, support for Nicaragua allows an outlet for that current of Swiss political culture which seeks to be part of "Europe," which is to say, the Europe of the Socialist International. Two Swiss development workers have recently been killed in Nicaragua, presumably by the contras, a traumatic event in a country which has not heard a shot fired in anger in many, many generations. It has provoked, naturally, prolonged and sometimes heated exchanges between our embassy, on the on hand, and the unions, churches, and the Foreign Ministry on the other. Switzerland gives economic aid to Nicaragua, almost to the exclusion of other Central American countries—a most un-neutral thing to do, one would think, unless one regards these matters as totally outside the realm of East-West relations, or even of broader political values. A senior official of the Foreign Ministry who has just returned from Central America is pessimistic about the Sandinistas; he depicts the Ortega brothers as committed to the militarization of the country ("never mind whether or not the people starve"), but is quite vague as to what policy responses are appropriate. My guess is that aid to Nicaragua will probably be increased next year.

Switzerland is odd in that it is highly cosmopolitan and remarkably provincial, all at the same time. At a dinner for journalists at the embassy residence one hears notions positively quaint in their antiquity (the need for the U.S. to abandon *le grand bâton* in Central America: the need to be concerned about democracy in other countries, not just or even especially in Nicaragua; the need to emphasize economic as opposed to military aid, and so forth). These people are not stupid, and they are not ignorant. But at a certain point one begins to find it difficult to take some of them seriously. Here criticism of our Central American policy appears to be a shell game played for the sheer amusement of it, and if that bothers us, so much the better.

Stockholm, May 25–27

This stunningly beautiful city is the capital of bad news. Last year Sweden gave Nicaragua $25 million in aid, making that Central American country one of its most important welfare clients. This should neither surprise nor shock, since, after all, Sweden is still giving enormous amounts to Vietnam. The Swedes built a paper factory for Hanoi. In spite of the fact that it uses slave labor, the enterprise still loses vast sums. The Swedes have poured literally millions, perhaps even billions, down this rathole. They recently expressed some vague unhappiness with the Vietnamese occupation of Cambodia, and as a sign of their displeasure announced they would give aid for only two years more.

The Vietnamese appear unworried. Perhaps they know something the Swedes do not.

All of this has a simple explanation. Swedish politicians like to discover and "adopt" Third World revolutions—Olof Palme found Vietnam, and Pierre Schiori, the current permanent undersecretary of the Foreign Office, has taken Nicaragua under his wing. When their protégés turn out badly, the Swedes continue to fund them anyway, out of arrogance and false pride, as well as a certain pathological hatred of the United States. The latter seems to occupy a disproportionate role as an organizing principle in the sorting out of priorities; why else would Vietnam and Nicaragua be so heavily favored, when there are so many other, presumably worthy, candidates for Swedish munificence? South Africa, however, is also a huge bugaboo. Much money goes to the so-called frontline states, corrupt Marxist dictatorships like Mozambique and Angola, or just plain corrupt dictatorships like Zimbabwe and Zambia. When I ask a member of parliament whether, in his view, such countries have good development projects which justify such preferential treatment, he replies without hesitation, "Oh no, not at all. We just do it for political reasons."

Basically Sweden could be described as a First World country in most important respects, and certainly as far as Europe is concerned, Sweden operates on the assumption that its interests lie within the broad political community we call the North Atlantic Treaty Organization (NATO). The Swedes even imagine that, neutral or not, if the Soviets try anything funny, the United States will come to their aid. This view, explained to me on my first night by members of our embassy staff, leaves me frankly breathless.

Meanwhile, in the Third World the Swedes are following a Soviet-bloc policy, in effect if not in specific intent. That is, they favor communism in Central America, and they prove it by aiding not only the Sandinistas but the Salvadoran guerrillas. If they do not perceive our displeasure with this in sufficient degree, it is certainly our fault, not theirs; we haven't yet made it expensive enough in Volvos and Electrolux vacuum cleaners. On the basis of a brief chat with our ambassador, I gather nothing of the sort is in prospect. Quite the contrary: for the first time in more than twenty-five years, a Swedish prime minister is set to visit Washington, and—another feather in the envoy's cap—Mrs. Reagan is due here in a couple of weeks.

One might well ask, why are the Swedes so anti-American? After all, unlike the British, they haven't been displaced in recent memory from great-power status and cultural hegemony within their language area; and unlike the Germans, they do not have to tolerate more than a quarter of a million American soldiers and their families in their midst, who thereby prevent them from reunifying with their brethren in the East and living peacefully ever after. The answer would seem to be this: Sweden and the United States comprise opposite poles of the continuum of Western utopias. Both have managed to combine a high standard of living with political democracy and pluralism, with the United States representing the individualist end of the continuum, Sweden its collectivist antipode. The problem is that in consumer preferences and styles of life, most younger Swedes are less and less drawn to their own traditions; the U.S. pole is a stronger one in many ways, and intellectuals and Social Democratic politicians feel the need to resist it in any way they can.

Put another way, the United States is a permanent temptation against which Swedish leaders must protect their people. In the 1940s Gunnar Myrdal discovered our racial problem; in the 1960s Olof Palme discovered Vietnam; now they Nicaragua to play with. Presumably in a Biden administration there would be something else—one hopes so, for the Swedes' sake.

Of course, there is nothing the Swedes could have done to prevent us from passing the Civil Rights Act, or, for that matter, from withdrawing from Vietnam, but in Central America they have a concrete opportunity to add fat to the fire, and within the boundaries of their deepest politico-cultural needs they would be rather silly not do so.

Concluding Notes

Though the Europeans can pretend the Third World is far away, it is becoming less so every day. Of course, in France the African, North African, and Asian presence has always been great, but now societies which until yesterday were racially homogeneous have begun to harbor significant minorities. The woman who cleans my hotel room in Vienna is clearly Indochinese, and all the newspaper vendors are Indians or Pakistanis. There are 10,000 Tamils in Switzerland—causing no small amount of anxiety among the Swiss, since each one has many relatives at home who would also like to live there, and in fact plan to do so at the earliest opportunity. Even Sweden is now the home of thousands of Chileans, Iranians, Iraqis, Kurds, and others. Not all of these coexist in perfect cordiality; Stockholm has, in fact, become the site of some ugly confrontations along sectarian lines. Quite recently a street confrontation between pro- and anti-Khomeini Iranians has erupted into violence, with each side throwing paper bags of human excrement at the other. Unfortunately Gunnar Myrdal is no longer alive to provide us with the fullest possible documentation of this very interesting phenomenon.

It is not difficult to see what attracts these people to Western Europe—it is orderly and prosperous, with a style of life which has many refinements unavailable elsewhere, certainly not in the "developing" countries from which the immigrants have come. In the nineteenth century people like Henry James felt as drawn to Europe as Asians, Africans, and Latin Americans do today, but a hundred years later he might view matters from a slightly different perspective. The countries of Central and Northern Europe have become what might be called societies of predetermined outcome. That is, a concrete decision was made a generation or more ago to level economic differences and guarantee that there would be no poverty and little real wealth.

This has brought about a remarkable state of affairs, where the really important question facing most Europeans at this season of the year is where to spend their four weeks of paid vacation (six weeks in Sweden)—in Spain, Italy, Greece, or the United States, or even in the Seychelles, Cuba, or Tahiti. Such is the final destiny, then, of the peoples who produced Strindberg and Sibelius, Mozart and Haydn, Jacob Burkhardt and Jean-Jacques Rousseau. Only the French are capable of looking up from their immediate environment and seeing the world as an interrelated whole.

I do not mean to be condescending or negative. There are good and ample reasons to celebrate this consummation; the entire modern history of many countries was one long class war. The walls of the Karl Marx Hof in Vienna, one of the first public-housing projects in Europe, are still disfigured by mortar shells expended in the civil war-cum-coup of 1934, which brought to an end the first social democratic period of Austrian politics. The shift reminds me that this placid republic was once as unstable, or at least as politically problematic, as some Latin American countries are today. For all I know the decision to create static societies at a high level of relative egalitarian distribution was the right one, particularly since the United States seems so anxious to assume responsibility for their defense and security. (I leave aside the whole question of whether the juggling act of egalitarian distribution and high productivity can continue indefinitely; most economists now believe that it cannot, and that difficult choices lie not far ahead).

But in such societies there is no place for two kinds of people— the idealist and the go-getter. Now, in the United States, when you feel in a guilty mood and want to have a good cry, you can start talking about the homeless, or the shamefully small number of Asian-American women who have been selected to be astronauts. But what do you do in Switzerland? One person sprayed onto the wall of the Cathedral in Bern, LIBERTY FOR POLITICAL PRISONERS IN SWITZERLAND: a perfect example of what might be called "repression envy." All of the great battles for social equality have been won here, and those who feel called upon to right the wrongs of society must either pretend they still exist, or go abroad to look for them—picking cotton and coffee in Nicaragua, or working in one of the "development" agencies busily undermining the economies of Sub-Saharan Africa. As for the go-getters, in Austria and German Switzerland they flee to West Germany, everywhere else to the United States.

Indeed, one senses that Europe needs the United States very badly—not merely for defense, and for someone to blame for the loss of cultural and international predominance, but also as a final escape hatch in case things turn out badly at home. If there is one thing Europeans fear more than U.S. hegemony it is the opposite—the lack of U.S. interest and involvement in European affairs. For too many people, the whole Nicaragua question— whether the Sandinistas are good or bad, or whether they are bad or because we are making them bad—is merely symbolic, and lacks all substance. Central America is seen as an undesirable distraction, unworthy of our attention, which should, in their view, be focused exactly where theirs is—on themselves.

Acknowledgments

Acknowledgments are made to the following publishers for permission to reprint material which formerly appeared in their pages.

To *The New Criterion* for
"Literature and Politics in Latin America"
"'An aristocrat in the public square': José Ortega y Gasset"
"Victoria Ocampo's *Sur*"
"García Lorca and His Times"
"Gerald Brenan"
"Carlos Fuentes Discovers America"
"The Doleful Legacy of Carlton Beals"
"Orphans of Utopia"

The Times Literary Supplement for
"Beyond Bilingualism"

Commentary magazine for
"The Only Hope for Latin America"
"Why Europeans Support the Sandinistas"

World Affairs Quarterly for
"U. S.-Cuban Relations: Back to the Beginning"

Freedom House and *Freedom Review* for
"America's Culture Wars and the Cuban Revolution"
"The Strange Case of Erich Honecker"
"Franco, Trujillo, and the CIA"

The National Interest for
"The Cuba in Our Mind"

The American Enterprise for
"Why the Latins Still Love Fidel"

The National Review for
"The Other Cuba"

The American Scholar for
"Orange Juice with General Perón"

Johns Hopkins Foreign Policy Institute for
"Between Two Fires: Terror and Counterterror in Argentina,
1970–83"

Global Affairs for
"The Falklands Conflict Revisited"

Index